THE DESIGN OF SAILING YACHTS

THE DESIGN OF SAILING YACHTS

Pierre Gutelle

INTERNATIONAL MARINE PUBLISHING COMPANY
Camden, Maine

© 1979 by Editions Maritimes et d'Outre Mer
English language translation © 1984 by Macmillan London Ltd.
Library of Congress Catalog Card Number 83-82851
International Standard Book Number 0-87742-183-8

Printed and bound in Hong Kong

Published by International Marine Publishing Company
21 Elm Street, Camden, Maine 04843
(207) 236-4342

Contents

FOREWORD

We, today, are witness to an accelerating application of theoretical and research hydro- and aerodynamics to the development of sailing yachts. Research programs, plus the lessons from marine and aerospace advances, now augment the traditional naval architectural disciplines. The results, when applied to yachts, form the threshold for exciting advances on the horizon.

To provide understanding of this new technology, Pierre Gutelle has written a state-of-the-art review of theory and practice in sailing yacht design.

The book is logically organized to explain the principal considerations for design and performance. Theory and formulae are included, with very satisfactory explanations for the nontechnical reader. Thus, the book is of interest to practicing naval architects, sailors, and those just interested in the whys and hows of sailing.

Gutelle draws from all the better research in the field to buttress his own clear explanations. He provides physical reasons as well as conclusions for understanding the flow of water about the hull and the flow of air about the sails that control our destinies at sea. And he discusses both definite practical results and unanswered questions.

Following his introduction of the physical and environmental considerations, the author explains yacht stability and control. The core of the book is the division of hydrodynamic forces into distinct components that indicate the intricate trade-offs for design and competitive sailing. Aerodynamic counterparts for sails and rigs complete the discussion of forces generated against a sailing yacht. The implications of these forces for design and performance are summarized, including the effects of unsteady conditions in the real world. Many of the excellent illustrations and diagrams are drawn from the literature, for which complete references are given.

I like the philosophy of this book: to locate and apply pragmatically the best available knowledge to the fascinating topic of sailing yacht design.

Halsey C. Herreshoff
August 1983

INTRODUCTION

Although there are many standard text books and every year a number of papers on ship design and naval architecture, the available books specifically on the design of *sailing yachts* are very few indeed. Skene's, often quoted as the standard reference work, was first published in 1927 and works by Phillips-Birt, if in print, date from the 1950s. If one turns to Baader, originally in the Spanish language, there is little technical substance for the professional, while Marchaj and a book by the Canadian Kay are both highly authoritative, but treat many individual aspects of sailing motion and do not pretend to be a treatise on the design of yachts.

In order to remedy this defect in a systematic way, the chapters that follow are not so much a personal work as an analysis and a synthesis of the many studies with which I have become aquainted. The book was first published in the French language in 1979, but the opportunity has been taken, while translating it into English, of correcting and updating minor points, and in particular adding a section following the considerable number of reports and papers after the Fastnet race of 1979, when the stability of racing yachts in extreme conditions came under scrutiny.

A most important step in Europe since the publication of the earlier works mentioned above was the formation of the Department of Naval Architecture at Southampton University with its wind tunnel and towing tank; and specifically the Wolfson Marine Craft Unit which carries out continual work on yachts and small craft, both sail and power. The difficulty here for the general student is that the unit's work is done to the order of commercial concerns, which then remains confidential and is seldom if ever released. Much work on small craft, including sailing yachts, is also done at Delft University in Holland and both here and in the USA there are regular symposia of naval architects and yacht designers which produce most helpful papers. At the end of this book will be found a list of works and papers to which reference has been made.

There have certainly been excellent yachts designed by persons with no formal training, and with a 'seat of the pants' instinct for the dynamics of sailing yachts. Yet precious time can be saved and major errors avoided by most students if one at least has a minimum of theoretical knowledge about the behaviour of a sailing boat. This book is intended to be the first volume, where the second would deal with drafting, calculations and construction. The original edition of this first volume took five years to write and so you may have to be patient before you see a further work: this book is, however, complete in itself.

Would-be designers and established ones as well should not be the only ones interested in the subject of theory, because this also serves to explain the phenomena which the sailor observes when he is on the water under sail. For instance, how can one fit out and load a cruising boat correctly, make her comfortable at sea, without knowing the factors which affect behaviour in waves? Bernard Moitessier's first circumnavigation of the world would certainly have been less arduous and dangerous if he had known beforehand how important it is to distribute the weight and to avoid overloading the boat, instead of discovering this later.

It is therefore just as important to be aware of the many factors that affect the behaviour of the boat as to study astronavigation or meteorology. Is not safety largely a question of seeing that the boat is in such a good condition that it is possible to get the most out of her?

A number of new designers have appeared on the scene over the past few years, not all of whom are without talent; others however, have had the idea that this was just the profession to enable them to combine work with pleasure. How many professions are there that can be followed absolutely freely with no need for a diploma or licence? The customer on the other hand is often disarmingly naive, with a vague idea of what he wants and what is actually possible; he is badly informed as to costs and the realities of construction, and leaves himself wide open to abuses and sharp practice.

As to builders and boatyards, some of the newcomers have so little experience or qualification that they are incapable of judging the real value of a design that has been supplied, of correcting it if need be and, especially, of making any additions that are essential. Between them these three make up a trilogy which results today, certainly on the continent, in a greater number of court cases than has ever been known in the sailing boat field.

It is obvious that it takes more than the ability to design an attractive letter head to become a naval architect, however much you love the sea and boats! A great many qualities are needed when it comes to the point.

First and most important, in spite of all scientific knowledge and the technical know-how at one's disposal today, it is a gift for design that it required, and this is what will decide the answers when sitting in front of a drawing board and having to choose to right value, which measurement, and whether this curve or that curve is preferable to another.

However sophisticated the facilities at you disposal may be — towing tank, wind tunnel computer programming — it is only the flair of the man holding the pencil that enables the right compromises to be made between the various contradictory factors involved in the design of a sailing boat. Although flair can be cultivated, as it can in relation to any other art, it is the basic essential. Studying literature, and careful and critical observation are indispensable tools, but they do no more than improve on flair.

Some consider that the designer must have first-hand knowledge of sailing. Personally I do not think so; you can sail for years without understanding what makes a boat sail. Besides, the best place to make judgments is not on board.

What one does learn on the water are the conditions under which life is lived on board, and the two basic ingredients: firstly motion and heeling, secondly damp. These are also as much the concern of the builder guided as he may be by the designer. So is experience of the forces to which a boat at sea is subject, and the convenient placing of fittings.

First and foremost, then, the budding designer must have the flair which includes a feel for water and the sea. But is this enough? Definitely not, because designing is not just a question of working out measurements and drawing lines, and this is where the extempore designers fall down; it must be possible for the abstract idea to be converted into a cohesive and lasting construction, and the designer must therefore be capable of translating his idea into an actual creation by means of his drawings by providing all the details required by the builder.

There is no other vehicle or structure that requires such varied and thorough knowledge, both of techniques and technology as a sailing boat. The plumber does not need to know much about masonry or carpentry when he goes to work in a house, and the carpet fitter does not have to worry about what the electrician has done. The naval architect, however, has to know everything, from working with wood and metal to weaving sailcloth, from electricity to the chemistry of plastics; furthermore every technique, which elsewhere would be the concern of a specialist, has to be adapted to the special conditions imposed by a marine environment, quite apart from specific specialist fields such as the rigging. The world of boat is so confined that the component parts are endlessly intertwined.

Again, the aspiring designer cannot study each of the different techniques needed in turn, in the normal way, because it would take far too long and would not really be suitable for his needs anyway; he has to teach himself parts of all aspects as he goes along.

The experience he gains is acquired at the expense of the client who pays the fees, and these can sometimes be very high. The designer rarely reaps much financial benefit; mostly his clients consider that the small number of pieces of paper handed to them are far too expensive — but the same clients will probably not hesitate to pay very dearly for standard plans, often out of date, from some well-known foreign designer!

This situation particularly favours the cut-rate designers who provide only the lines drawing, the sail plan and a vague sketch suggesting the accommodation, and they do very well out of it themselves because the fee is high in relation to time taken. It is then up to the builder and the client to get themselves out of the mess, if they can.

The aim of this book is therefore not only to introduce prople to the profession about which they dream, but to enable anybody interested to acquire a deeper knowledge of the modern sailing vessel.

Pierre Gutelle
Paris, 1983

I

The Environment of the Sailing Boat

There is no doubt that the behaviour of the sailing boat is more complex than that of any other type of vehicle. Whereas the aircraft and the submarine moving through their media depend on air and water respectively, both for propulsion and for support, a sailing boat can only use the energy imparted by air in motion by thrusting her way through the water which, additionally, provides her support. Her behaviour on the water is also affected by the forces developed by air on her sails. There is therefore constant interaction between these two media, and the sailing boat is able to move on account of the combined effects of both fluids. Before examining the way in which a sailing boat functions, it is necessary to become rather better acquainted with the properties of the two media.

Air and water are both fluids, that is to say they are bodies that have no fixed shape. They change shape easily, but doing so does absorb a certain amount of energy. The molecules of which they are made up react upon each other as a result of both pressure and friction. An action that disturbs one molecule is transmitted to neighbouring molecules, the energy being absorbed progressively as it is transformed into heat. Viscosity is the property of a fluid whereby it resists deformation, and, whereas the purely theoretical 'perfect' fluid has zero viscosity, air and water are described as 'imperfect' fluids.

A Air and wind

1 Air

Air is a mixture of gases and is therefore compressible but this property, which complicates the study of flow, is not of interest at subsonic speeds or at ambient temperatures. If a variation in specific volume of 1% is ignored, at normal temperatures the flow of air up to a speed of 50 m/s is the same as the flow of water:

$$50 \text{ m/s} = 180 \text{ km/h} = \text{Beaufort force } 15,$$

which is of course far faster than the speeds normally involved when sailing. In consequence, all aeronautical research relating to flight at slower speeds is relevant to sailing boats, and the aerodynamic and hydrodynamic laws are the same.

The relative density of pure dry air is 0.001 225 at sea level at a temperature of 15° C. Mass density, ρ, which is important when calculating resistance or the dynamic pressure of a fluid in motion, is the ratio of weight to gravity acceleration, g; the value of ρ is 0.125 kg/m^3. Air pressure at sea level is 1 034 kg/cm^2, and viscosity at 15° C is 0.000 001 81 (unit kg sec/m^2). Kinematic viscosity, which is required for the study of flow and frictional resistance, is the ratio of the coefficient of viscosity to fluid density, and is 0.000 145 m^2/s.

All these values vary with temperature, atmospheric pressure and humidity, and this is why appreciable differences may sometimes be found between an area where the winds are of continental origin, dry and hot (in summer), and on the other hand maritime, in which case they are humid and fresher. Helmsmen report that in winter winds are 'stronger' for the same recorded speed.

2 Wind in nature

The intention here is not to delve into details of the meteorological phenomena that give rise to winds; that subject is well covered by books that not only go into the physics involved, but also consider the implications of weather on strategy and navigation. It is enough to remember that wind is air which is in motion because variations in pressure or in temperature cause the density of air masses to differ; heavier masses (colder temperatures or higher pressure) chase the lighter masses.

The mean wind is not constant. In the case of gusts and squalls it varies for meteorological reasons, but it also varies in accordance with the laws of physics, surface eddies being caused by frictional resistance as air passes over the earth. Characteristically, the disturbances that affect the mean wind for meteorological reasons, in an unstable airstream occur in bands of 1000–2000 m and 10–30 km and are large enough to cause the helmsman to consider altering course, or perhaps even to go about onto the opposite tack when beating. On the other hand, when disturbances are of physical origin the intervals between them are too small to be registered by the helmsman, and they will therefore adversely affect the total driving force produced by the sails.

Although frictional eddies are of interest only in the layer up to about 10 m above sea level, the effect of both types of disturbance combined may extend as high as 1500 m, the mean height being 600 m. The more uneven the surface (land has a rougher surface than the sea) and the more unstable the airstream, the higher is the turbulent layer. The regime is unstable when the air is colder than the surface beneath, as in the evening. Table I.I shows these differences clearly.

The lighter the mean wind, the greater is the difference in gusts between mean wind speed and maximum wind speed; the difference is also greater in daytime than at night, and in an unstable rather than a stable airstream. The mean wind speed, as quoted by weather stations, therefore has to be multiplied by a certain factor to obtain either the gust maximum speed or gust mean speed, or a more realistic yacht mean speed. It is this last wind speed that is generally felt on board, and this is why the wind experienced seems stronger than was forecast.

TABLE I.I

HEIGHT IN METRES AFFECTED BY TURBULENCE

NORMAL AIR FLOW			SETTLED AIR FLOW		
Wind force	Land	Sea	Wind force	Land	Sea
1	150	100	1	65	30
2	350	200	2	200	100
3	600	400	3	400	250
4	900	600	4	500	350
5	1200	900	5	650	500
6	1500	1200	6	800	600

TABLE I.II

COEFFICIENTS FOR THE CORRECTION OF WIND SPEEDS

Wind speed	Factor for maximum gust speed	Factor for mean gust speed	Factor for assessing yacht mean speed
Day			
3–4	2	1.6	1.8
5–6	1.8	1.5	1.25
7–8	1.6	1.5	1.25
Night			
3–4	1.9	1.5	1.5
5–6	1.8	1.5	1.5
7–8	1.7	1.5	1.5

Taken from A. WATTS – *Wind & Sailing Boats*

These factors are important when calculations are made for a wind of given strength. Table I.II gives the factors by which to multiply wind speed by day and by night.

The wind gradient, i.e. the way in which wind speed increases with height within the turbulent layer, is affected by two important considerations: the roughness of the surface and the stability of the airstream. Wind speed also increases more quickly with height when the mean wind is strong than when it is light.

Figure I.1 gives examples of the wind gradient in the layer up to 10 m above the surface, showing the difference between stable, neutral and unstable conditions. It is evident that the differences can be considerable when conditions differ, and this can lead to very diverse interpretations, for example when analysing mainsail twist.

Variations in wind speed are accompanied by modifications in direction. At surface level, such modifications can only be horizontal but there is a progressive reduction in the horizontal shift in direction as height increases, and a relative increase in the vertical element. Thus in the horizontal plane the ratio of average downwind longitudinal speed to transverse speed is 0.47 (averaged over 5 minutes) at a height of 1–2 m, and this decreases by 5% each time the height is doubled, up to a height of 50 m. The vertical ratio of only 0.2 reduces more slowly, but the less stable the conditions the more rapid is the change. If the variations are considered over a still shorter time scale, of several seconds, speed differences noted are of the order of about $\pm 15\%$, and shifts in direction are of about $\pm 5°$, with a periodicity of 8–12 seconds.

This again verifies how the disturbances arising solely as a result of friction and those due to meteorological phenomena interact.

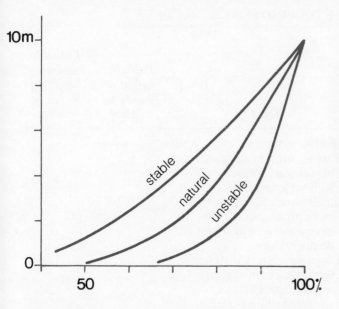

Figure I.1 *How the wind gradient varies with the stability of the airstream.*

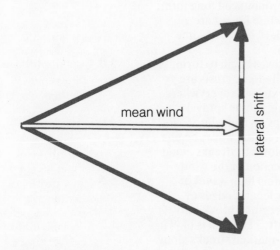

Figure I.2 *The true wind shifts constantly either side of its mean direction.*

In the northern hemisphere, when the wind direction varies for longer periods of several minutes it veers as it freshens, changing direction clockwise, but it will back and return to its initial direction when it eases. This is why it is always best to be on starboard tack in the gusts.

Clearly the structure of the true wind is far from uniform, and the result is that there are often discrepancies when the performance of the boat herself is compared to calculations obtained by testing a model in a towing tank or wind tunnel.

Wind speeds, measured at a height of 10 m, were classified at an international congress held in 1946.

They are graded in forces in accordance with the Beaufort Scale, originally devised by Admiral Sir Francis Beaufort in 1806, based on the amount of sail that a full-rigged frigate could carry.

Table I.III gives the wind speeds in knots that correspond to the various forces. Mean dynamic pressure is given by $q = 0.5\ \rho V^2$ in kg/m². The force $F = C \times q \times A$ on any profile can be calculated from this, assuming that the coefficient C, which corresponds to the particular angle of incidence of the wind to the profile, is known. For example, in the case of a flat plate 1 m² in area, placed at right angles to the wind, with a drag coefficient of about 1.17, dynamic pressure results in an aerodynamic force of 0.06 kg in a force 1 wind, 1.4 kg in force 3 and 6.3 kg in force 5.

Note that dynamic pressure increases as the square of speed, which means that when wind speed doubles the force exerted on the sail is four times greater. This explains why a gust always feels so violent.

When no instruments for measuring wind speed are at hand, the signs listed in Table I.IV indicate the strength of the wind; the actions to take are also given in this table. However, as we have just seen, wind is far from constant and the fact that the actual wind speeds encountered will gust to a maximum of about one and a half to twice mean wind speed has to be taken into consideration.

3 The apparent wind

It is not the true or atmospheric wind that acts on the sails, however, except when the boat is at a stand-still. She creates her own apparent wind the moment that she starts to make way.

When you are running, riding a bicycle or driving in an open car, you feel wind on your face even on a dead calm day. This wind, which you feel because you are moving over the ground, blows at a speed equal to your own velocity, but in the opposite direction (fig. I.3).

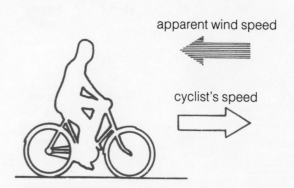

Figure I.3 *When a cyclist is riding his bicycle on a calm day, the apparent wind speed matches his own speed but blows in the opposite direction to that in which he is travelling.*

TABLE I.III

BEAUFORT SCALE OF WIND FORCE

Beaufort wind force	Mean wind speed in knots	Limits of wind speed in knots (Measured at a height of 10 metres above sea level)	(Description)	Sea state	Probable height of waves in metres	Probable maximum height of waves in metres
0	0	Less than 1	Calm	Sea like a mirror.	—	—
1	2	1–3	Light air	Ripples with the appearance of scales are formed, but without foam crests.	0.1	0.1
2	5	4–6	Light breeze	Small wavelets, still short but more pronounced, crests have a glassy appearance and do not break.	0.2	0.3
3	9	7–10	Gentle breeze	Large wavelets. Crests begin to break. Foam of glassy appearance. Perhaps scattered white horses.	0.6	1.0
4	13	11–16	Moderate breeze	Small waves, becoming longer; fairly frequent white horses.	1.0	1.5
5	19	17–21	Fresh breeze	Moderate waves, taking a more pronounced long form; many white horses are formed. (Chance of some spray.)	2.0	2.5
6	24	22–27	Strong breeze	Large waves begin to form; the white foam crests are more extensive everywhere. (Probably some spray.)	3.0	4.0
7	30	28–33	Near gale (US: Moderate gale)	Sea heaps up and white foam from breaking waves begins to be blown in streaks along the direction of the wind.	4.0	5.5
8	37	34–40	Gale (US; Fresh gale)	Moderately high waves of greater length; edges of crests begin to break into spindrift. The foam is blown in well-marked streaks along the direction of the wind.	5.5	7.5
9	44	41–47	Strong gale	High waves. Dense streaks of foam along the direction of the wind. Crests of waves begin to topple, tumble and roll over. Spray may affect visibility.	7.0	10.0
10	52	48–55	Storm (US: Whole gale)	Very high waves with long overhanging crests. The resulting foam in great patches is blown in dense white streaks along the direction of the wind. On the whole the surface of the sea takes a white appearance. Tumbling of the sea becomes heavy and shock like. Visibility affected.	9.0	12.5
11	60	56–63	Violent storm (US: Storm)	Exceptionally high waves. (Small and medium-sized ships might be for a time lost to view behind the waves.)	11.5	16.0

| | | 12 | — | 64 and over | Hurricane | The sea is completely covered with long white patches of foam lying along the direction of the wind. Everywhere the edges of the wave crests are blown into froth. Visibility affected. The air is filled with foam and spray. Sea completely white with driving spray; visibility very seriously affected. | 14 or over | — |

(continued from previous)

The sea is completely
covered with long white
patches of foam lying along
the direction of the wind.
Everywhere the edges of the
wave crests are blown into
froth. Visibility affected.

12 — 64 and over Hurricane The air is filled with foam and 14 or —
spray. Sea completely white over
with driving spray; visibility
very seriously affected.

TABLE I.IV

INDICATIONS OF WIND STRENGTH

Force on land	At sea	Mean wave height	Boats out for a sail or cruising
0 Smoke rises vertically.	Flat calm, no ripples, like a mirror.	0 m	Ideal for motorboats.
1 Leaves move on trees.	Small ripplies without crests.	0.1 m	Sailing boats start to make way.
2 Flags unfurl.	Small wavelets with glassy crests; the sea darkens.	0.2 m	Dinghies with outboards affected by the popple, motion in small cruisers still pleasant. Sailing dinghy crews sit to windward. Cruising boats carry full sail with light genoas.
3 Longer branches are set in motion.	Larger wavelets with crests starting to break. Scattered white horses.	0.6 m	Dinghies with auxiliaries reduce speed. Sailing dinghy crews start to sit out. Light genoas are replaced by heavier ones.
4 Poplars start to sway, dust flies.	Small waves becoming longer. More frequent white horses.	1 m	Dinghies with auxiliaries have to turn back. The motion of small motor cruisers starts to become unpleasant. Sailing dinghy crews sit right out or use the trapeze. Cruising boats change down from genoas to jibs; one reef in the mainsail.
5 Wind whistles in the telephone wires.	Moderate waves, longer, with many white horses. Some spray.	2 m	Small launches take shelter or head into the waves at reduced speed. Sailing dinghies roller reef, and the crew stays out on the trapeze. In larger boats, smaller jibs are set and mizzens handed.
6 All trees in motion, wind whistles loudly in the telephone wires.	Large waves with extensive white foam crests. Some spray.	3 m	Apart from large launches, motorboats take shelter. In small sailing dinghies, the crew reef the mainsail. Small cruisers — two reefs in the main and a No.2 jib; larger boats — reefed mainsails, jibs changed down.
7 Trees agitated violently.	Sea heaps up, the white foam from breaking waves starts to be blown in streaks.	4 m	Larger launches heave to if unable to take shelter. Sailing dinghies are under reefed mainsail alone, or jib alone. Larger boats under way with three reefs in the mainsail and a storm jib.
8 Branches torn off trees, shutters clatter, small branches and light objects blown about.	Moderately high waves of greater length. Edges of crests break into spindrift, foam blown in long, well-marked streaks by the wind.	5.5 m	Only large sailing boats still under way; most are hove to or running before the wind.
9 Chimneys blown down, 10 small trees uprooted, roofs may be damaged.	Waves increasingly high, breaking everywhere, visibility reduced by spray. Sea rolls, surface white as patches of foam are blown in very dense streaks.	7–9 m	It becomes dangerous to stay at sea. Large vessels heave to or run downwind.
11 Trees uprooted, roofs 12 blown away. Dikes damaged. In harbours mooring ropes part.	Sea completely white with driving spray, blown in the wind. Small and medium ships might be lost to view behind waves. Visibility greatly reduced. Air filled with foam and spray.	11–14 m	Large ships may suffer damage to their superstructure.

On the other hand, when an atmospheric wind is blowing, its direction and speed combined with your direction and speed of motion results in the apparent wind, which is the wind that you actually feel on your face (fig. I.4).

Figure I.4 *The same cyclist, riding on a day when the wind is blowing at about 45° to the direction in which he is moving. The apparent wind is the resultant of the true wind and his own speed.*

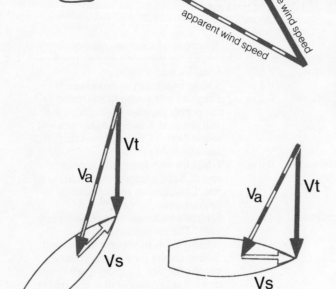

The direction and speed of the apparent wind are governed by the relative direction and speed of the true wind and those resulting from your own motion (that is boat speed, fig. I.5). Furthermore, a variation in either of the two component winds affects the apparent wind (fig. I.6). As can be seen in the figures, as a general rule the apparent wind blows from nearer the bow than the true wind, and its speed is greater than that of the true wind when it blows from forward of the beam; when blowing from abaft the beam it is less strong than the true wind, but the actual line where the two blow at the same strength depends on the relative speeds of the true wind and boat speed.

Figure I.5 *Given constant values for true wind and boat speed, the speed and direction of the apparent wind changes according to the point of sailing; it will blow from nearer the bow, and will be stronger than the true wind when the boat is close-hauled, but less strong when the boat bears away beyond a beam reach.*

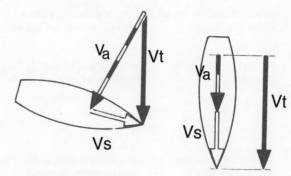

Figure I.6 *Any variation in the speed of the boat or of the true wind will always cause an alteration in the speed and direction of the apparent wind. Here are four examples:*
a When the true wind increases, the apparent wind increases and frees: the helmsman can choose whether to luff up or to stay on course, easing the sheets and accelerating.
b When the boat is slowed by a wave, the apparent wind decreases but frees. This is why the helmsman should luff up when climbing a wave.

c When the true wind eases, not only is apparent wind speed reduced but the boat is headed as well: if the boat is already hard on the wind there is no alternative but to bear away.
d When the boat accelerates (say on the back of a wave), the apparent wind increases but heads. The sails must be hardened in, but if the boat is already close-hauled the helmsman has to bear away.

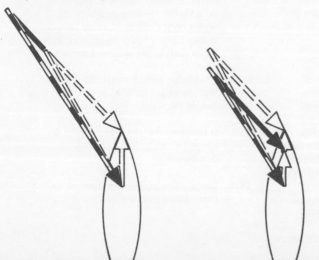

Turbulence and variations in the true wind are therefore amplified at those apparent wind angles where sail trimming has to be most precise.

There are mathematical relationships between the following vectors and angles: the three vectors are true wind velocity V_t, apparent wind velocity V_a, and boat speed V_s; the angles are γ between the true wind and the course, β between the apparent wind and the course, $(\gamma - \lambda)$ between the true wind and the boat's centreline, and $(\beta - \lambda)$ between the apparent wind and the centreline. Thus, when the

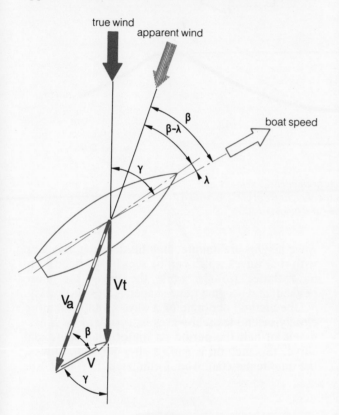

Figure I.7   *The speed vectors and angles involved in the true wind–apparent wind–boat speed triangle.*

value of V_s can be obtained from the speedometer, that of V_a from the anemometer and $(\beta - \lambda)$ is indicated by the wind vane (λ being estimated), V_t and γ can be calculated:

$$\tan \gamma = V_a \sin \beta/(V_s - V_a \cos \beta)$$
$$V_t = \sqrt{V_a^2 + V_s^2 - 2V_aV_s \cos \beta} = V_a \sin \beta/\sin \gamma.$$

Equally, the strength and direction of the apparent wind V_a and angle β can be calculated when the value of the true wind V_t and the angle γ are known, as well as the anticipated boat speed, V_s.

$$\left.\begin{array}{l} \text{Tan } \beta = V_t \sin \gamma/(V_s \pm V_t \cos \gamma) \\ V_a = \sqrt{V_t^2 + V_s^2 \pm 2V_tV_s \cos \gamma} \\ \quad = V_t \sin \gamma/\sin \beta \end{array}\right\} \begin{array}{l} + \text{ if } \gamma < 90° \\ \\ - \text{ if } \gamma > 90°. \end{array}$$

B Water and waves

1 Water

The same details relating to the properties of water are required as for air, but the difference between fresh and salt water has to be made. Given a temperature of 15° C, the relative density or specific gravity of fresh water is almost 1 (0.998 to be exact), while that of salt water with a salinity of 35°/∞ is 1.026. A body floating in fresh water therefore displaces a greater volume of water than it does in salt water.

Variations in temperature affect density more than do variations in salinity, and density is greatest at the North Pole where temperature is low (approximately 4°) and salinity is also low on account of the large amount of fresh water that comes from melting ice.

Mass density, ρ, is 102 for fresh water and 104.6 for salt water. When these values are compared with those for air it is evident that resistance to motion (which is a function of ρ) is 816 times greater in water than in air; to put it another way, the value for air drag is equal to that of hydrodynamic drag when speed (which is squared) in the air is 28.6 times greater than speed in the water.

The viscosity, μ, of sea water at 0.000 116 kg s/m² is of course greater than that of fresh water, 0.000 122, but again viscosity varies more with temperature than with salinity. At 15° C kinematic viscosity, υ, is 0.000 001 14 m²/s and 0.000 001 19 m²/s for fresh and salt water respectively.

The viscosity of water is some 65 to 70 times greater than that of air, depending on temperature, pressure and salinity.

2 Waves

The naval architect is concerned with two different types of waves: the natural waves that occur in the seas and oceans, and those that are formed when the hull moves through the water, absorbing a considerable amount of the power required for propulsion. These two types of waves have a certain number of theoretical factors in common, and these should be known, whether it is the resistance of a hull to movement through the water that is being studied, or the motion of the vessel, or the effect that each has on the other. The speed of a sailing boat, whose propulsive power is limited to the driving force produced by the wind on her sails at any particular instant, is in fact reduced as soon as her equilibrium is disturbed by the slightest wave.

Furthermore, a vessel's safety can be said to be limited by the size of waves, and the various factors associated with them.

Whatever its origin, a disturbance of a mass of liquid causes the formation of a progressive wave which spreads out from the centre of the distur-

17

bance, oscillating freely. In the oceans these oscillations are seas which, when they have travelled sufficiently far, can be seen as straight transverse waves parallel to each other and at right angles to the direction in which they are travelling (fig. I.8). The parameters of such a wave are its length, λ, the distance between two successive crests (or troughs); its period, T, the time interval between the passage of two successive crests past the same point; its velocity, C, the speed at which it travels; its height (or depth), H, double the amplitude A of the vertical displacement of the water particles.

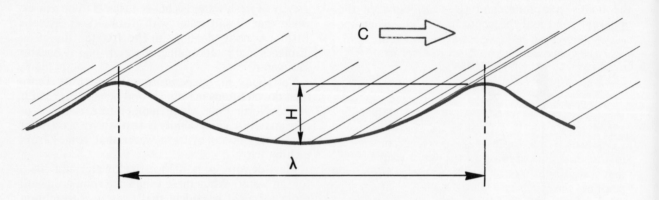

Figure I.8   *Wave profile measurements. C: velocity of propagation H: twice amplitude, height from crest to trough λ: wavelengths between crests (or troughs)*

a Wave form

In theory, the forms of waves are taken to resemble several different mathematical curves. The simplest of these, a sine curve (fig. I.9), can be applied regardless of the ratio of wave height to length. Although it does not correspond exactly to the shape of a real wave, the sinusoidal wave form makes it easier to study the different components of the irregular wave patterns met at sea, and the relationship between wave encounter and the motion of the boat. Sine curves can be drawn to the point where wave heights are infinite, and this does not match up with real waves which can be seen, in particular, to have flatter troughs while the crests are more peaked, and become ridge-shaped relatively quickly.

One method of obtaining a wave profile that more closely resembles real waves is to superpose a harmonic of half the period on the original sinusoidal curve; this method is named after Sir John Stokes, the mathematician who formulated it (fig. I.10).

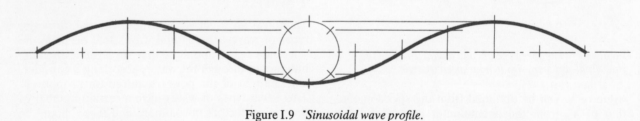

Figure I.9   *Sinusoidal wave profile.*

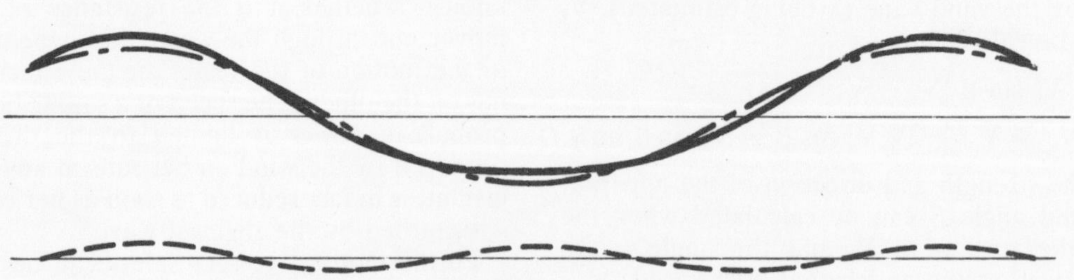

Figure I.10   *Pure sinusoidal wave profile (dash-dotted curve) compared with a Stokes wave, formed by superposing a wave with a length equal to half wavelength, λ/2.*

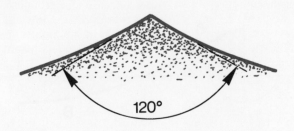

Figure I.11 *The limit of the Stokes wave form occurs when wave height reaches the critical value of 0.14λ: the crest then forms an angle of 120°, which is similar to that of a real wave.*

When height H reaches the critical value of 0.14λ, the curve peaks to reverse at an angle of 120° (fig. I.11).

With this wave form, the longitudinal movement in the direction of wave propagation, superposed onto the orbital motion of the water particles, can amount to as much as 2–3% of wave velocity, and in consequence can greatly modify the speed of the particles which would no longer follow a circular orbit. This disadvantage is usually avoided by turning to a third curve, Gerstner's trochoidal wave form, which is one of the cycloid family.

The trochoidal wave (fig. I.12) may be defined as the path traced by a point on a circle with a radius r = H/2, within a circle with a radius R = λ/2π rolling along and beneath a straight line parallel to the still water surface.

Fig. I.13 shows that, as the wave passes on, a particle on the surface does indeed follow a circular path, the diameter of the circle being equal to the height of the wave; rotation is in the same direction as that in which the wave is travelling. Thus a cork, floating on the surface, moves forward on the crest of the wave, back again in the trough to a point vertically beneath its starting point, and then back further after the trough has passed before finally advancing again to its starting point as the next crest approaches. It therefore moves horizontally and vertically around a fixed point.

The limit to the trochoidal wave form occurs when r = R (fig. I.14) and, consequently r = λ/2π or 0.16λ. The crest is much more pointed than in the Stokes wave (fig.I.11). In order to maintain equal volume despite the vertical asymmetry of crests and troughs in both the trochoidal and Stokes wave forms, the line of the orbit centres must be above still water level by a quantity $h = r^2/2R$ or $\pi r^2/\lambda$ (fig. I.15). In all other respects the wave characteristics are similar to those of a sinusoidal wave form.

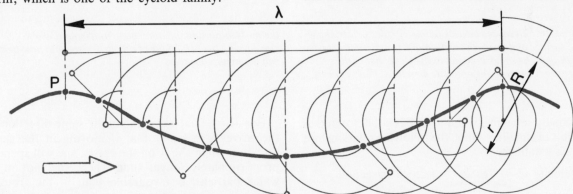

Figure I.12 *Gerstner's trochoidal wave form is the path traced by point P at the end of radius r = H/2 of a circle that is within a circle of radius R = λ/2π, which is rolling* beneath a straight line in a direction parallel to the displacement of the wave.

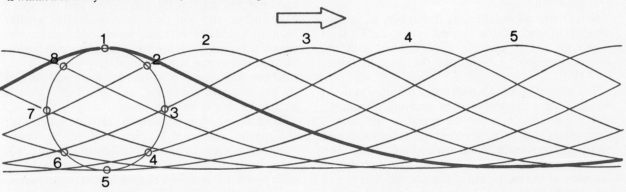

Figure I.13 *As a wave passes, a point on the surface moves progressively from position 1 to position 8 around* the circumference of a circle, the diameter of which is equal to wave height.

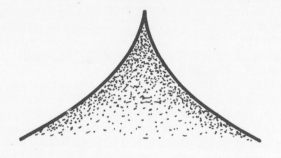

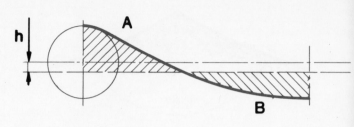

Figure I.14 *The limit is when r = R: the trochoidal form becomes a simple cycloid with a reversal point corresponding to the crest; this is most unrealistic when compared to an actual wave.*

Figure I.15 *To equalize areas A and B, namely the volumes above and below still water level, the line of the orbit centres of the trochoid must be raised by a height $h = \pi r^2/\lambda$.*

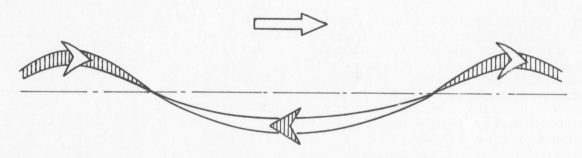

Figure I.16 *Because particles follow circular orbits, those at the surface and inside the wave move fastest on the crests, travelling in the same direction as the wave, but in the troughs they move in the opposite direction. This is one of* the most important phenomena to understand when considering the behaviour of a boat in seas, and how best to sail her through waves.

Broadly speaking, when a wave is not deformed as a result of shoaling water, the following relationships can be established:

Velocity $C = \sqrt{g\lambda/2\pi} \simeq 1.25\sqrt{\lambda}$ m/second

Wavelength $\lambda = C^2 2\pi/g \simeq 0.64C^2$ metres

Period $T = \sqrt{2\pi\lambda/g} \simeq 0.8\sqrt{\pi}$ seconds

(in metres and seconds; g, acceleration due to gravity = 9.81 m/s^2).

Sometimes wave (angular) frequency, ω, is considered instead of the period; $\omega = 2\pi/T$. It is important not to confuse wave velocity with the orbital speed of particles on the circumference, $v = H/T$.

The orbital speed at which water particles move in waves is very important when studying directional stability in seas, because the speed of the boat is composed partly of the speed of the water itself, and major differences in relative speed are found. The particles at the surface move in the same direction as the wave at the crests, but in the reverse direction in the troughs (fig. I.16). The motion of water particles must not be confused with surface flow caused by wind, which will be considered later.

Because a boat travelling in the same direction as the wave is in water that is moving in the same direction when she is on the crests, she will spend a proportionately longer time where the motion of water particles is favourable than in the troughs where the direction is adverse and, consequently, she benefits from an overall increase in speed. At best, when the sum of the boat's speed through the water and that of orbital speed equals wave velocity, the boat will stay on the wave crest and her speed over the ground will then be considerably greater than it would be in calm water. Of course, the opposite occurs when the boat is heading into waves, but the difference is proportionately smaller.

These differences in speed are increased further by the slope of the wave, the effect of which is similar to that of orbital motion.

Theoretically it is possible to calculate speed over the ground, corrected for each point of the wave.

Between these extreme positions (high and low), the velocity of the particles varies in direction, but at each position it is always perpendicular to the radius, as illustrated in fig. I.17. The direction of water particle flow has a major effect on sailing boat behaviour, as will be seen in Chapter VIII.

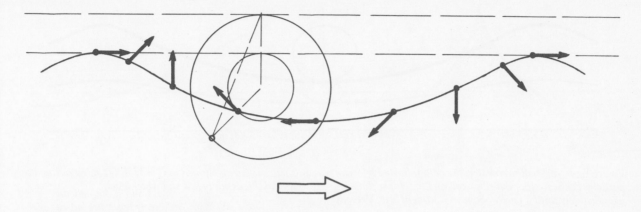

Figure I.17   *Direction of water particle flow at various points of the wave.*

It is also important to understand the effect that orbital motion has on the acceleration to which a vessel is subject. When a body rotates in a circle about a centre point, centrifugal acceleration acts outwards. It is known that, in the case of water particles in a wave, the direction in which the resultant of centrifugal acceleration and gravity acceleration acts is perpendicular to the surface at every point of the wave; resultant acceleration is less than g at the crest, but greater than g in the trough. Given a wave of 36.0 m, moving at 18.9 knots for example, the centrifugal acceleration to which a particle is subject at the surface will be 0.2 g ; the resultant acceleration will vary from 0.8 g at the peak of the crest to 1.2 at the bottom of the trough. The consequence is a reduction in the boat's apparent weight on the crests (she will float higher in the water and be less stable) while the reverse occurs in the troughs (fig. I.24). This difference can be as much as 1.5 to 1.

These diverse effects, due to the orbital motion of water particles in waves, explain the phenomenon of 'surfing', and the major increase in speed involved, as well as the many disturbances met when determining the horizontal, which cause wave heights to be overestimated so frequently.

The orbits in which the particles move decrease with depth; every time depth increases by λ/9, the radius of the orbit is approximately halved, to the point where orbital motion ceases at a depth equal to λ (fig. I.18). Thus, at every depth, curves of equal pressure, which are trochoidal like the surface curve, are traced by the water particles as they execute orbits of continuously decreasing diameter.

When water shoals, the circular orbit is modified and becomes elliptical in shape; this ellipse becomes progressively flatter until finally, when velocity reaches a critical value equal to $\sqrt{gH}$, or when wavelength λ = 2πH, movement is simply back and forth in a straight line (fig. I.19).

As depth decreases progressively, for example when a wave reaches a beach, all the energy stored in the wave is transmitted to a smaller volume of water; wavelength and velocity are reduced by friction but wave height increases, causing the crest to become unstable and break (fig. I.20).

The same occurs when a wave encounters a current that is flowing in the opposite direction and which reduces its velocity. Generally waves start to break when the current velocity is a quarter of wave velocity. Conversely, wave heights are reduced when current and wave are both moving in the same direction. Such modifications to wave shapes are often met at sea, and are due to the conservation of the energy stored in the wave, in other words the value of the energy does not alter.

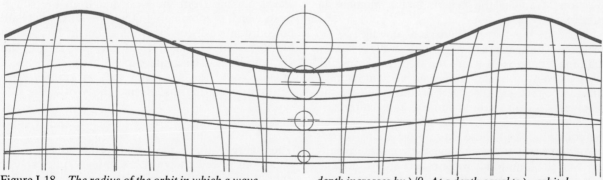

Figure I.18   *The radius of the orbit in which a wave particle moves decreases with depth, being halved each time depth increases by λ/9. At a depth equal to λ, orbital radius is equal to amplitude/512, a = A/512.*

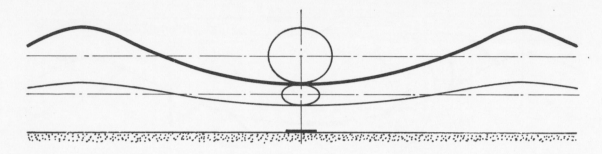

Figure I.19   *In shallower water, the path followed by wave particles is not circular but elliptical, and the ellipse flattens progressively until it finally becomes a straight line. Velocity* *in shallow water is limited to C = √gh (g, acceleration due to gravity, h, depth below still water level).*

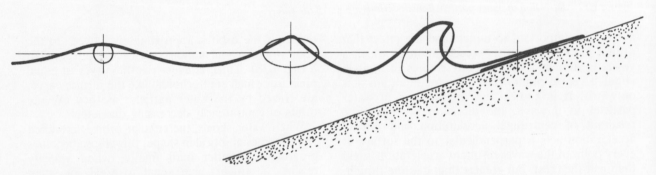

Figure I.20   *When the wave reaches a beach, the reduction in the depth of the water causes the orbit to be transformed from circular to elliptical, the axis of the ellipse tilting* *forward to the point where the crest becomes unstable and breaks. The motion of the particles then ceases to be orbital and becomes reciprocating.*

b Compound wave patterns

The single wave that we have so far been considering is found only in exceptional circumstances. Normal waves met at sea result from a number of wave trains, of varying speed, height and direction.

In the case of trochoidal waves, the wave movements combine at the level where particle motion is orbital in a relatively complex form which introduces horizontal displacement in addition to vertical motion. Consequently, in order to simplify the problem, seas are assumed to be sinusoidal in form, there being relatively little difference between the two wave forms when the steepness ratio H/λ is small. The superposition of waves is then simply a question of adding the heights at the moment in question, t.

The three wave forms illustrated in   fig.I.21 could be, for example, 1 ground swell, 2 waves resulting from a local wind, the direction being the same as that of 1, and 3 a swell, arriving from a different direction, generated as the result of the passage of a depression at some distant latitude.

It can be seen in 4 that the pattern produced by the combination of these three wave trains is irregular; some waves become higher than those resulting from the local wind, while others are lower. The way in which real waves combine can easily be observed on beaches where there are almost always at least two components; one wave train arrives from the open sea while the other is reflected by the shore.

This also explains why waves of exceptional height are sometimes encountered.

When compound wave trains are considered in the horizontal plane instead of vertically, it can be seen that the wave patterns which emerge correspond to what actually occurs at sea, with patches of calmer water as well as other areas where waves are steeper.

Given a sufficiently long swell initially, as occurs in high latitudes in the southern hemisphere, it can be readily understood that the superposition of waves coming from the west and from the southwest, which predominate in these regions, can result not only in waves of exceptional height but also in the formation of 'corridors' where wave heights are very different. This could explain the differences of opinion as to the sea states met by various competitors during the first Round the World Race.

c Wave energy

The energy stored in a wave (that this can be enormous is well known) is a combination of kinetic energy, due to the orbital motion of the water particles, and potential energy, due to the difference

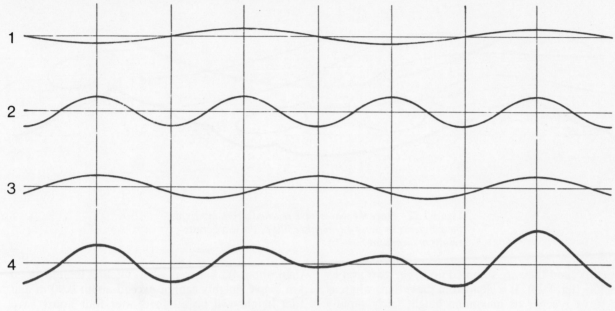

Figure I.21 *When several sinusoidal wave forms are superposed, their heights at a given moment, t, are added together.*

in the heights of wave crests and troughs. Equal quantities of kinetic energy and potential energy make up total energy, E, which is equal to

$$1/8 \; \rho g \lambda H^2 \simeq 125 \lambda H^2.$$

In the case of a wave 50 m long and 2.5 m high, total energy is 20 060 kg/m or 267 hp per metre of crest. It is easy to appreciate how destructive waves can be when their progress is halted by an obstacle, and why they can shift enormous rocks. At St-Jean-de-Luz, for example, a block of concrete weighing some tens of tonnes was carried from the outside of the Socoa jetty to the inside, where it can still be seen. In addition, the pressure exerted on an obstacle fluctuates wildly, and has been found in experimental tests to vary from 0–70 tonnes per m² in the space of 1/100th of a second.

d Wave generation

Apart from astronomical forces which act on the water of the oceans and raise the tides, the main reason for the formation of waves is friction, which occurs when air moves over the water's surface. Because wind has travelled for a considerable distance, air flow is inevitably turbulent (Chapter II.3b, p. 34), and the resulting variation in pressure at the interface of the two fluids causes waves of very small amplitude to form. However, if these small waves are to continue to grow, their length must exceed about 17 mm, and this corresponds to a velocity of about $\frac{1}{2}$ knot. Below this figure the surface tension of the water prevents the formation of waves. Surface tension may be modified in certain circumstances, such as by a film of oil or a sprinkling of

dust, and this is why, in a calm, ripples do not form over the entire surface but are interspersed with patches of absolutely unruffled water. The wind must be blowing at least at about 4 knots if it is to generate waves large enough to grow in size.

It may also be assumed that at lower speeds air flow low remains laminar.

Once in motion, the two fluids (air and water) react upon each other, and this increases the size of the waves. When they have reached a certain height, air flow becomes unstable and separates from the surface of the water; this causes an eddy, which forms to leeward of the crest and moves in the reverse direction. As this eddy passes over the surface of the water, friction accelerates the orbital motion of the water particles, and this increases the length of the wave (fig. I.22).

The confused small waves that are formed initially gradually become more ordered. The relative speed of the shortest of them differs more from wind speed than the relative speed of the longer waves; the shorter waves grow rapidly and break, disappearing and leaving room only for the longer waves. This process continues as long as the energy of the wind exceeds the energy absorbed by frictional resistance, to the point where wave velocity reaches about four-fifths of wind speed.

Thus the height of waves, ignoring all other external factors such as geographical features,tidal streams, depths etc., is governed by wind speed, the length of time that the wind has blown, and the fetch, the distance of open water over which it has blown. The Norwegian oceanographer Harald Sverdrup, after years of work, established laws that determine wave heights as a function of these

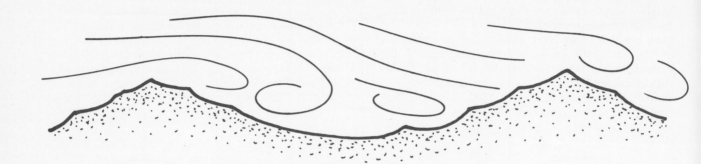

Figure I.22 *Once the waves have reached a certain height, the difference in pressure on either side of the wave crests results in form drag.*

factors, and they are summed up in the two graphs below (fig. I.23). It is clear from these that, whereas a wave reaches its maximum height fairly rapidly (after 25–30 hours), wavelengths continue to increase for a much longer period. For example, the graphs show that a 30 km/h wind, blowing for ten hours, will raise 1.50 m high seas if fetch is greater than about 90 km, but when fetch is limited to 20 km, wave heights cannot exceed about 0.90 m and that height will be attained after four hours have elapsed. This explains why the seas in latitudes near 40° S can become so enormous: quite apart from the particular conditions of wind and current in those waters, fetch is virtually unlimited.

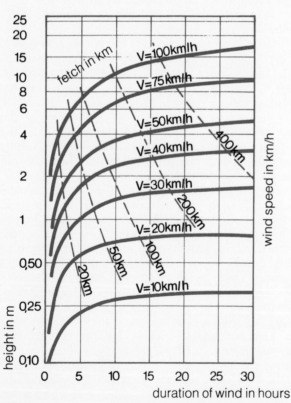

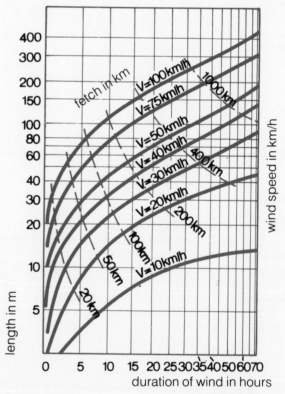

Figure I.23 *Graphs reprinted from J. Baader's* Cruceros y lanchas veloces, *which enable wave height and length to be determined given (a) wind speed, (b) duration of the wind,* (c) fetch, or distance of open water to windward of the observer.

Once a wave is steep enough (steepness is the height : length ratio) for the wind to create a sufficient difference in pressure between the face and the back (fig. I.24), the crest will rise and the steepness of the face will increase considerably until the moment comes when the crest breaks on account of the direction of action of the resultant of gravity and centrifugal acceleration due to orbital motion on the one part and the force of the wind on the other.

The steepness of the wave face, and the difference in the speed of the surface water at the bow and at the stern due to orbital motion, can cause a boat to pitchpole, that is to say, to be turned over completely stern over bow by a following sea (fig. I.25). Pitchpoling only occurs when waves are able to grow to a huge size. Miles Smeeton has described the experience, which he suffered aboard *Tzu-Hang* 1 600 km from the coast of Chile.

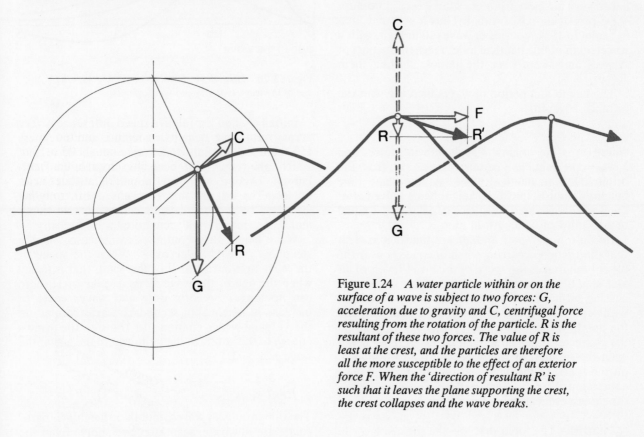

Figure I.24   *A water particle within or on the surface of a wave is subject to two forces: G, acceleration due to gravity and C, centrifugal force resulting from the rotation of the particle. R is the resultant of these two forces. The value of R is least at the crest, and the particles are therefore all the more susceptible to the effect of an exterior force F. When the 'direction of resultant R' is such that it leaves the plane supporting the crest, the crest collapses and the wave breaks.*

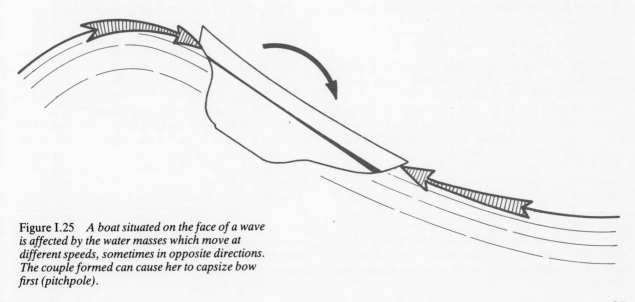

Figure I.25   *A boat situated on the face of a wave is affected by the water masses which move at different speeds, sometimes in opposite directions. The couple formed can cause her to capsize bow first (pitchpole).*

The amount of energy that is dissipated when a crest breaks is enormous, as can be imagined when it is remembered that the tons of water that break per metre of crest can move at a speed of as much as 30 knots down a slope of some 30°.

The waves that spread outward from the zone where the wind is blowing decay progressively as they are attenuated by the viscosity of the water and by surface tension, but major swells can be experienced very far away from the source region because wave propagation is so rapid. Thus it was that, in a flat calm in 1934, a series of waves 10 m high, with a wavelength of one nautical mile, reached the port of Algiers and swept over the jetties, shifting them 400 m.

The length and period of waves increase with the distance covered:

$$\lambda_d = \lambda_o + 0.0018 \ D$$

where λ_o is the original wavelength in metres and λ_d the wavelength at a certain distance, D, from the origin; D is in nautical miles. At the same time heights diminish, the initial height being halved after the wave has covered a distance in miles that is equal to one third of its length in metres.

Because both water and air are fluids, it is clear that the friction occurring when one passes over the other both brakes the speed of the lower layers of air and sets the surface layer of the water in motion, causing surface currents, the speed of which reduces with depth. The speed of flow of such a current, and the depth of the layer of water affected, depend on the character of air flow (laminar when there is not even the smallest of wavelets, and then turbulent), on the speed of the wind and on the stage of wave generation. Broadly, surface flow is proportional to the square of mean wave height, and it is affected by the fact that the face and back of a wave are asymmetric. The force that sets the surface layer in motion therefore results not just from friction but also from pressure differences or form drag, and can be expressed as

$$F = \rho_{air} \ KV^2 = \rho_{water} \ K'(V - C)^2$$

K and K' being the coefficients of frictional resistance and form drag, while V is wind speed at the reference level fo 10 m above sea level.

Clearly a relatively greater force will be exerted on small waves because their relative speed (V − C) is greater, and this indicates clearly that it is small waves that create larger waves.

Wave generation can also be explained as the transfer of energy from the air to the water due to the forces of frictional resistance and form drag[10]; figure I.26 shows how the different characteristics of waves vary with their growth, in other words, with increasing wavelength and wave velocity and, consequently, with the increase in the ratio of wave speed C to wind speed V, C ÷ V being termed the age of the wave.

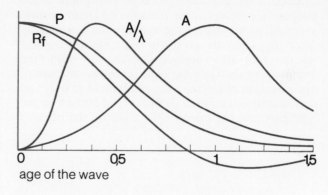

Figure I.26 *How wave characteristics vary with the age of the wave (wave speed/wind speed).*

Initially, when the relative speed difference is very great, form drag is at its maximum and steepness H/λ increases rapidly to a value of about 0.1, at which point the crest becomes unstable and collapses, forming what are popularly called white horses. The energy that is released can only be absorbed by a more rapid increase in wavelength and, consequently, an increase in wave velocity.

Wave height then continues to increase, but the steepness ratio H/λ decreases. When the speed of the wave approaches that of the wind, that is to say when the age of the wave nears a value of 1, there can no longer be form drag and waves cease to increase in height, but secondary waves formed on the original wave continue to transfer the wind's energy to the latter, to the point where the age of the wave is 1.5–2.

e Real seas

The dimensions of waves, and their heights in particular, are always exaggerated by sailors. Even the most respected, like La Pérouse, speak of 60 m seas; Dumont D'Urville is much closer to the truth when referring to 30 m waves, although these can only occur in the desolate Antarctic Ocean. In fact, from the deck of a boat that has just passed the crest and is sailing down the sloping face of a wave, a false impression is obtained of the height of the next wave ahead, and a good deal of experience is required to adjust the apparent height to a realistic value.

True heights vary from the few millimetres of ripples to about 30 m in the great storms of the Roaring Forties, but 94% of ocean waves are under 5 m high; those most frequently observed are about 1.5 m.

Length, which varies from a few centimetres to a mile, is hard to measure and waves are therefore generally classified by their periods, measured in seconds, that of capillary waves being 0.07–2 s, small waves 2–5 s, larger waves 5–15 s, and ocean rollers 15–30 s. Most of the sea's energy is stored in waves with a period of 5–50 s. Broadly speaking, storms produce waves with a 12–15 s period, while 6–9 s waves are common in the Atlantic. The period of the tides is about 10 000 s, and that of tsunamis (often wrongly referred to as tidal waves) resulting from submarine earthquakes 1000 s.

Sea states are classified as shown in Table I.V, just as winds are classified in forces.

TABLE I.V
DOUGLAS SEA SCALE

Degree	State of sea	Height of wave from crest to trough in metres
0	Calm	0
1	Smooth	0 –0.10
2	Slight	0.10–0.50
3	Moderate	0.50–1.25
4	Rough	1.25–2.50
5	Very rough	2.50–4.00
6	High	4.00–6.00
7	Very high	6.00–9.00
8	Precipitous	9.00–14.00
9	Vast	> 14.00

f Statistical representation of waves

We have been considering only individual waves up to now, but reality of course is very different; waves come in groups of varying heights and lengths as a result of wave trains combining with each other. Fig. I.27 shows the waves that passed a particular point, as measured by a wave-recording buoy. Except for the height : length ratio, the overall profile is the same as that of the various individual waves that followed each other past this point.

Similarly photogrammetric analysis showing the contours of part of the surface of the sea (fig. I.28), or just an aerial photograph, indicate clearly how irregular waves are, not only when considered parallel with the wind direction but also at right angles to it. A crest never extends far, and disappears rapidly when another appears. Nevertheless, the observer is often struck by the fact that, over a period which is often of considerable length, the surface appears almost to have a regular pattern to it. This enables oceanographers to describe waves statistically, to forecast the seas that will occur, and to study the behaviour and motion of a boat.

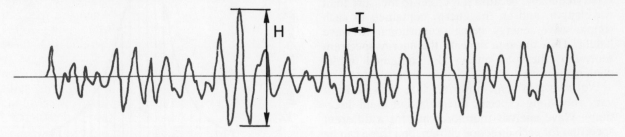

Figure I.27   *A record of individual waves, from which the seas can be studied. H = height   T = period, the time interval in seconds between the passage of two crests*

Figure I.28   *Photogrammetric relief showing the superposition of three wave trains with wavelengths of 36 m, 122 m and 72 m, and heights of 1.20 m, 2.40 m and 1.80 m respectively. Each line corresponds to a certain contour level above or below still water level; the continuous lines are heights and the broken lines troughs.*

Such studies are based on particular wave characteristics extracted from records of actual seas, generally on the actual height (the vertical distance from crest to trough), the average height of all waves, or the average height of the highest one-third of the waves (termed significant wave height by the oceanographers). Similarly a distinction is made between the period and the average of all periods.

Given these details, various aspects of waves can be studied. First there is the frequency with which the different waves occur — in other words, the percentage distribution of waves of different lengths or periods (fig. I.29). The distribution of waves of different heights as a function of wavelength is important. Take, for example, a wave that is a compound of two simple waves, one long and high, the other shorter and smaller. As in the line spectrum in fig. I.30, the lengths of the two ordinates H1 and H2 are proportional to the heights of the waves, and the abscissae to wavelengths λ1 and λ2.

If a sea formed by the compounding of a great number of different waves is now analysed, a continuous spectrum is obtained by connecting the ends of the ordinates of the waves (fig. I.31).

Oceanographers generally base their studies on wave frequency, because it is easier to measure than wavelength, and on the energy contained in each simple wave, energy being proportional to wave height. Thus the area beneath the energy spectrum represents the total energy, E, contained in the composite wave.

We have also seen, however, that waves do not vary only along a specific direction, but in all directions. Wave analysis therefore calls for a different spectrum for each direction chosen, and these can be presented in two- or three-dimensional form (fig. I.32).

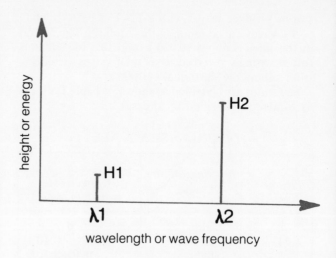

Figure I.30 *Line spectrum of constituent waves, based either on their length and height, or on wave frequency and wave energy.*

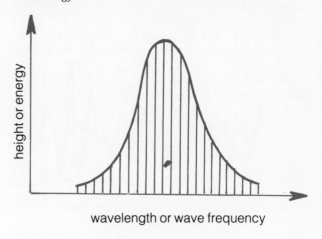

Figure I.31 *Continuous spectrum.*

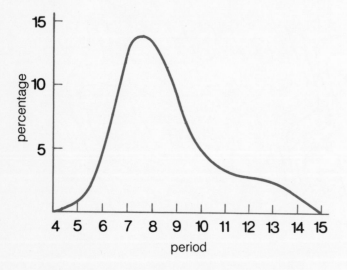

Figure I.29 *Percentage distribution or spectrum of the periods of the waves that make up a sea: e.g. here 14% of waves have a 7.6 second period.*

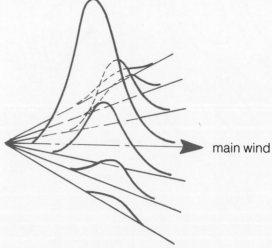

Figure I.32 *Spacial spectrum showing how waves spread out to either side of the main wind direction.*

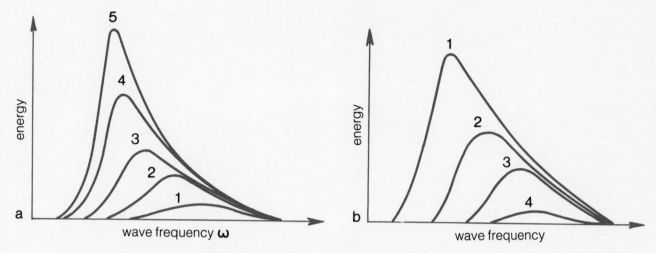

Figure I.33 *Growth (a) and decay (b) spectra.*

Lastly, the strength of the wind of the moment has to be considered, and a number of spectra obtained, each corresponding to a different wind force. The growth of waves over a period as a function of the duration of the wind can be studied in the same way, as can their progressive decay after the wind has dropped (fig. I.33). It is clear from these graphs that large waves (decreasing values of wave frequency ω) do not occur before a certain time has elapsed and, equally, that they are the first to disappear when the wind drops.

The statistics needed for calculating wave spectra are provided mainly by weather ships, but local research (for example in waters where racing takes place, or prior to building a marina) can be undertaken with special wave-recording buoys anchored offshore; the information obtained is transmitted by radio and recorded on shore. It can then be processed mathematically to provide the wave spectra required so that the conditions to which the boat or the marina will be subject can be reproduced in a test tank or for a model.

II
Aero- and Hydrodynamics

Now that we know the characteristics of the two fluids that concern the sailing boat, it is a question of seeing how they affect her, and we therefore have to touch on the two fields of fluid mechanics, namely aerodynamics and hydrodynamics.

Because the speeds involved here are relatively low (below 50 m/s), and the variation in pressure cannot produce appreciable variations in the volume of the air, the phenomena with which we are concerned can be considered as similar for both air and water.

Equally it can be stated that it makes no difference whether the body moves through the fluid, or whether the body is motionless and the fluid flows past it, assuming of course that speeds are the same and flow is steady.

1 Streamlines

When flow is steady (stable and of uniform speed), particles in the fluid follow a constant course along streamlines, and these streamlines can be made visible in a test tank or a wind tunnel by introducing coloured liquid or smoke into the fluid. When flow is being studied in two dimensions only, that is in plan, the surface can be powdered with grains of aluminium; a photograph, with exposure timed to match the speed of flow, shows the direction of motion of the grains, and their speed can be calculated from the distances that they have moved.

An alternative method is the electric analogy process, perfected in France by J. Pérès and L. Malavard. An electric current establishes a potential difference between the upper and lower edges of a piece of special conducting paper. It can be confirmed with a sensor that constant potential differences are shown by lines running parallel to the edges, and these equipotential lines correspond to the streamlines.

When a curved profile of some sort is marked out on the sheet with conducting material, and a wire is run from a point on the shape to a resistor which connects the upper and lower edges (fig. II.1), the shapes of the equipotential lines change in accordance with the pattern of flow around the profile. The exact shape of the equipotential lines can be found with the sensor, that is to say the path followed by the streamlines; the differences in speed and the corresponding pressure differences can then be calculated mathematically.

This process does not of course take account of the effects of friction or the turbulence that results from friction, and it is therefore only used in connection with perfect fluids. Nevertheless, it makes it possible to explain a number of basic concepts.

2 Theory of flow in perfect fluids

In fluid mechanics, flow in a perfect fluid is not affected by viscosity, and is called potential flow. The theory of potential flow makes it possible to resolve problems relating to flow around an object, either mathematically or by the electric analogy process just described, or by a combination of the two.

Theoretically the fluid flows along streamlines, one of which is the dividing streamline between the two streams which pass on either side of the object or, if flow is studied in the vertical plane, one above the upper surface, the other below the lower surface.

The dividing streamline terminates at the stagnation point (fig. II.2) where velocity is zero. Total pressure p_t is equal to the sum of the static pressure of the fluid, p, and the dynamic pressure q, and $q = \frac{1}{2}\rho V_0{}^2$; this is derived from Bernoulli's principle, $p + \frac{1}{2}\rho V^2 = $ Constant. V_o is the free stream velocity of undisturbed flow well upstream of the stagnation point.

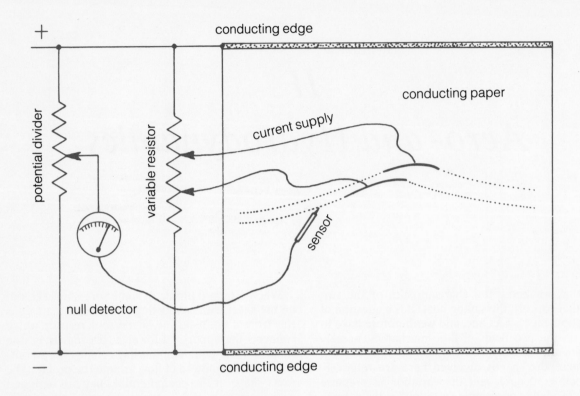

Figure II.1 *The shape of streamlines can be determinated by the electric analogy process. When an electric current is passed through a sheet of special paper, a potential difference is created between its two sides. When there is no disturbing influence, the equipotential lines run parallel to each other and to the edges at top and bottom, but when the profile to be studied is marked out on the paper, it causes the equipotential lines to alter their shapes. In order to simulate the pattern of flow, the profile is connected to a current which is adjusted so that the shape of the dividing streamline, on either side of which flow divides, is satisfactory. The equipotential lines that correspond to streamlines are found with a sensor and a null meter.*

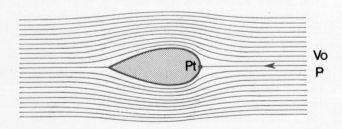

Figure II.2 *Streamlines around a body. The dividing streamline terminates at the stagnation point where speed and dynamic pressure are zero. Total pressure, P_t, is equal to static pressure, p, plus dynamic pressure q, and $q = \frac{1}{2}pV^2$.*

Total pressure $p_t = p + q$ can be measured with a manometer at the stagnation point. A pitot tube may be used, with a small bore so that flow is not disturbed. V_o velocity can be determined with this when the value of p is known (fig. II.3). The speed of fast power-driven vessels may be measured with a simple pitot tube; sited close beneath the surface, the value of p is negligible by comparison with p_t. With a sailing boat, however, p cannot be neglected because the depth of the instrument varies considerably, and a pitot-static tube is therefore required. This has a second tube which measures static pressure, the two tubes being connected one to each end of a manometer, which gives the difference between p_t and p (fig. II.4). The graduation gives a direct indication of speed, V.

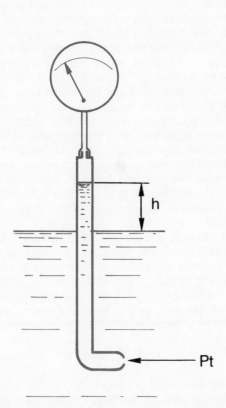

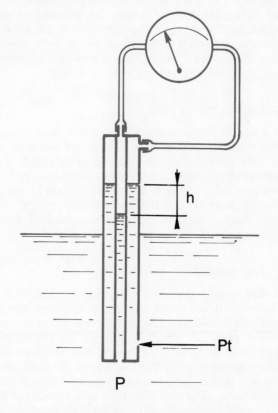

Figure II.3 *Pitot tube. The nose of the tube is connected to a manometer which indicates the total pressure $P_t = p + q$ at a certain height, h, of fluid, corresponding to static pressure plus dynamic pressure.*

Figure II.4 *A speedometer consisting of a pitot tube, plus a static tube which measures static pressure, p. The manometer indicates dynamic pressure, q, which is the difference between total pressure and static pressure at a certain height, h. The manometer dial can be graduated so as to indicate speed directly.*

3 Flow in real fluids

As we have already mentioned, there is a difference between a perfect fluid and real fluid in that layers of fluid retard or accelerate their neighbours due to shearing stresses, the velocity gradient relating to the fluid layers being proportional to the coefficient of viscosity, μ.

a Viscosity

In fluid dynamics, it is only kinematic viscosity, υ, the ratio of viscosity to fluid density, μ/ρ, that is of interest. It is kinematic viscosity, together with the two other factors that affect flow, namely flow velocity (V) and the length of the body (L), that are the three variables found in the Reynolds number,

$$R_e = \frac{V \times L}{\upsilon},$$

named after the English physicist Osborne Reynolds.

The Reynolds number is dimensionless, coherent units being used such as υ in m^2/s, L in m, and V in m/s, and is a major factor of dynamic similitude, the character of flow being the same whenever the Reynolds number has the same value.

Thus, for example, in the case of a centreboard 0.50 m in breadth, moving in fresh water at a velocity of 3 m/s, the Reynolds number will be $3 \times 0.5/0.000\,001\,14 = 1\,315\,789$. With a scaled-down centreboard 1/5th of the size and therefore 0.10 m in breadth, still in fresh water, velocity would have to be equal to

$$\frac{R_e \times \upsilon}{L}$$

if flow were to be similar;

V = $1\,315\,789 \times 0.000\,001\,14/0.1 = 15$ m/s.

Equally, if this model were to be studied in a wind tunnel, as happened with *Pen Duick III* in Nantes, velocity would then be equal to

$1\,315\,789 \times 0.000\,014\,5/0.1 = 190$ m/s.

33

In practice, however, the effective Reynolds number is almost always greater on account of the turbulence of the fluid. In wind, for example, the effective Reynolds number can be 30–50% higher than its nominal value, depending on meteorological conditions and the type of terrain.

b Definition of flow

If a line of colour is introduced into a fluid flowing between two walls or in a tube, it will maintain its identity when velocity is low, indicating that flow is laminar. If velocity then increases it can be seen that at a particular moment, although a certain length of the upstream part of the line remains straight, the rest merges rapidly with the surrounding fluid, showing that flow has become turbulent.

c The boundary layer

If flow over a flat plate immersed in a current is observed, it is evident that there is a thin film of motionless fluid immediately adjacent to the surface of the plate, to which it adheres on account of molecular attraction. Although the neighbouring layers are affected by the viscosity of the fluid, they are not subject to this attraction and can slip past one another. The transition from zero velocity at the plate to V (undisturbed free flow) is confined within the boundary layer, the thickness of which increases from the leading edge to the trailing edge of the plate, and in which there is progressively increasing agitation.

The character of flow within this layer of water was studied at the celebrated Göttingen laboratory by the German physicist Ludwig Prandtl, who named it the boundary layer, and later by Schönherr and others. Within this boundary layer, the energy absorbed by friction when fluid molecules rub against each other, is dissipated in the form of heat.

The cross-section of the boundary layer, greatly enlarged, is shown in fig. II.5. At the upstream end, the boundary layer is relatively thin and the molecules move regularly, as is characteristic of laminar flow. Further downstream, in the transition region, only the very thin sublayer in contact with the motionless film remains laminar, while the molecules in the neighbouring layers start to oscillate in a less regular way; downstream of this flow becomes fully turbulent.

Flow changes from laminar to turbulent at a point called the transition point, the position of which depends on a critical Reynolds number between 90 000 (9×10^4) and 1 100 000 (1.1×10^6), or roughly about 450 000 (4.5×10^5). Even in the case of a flat plate the position of the transition point, which is situated at a distance

$$L = \frac{R_{ecr}\,\upsilon}{V}$$

downstream of the leading edge, varies very considerably in view of the fluid's turbulence, and the term 'transition region' is therefore often preferred to transition point.

Thus, when a centreboard dinghy, 5 m long, is moving at 1 m/s (about 2 knots), the best that could

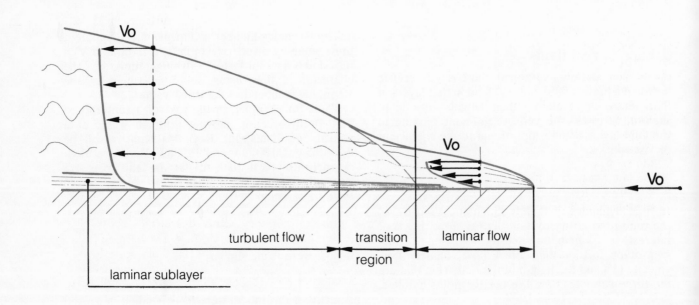

Figure II.5 *Characteristic elements of the boundary layer of a flat plate.*

be hoped for would be that flow over the hull would remain laminar for about 1/10th of her length. On the other hand, Reynolds number for the same boat's centreboard, 0.50 m in width, would be no greater than 450 000 (4.5×10^5) at the trailing edge, and it could be expected that flow would be entirely laminar.

Where flow is laminar, velocity in the boundary layer varies according to a parabolic law, and the same is true of the thickness of the boundary layer. At a point x, where the value of the Reynolds number is R_x, boundary layer thickness is about $4.92x/\sqrt{R_x}$. The stagnation point, where flow divides, is the starting point of the parabola that indicates the edge of the boundary layer. It is evident that the thinner the boundary layer, the greater is R_x, that is to say, either the length of flow or velocity is greater, or kinematic viscosity is lower. Consequently, when length and velocity are the same the boundary layer will be much thicker in air than in water.

Thus, when x = 0.5 and V = 1 m/s, R_x will equal $1 \times 0.5/0.000\,014\,5 = 34\,482$ for air, and

$$1 \times 0.5/0.000\,001\,14 = 438\,596$$

for fresh water; the thickness of the laminar boundary layer will be $4.92 \times 0.5/\sqrt{34\,482} = 0.013$ m in air, and $4.92 \times 0.5/\sqrt{438\,596} = 0.004$ m in water.

In the region where flow is turbulent, the thickness of the boundary layer increases much more rapidly. Given the same factors as for laminar flow, thickness = $0.38 \times \sqrt[5]{R_x}$. Functions of R_x vary as for laminar flow, but more slowly.

The laminar sublayer is extremely thin, about $16 \times \sqrt{C_f}/\sqrt{R_x}$, C_f being the mean coefficient of friction for the entire surface. Its value will be found later.

Calculation of boundary layer thickness can be simplified by assuming that the laminar sublayer increases as the function of $x^{0.1}$ (note: $x^{1/m} = \sqrt[m]{x}$), the laminar part of the boundary layer as $x^{0.5}$ and the turbulent layer as $x^{0.9}$.

Given a dinghy hull 5 m long with a perfectly smooth, even and polished surface, moving at 1 m/s or roughly 2 knots:
— the sub-layer would be 0.02 mm thick, 4 m aft of the stem;
— the laminar part of the boundary layer would be 0.12 mm thick, 50 cm aft of the stem;
— the turbulent layer would be 110 mm thick at the stern.

d Frictional resistance, roughness

The frictional forces that develop within the boundary layer make up skin friction, the value of which is $R_f = q \times A \times C_f$, q being dynamic pressure ($\frac{1}{2}\rho \times V^2$, see p. 00), A the area in contact with the fluid, and C_f the coefficient of friction. The value of C_f can either be that at a point on the surface, or the average value over the entire length; only the latter value is useful to us, and it is this that we shall consider.

The value of C_f depends on flow, that is to say on the Reynolds number, and on any imperfections that may mar the surface, whether due to roughness or unevenness. Surface irregularities cause shear stresses which increase turbulence in the boundary layer, and obviously there must be some connection between the thickness of the boundary layer and the permissible height, k, of roughness. In practice, the height of surface roughness can be taken as follows:
    rubbed down and polished: k 0.0005 mm
    smooth marine paint, rubbed down: k 0.05 mm
    galvanized metal: k 0.15 mm
    ordinary bare wood: k 0.5 mm
    average barnacles: k 5 mm

The curve in fig. II.6, based on Schönherr's studies, gives the values of C_f for a theoretically perfect surface, while Nikuradse and Schlichting's curves in fig. II.7 show how the coefficient of friction increases with the surface roughness, namely with the ratio of l, the representative length, and k, the height of the protruberances. The discontinuity due to the change from laminar to turbulent flow in the transition region can be seen again in the curve of fig. II.6. The C_f for laminar flow established by Blasius is $C_f = 1.327/\sqrt{R_e}$, and that of turbulent flow, studied by Prandtl and von Karman, is $C_f = 0.072/\sqrt[5]{R_e}$.

If the values shown in the curve of fig. II.7 are applied to our dinghy, based on a surface coated with rubbed-down paint that has a roughness of 0.05 mm, the degree of roughness 1/k will be 100 000 (10^5), and the coefficient of friction increases again above $R_e = 10^7$, or 2.22 m/s.

The shorter the length of the surface over which the fluid flows, the more important it is to reduce surface roughness so as to obtain a low skin friction coefficient, and particular attention should be paid to the fin keel, centreboard and rudder. For hulls, it is essentially the forward part that matters; in boats with accommodation, siting anything in this area that would protrude from the hull, such as water inlets or outlets, the echo sounder transducer, or the speedometer impeller, should be avoided. It is not just a case of reducing roughness to the minimum, however; above all the surface should be absolutely fair and even, because the smallest dent or the slightest hump can cause turbulence in the boundary layer, and may even cause separation.

The roughness of sailcloth is just as important. The mainsail of a 505, with a chord of 2 m, will have at half height a Reynolds number of only 690 000 in a 5 m/s wind. Were it not for the effect of the mast, flow might be hoped to be still laminar at

$$C_f = 0.0016$$

or, at worst, to be turbulent when $C_f = 0.005$. This means that the degree of roughness must be under

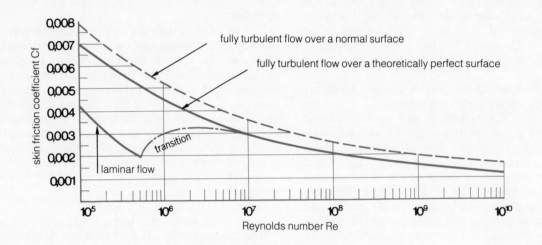

Figure II.6   *Curves of skin friction coefficient and Reynolds number (Schönherr)*

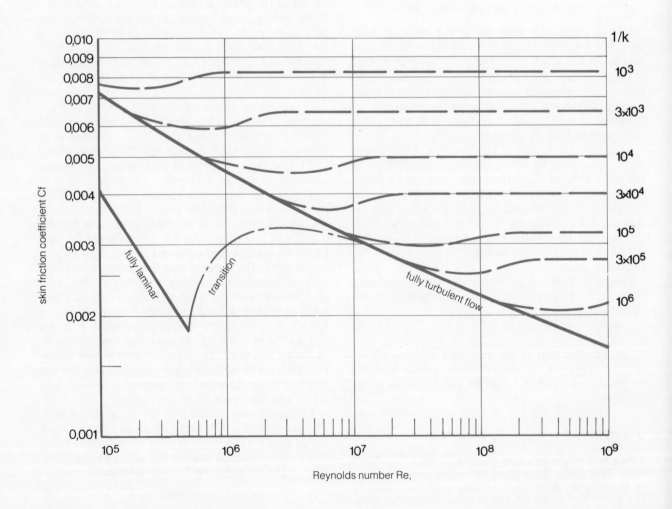

Figure II.7   *Curves of skin friction coefficient and Reynolds number for surfaces with a variable l/k ratio, l being length of the surface and k the height of the roughness.*

10^4, in other words k must be less than 0.2 mm — and this is a reasonable figure for today's polyester sailcloth when it has been fairly heavily calandered.

We will see later that roughness not only affects skin friction drag but has an adverse effect on the useful force developed by a lift-producing foil.

Because the Reynolds number is relatively low when models are used for tank testing, it is hard to be sure when flow is fully laminar, and even more difficult to fix the transition point with any accuracy. Therefore the method used is deliberately to prevent laminar flow by causing the entire boundary layer to become turbulent. A mean coefficient of friction can then be obtained more easily and, furthermore, the part of total resistance to forward motion that is due to friction can also be calculated. In order to stimulate turbulence, small studs or pins, or strips of sand glued to the hull, are placed close to the leading edge of the hull and fin keel.

For tank testing, the International Towing Tank Conference of 1957 defined the coefficient of friction as

$$\frac{0.075}{(\log R_e - 2)^2},$$

and the following ship model correlation values are generally taken for R_e:

for the hull $R_{eh} = V \times 0.7 \, L_h/\upsilon$
for the fin keel $R_{efk} = V \times C_{fk}/\upsilon$
for the rudder $R_{er} = V \times C_r/\upsilon$

C_{fk} and C_r are the mean chord in metres of the fin keel and the rudder respectively.

Researchers have long been considering the problem of how to reduce skin friction. Certain marine animals, both fish and mammals, but dolphins in particular, are known to be capable of speeds that are considerably greater than would be expected from their muscular structure, taking into account the coefficient of skin friction that results from their relatively rough skins. It has been observed that this coefficient is reduced in two ways: first, the shape of the body is adapted so as to try and retain the laminar boundary layer; second, substances of the polymer group are exuded, and these inhibit the laminar layers from becoming turbulent. There is no question of a waterproofing element being interposed between the surface and the skin.

Attempts have been made to reproduce both of these methods artifically: flexible rubber sheathing was fitted successfully (or so it would appear because this was military research) to torpedoes and nuclear submarines; and experiments with polymer additives were carried out with the Britton Chance 5.5-metre prior to the 1968 Olympic Games, and with the Dutch One-Tonner *De Schelde*, a polymer solution being ejected by a great number of small tubes that pierced the hull along the leading edge. Although a large quantity of the solution was required, the results seemed interesting, but the IYRU banned its use because competitors from countries where the level of technical research is high would gain an unfair advantage.

Since then research has continued in the laboratories of marine paint manufacturers with a view to perfecting a covering that will dissolve and release the necessary polymers into the water, but little progress has been made towards finding a product that is so effective that it does not have to be used in too great a quantity.

e Separation, ventilation, cavitation

Up to now we have considered flow over a flat plate. Obviously when fluid meets a curved surface flow will be changed on account of variations in pressure over the length of the body.

As in fig.II.8, the pressure P_t of a moving fluid at a point well upstream of a foil (point 1) is equal to p + q. As the leading edge of the body is approached, the streamlines are deflected to either side, and pressure p_t is increased by a quantity Δp (point 2), but as soon as the streamlines curve back in the opposite direction, differential pressure Δp becomes negative (point 3).

Fluid flow will remain attached to the surface provided pressure $p_t - \Delta p$ is sufficiently high at the rear of the foil; the moment that $p_t - \Delta p$ becomes too low, for example if there is too abrupt an alteration in hull form aft, the boundary layer becomes detached at a certain point (4) called the point of separation.

Eddies and reverse flow occur within the turbulent separation wake, the zone of dead air between the boundary layer and the trailing edge of the body, and the effect can be seen in the velocity profiles as in fig. II.9. It follows, of course, that there is an increase in resistance, but its coefficient will, however, be fairly constant — whatever the Reynolds number and speed.

On the other hand, it is clear that the occurrence of separation and the position of the point of separation must depend on the value of $p_t - \Delta p$.

The pattern of flow either side of the separation wake is as if the wake were an elongation of the body itself.

If we now consider a foil that is not entirely immersed in a single fluid of uniform pressure p, but partly in the air and partly in the water (fig. II.10), pressure p will depend on the depth of immersion and will therefore be the sum of p_o (atmospheric pressure) and p_h (hydrostatic pressure). Because p_h, and therefore $p_t - \Delta p$, decrease progressively towards the surface, separation will occur at points progressively further upstream; furthermore air may be sucked into a cavity in the middle of the wake. The point of separation will then travel further upstream as speed increases and, being a function of the Reynolds number, the phenomena relating to a full-size hull and its model will be the same when the Reynolds number is the same.

If the body is entirely immersed but not at all deeply, pressure $p_t - \Delta p$ can be so low that bubbles of air are attracted down from the surface, a phenomenon that is called ventilation (fig. II.11). In the case of a self-bailer, when $p_t - \Delta p$ is lower than P_o, the water inside the hull is sucked out (fig.II.12). Ventilation occurs relatively frequently, not only in connection with motorboat propellers, when it is often confused with cavitation, but with surface-piercing foils such as those used for hydrofoil craft, and transom-hung rudders, as in dinghies.

Wake or pressure drag can be considerably reduced by directly connecting the wake with the atmosphere, eliminating all that part of a body that is situated downstream of the point of separation (fig. II.13).

Quite apart from the fact that separation causes wake drag, it also has an adverse effect on the form drag of a totally submerged body, or the wave-making drag of a hull. It is difficult to determine the value of wake drag by itself, or of the two drag components just mentioned, and wake drag is therefore normally considered with form drag or with residual resistance.

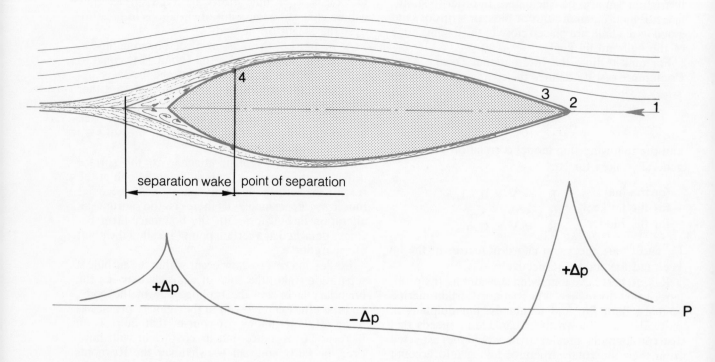

Figure II.8   *Separation of the boundary layer near the rear of a foil; below, pressure variation over the foil.*

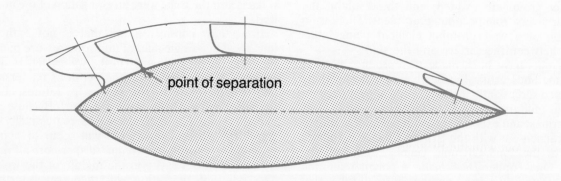

Figure II.9   *How the velocity profiles evolve when the boundary layer separates from the foil.*

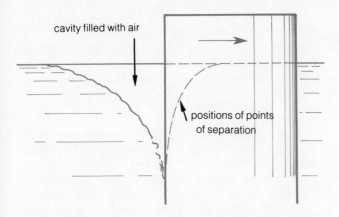

Figure II.10 *How the positions of the points of separation vary when a body is immersed partly in water and partly in air.*

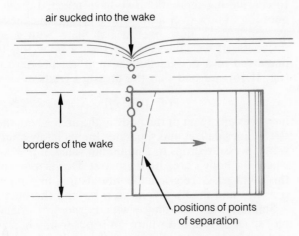

Figure II.11 *Ventilation in the wake of an object moving close beneath the interface between air and water.*

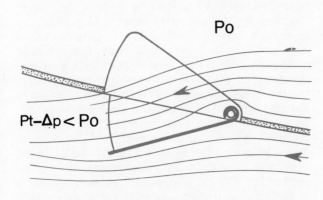

Po

Pt–Δp < Po

Figure II.12 *How a self-bailer works. When the flap is opened, pressure $P_t - \Delta_p$ in the wake created downstream of flap is lower than atmospheric pressure*

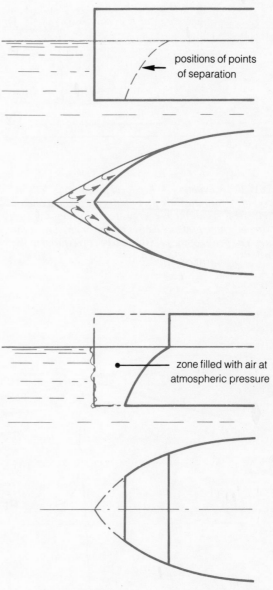

Figure II.13 *When pressure $P_t - \Delta_p$ in the wake of a semi-immersed body is lower than atmospheric pressure p_0, the rear end can be cut off along a line matching the curve of the points of separation. The pressure of the fluid that fills the eliminated area will be p_o and drag is reduced in consequence. This does not hold good at very low speeds if the height of the cut-off area is too great in comparison with its breadth. A further complication is that pressure is modified by waves made when the body moves through the water.*

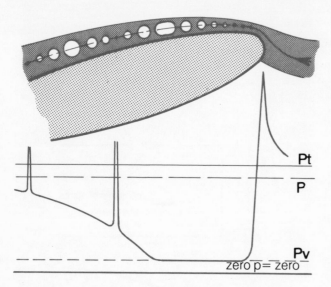

Figure II.14 *Cavitation. When local pressure, p, falls to the level of vapour pressure p_v, bubbles are formed and implode, freeing enormous energy at very localized points; the extremely high pressure causes pitting or erosion of the surface. The peaks of the pressure curve correspond to these implosions.*

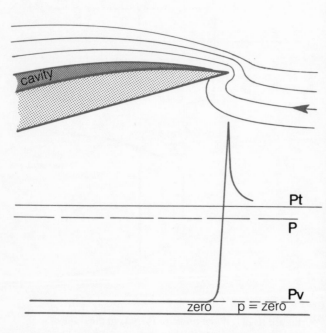

Figure II.15 *In the case of super-cavitation, the vast number of bubbles becomes a single cavity which entirely covers the back of the foil and terminates at the trailing edge. Erosion is avoided, and the flow is not separated from the cavity by a boundary layer.*

Suppose now that the body is so deeply immersed that ventilation cannot occur; when pressure at the point of contact with the boundary layer falls to a value close to zero, and lower than that of vapour pressure, bubbles form in the water and immediately fill with water vapour or gas, exactly as occurs when water is boiled (fig. II.14). This is called cavitation, and is the equivalent of what occurs when water is carried to a great altitude.

The bubbles implode rapidly and then re-form, and the process, which is too complicated to go into here, involves alternating differences in local pressure of some several hundred kg/cm^2; the result is rapid erosion of the body and pitting of the surface.

The term super-cavitation is used when the back of a foil is covered completely by a sheath of cavitation. This is of interest when fine-pitch propellers rotate at very high speeds, because pitting is reduced and surface friction is eliminated (fig. II.15).

f Form drag

In considering separation, we have touched on the question of flow over a foil with a certain thickness, as opposed to flow over a flat plate with zero thickness. If we now consider such a body totally immersed in a perfect fluid of uniform pressure p (fig. II.16), we find that the pressure gradient

$$p_t = p + \Delta p$$

increases upstream of the body in the area where the streamlines deflect and separate. Immediately afterwards pressure drops to a minimum value of $p - \Delta p$ where the body's breadth is greatest. Downstream of this point pressure gradually mounts to a maximum $p + \Delta p$, and finally reverts to p beyond the body.

Similarly, in accordance with Bernoulli's principle, speed is reduced where Δp is positive, whereas it exceeds V_o where Δp is negative.

In a perfect fluid of zero viscosity, the components of pressure at the front of the body balance those at the rear, and the body experiences no resistance to motion; this is d'Alembert's **paradox**. However, we have seen that in a real fluid the shape of the body is modified by the boundary layer, and possibly by separation as well, which affects the pattern of fluid flow. Over the front part of the body, flow is similar to flow in a perfect fluid, and an axial force is created the direction of which is towards the trailing edge, but this is not balanced by the axial force acting in the opposite direction because flow differs greatly further downstream near the rear of the body; the resultant of the axial components can therefore no longer be zero. Then again, although a foil and a flat plate may have the same chord length, the curved surface has a longer effective length and, because it is on this that frictional resistance calculations are based, it follows that both the speed of flow and friction increase. The combined effect can be expressed as the difference between the total drag that is measured and the frictional resistance that is

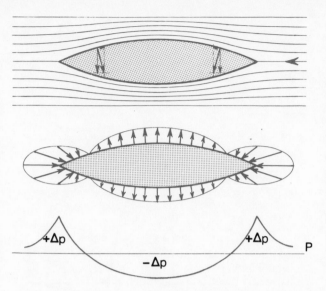

Figure II.16 *In a perfect fluid, there is no form drag because flow is absolutely symmetrical, and the resultant pressures at front and rear are balanced.*

calculated. Drag force D = q × S × C_d where q is dynamic pressure, S the frontal area presented to the flow and C_d the drag coefficient, i.e. the shape factor.

The drag coefficient C_d is constant in any given type of flow, regardless of the Reynolds number, but it will of course vary considerably with the shape of the body.

When a flat plate is placed perpendicular to flow (fig. II.17), frictional resistance is very much reduced. Separation being rapid and abrupt, the drag coefficient has a virtually constant value of 1.15 if the plate is square, 1.16 if it is a round disc, and 1.2 − 2 if it is rectangular, depending on the ratio of its height to its breadth.

When a streamlined body or even a simple cylinder are considered, the pattern of flow is very different.

Fig. II.18 shows variations in the coefficient of total resistance C_t (that is to say $C_f + C_d$) of a cylinder which is extremely long by comparison with its diameter, for example a shroud. The different types of flow matching the Reynolds numbers are shown beneath the scale.

When Reynolds number R_e is under 1, Stokes's Law of Drag for very low Reynolds numbers is valid, the streamlines remain attached, and flow is fully laminar throughout.

Up to $R_e = 15 − 20$ (a), the boundary layer downstream of the cylinder becomes thicker. Above $R_e = 20$, streamlines start to separate at a point upstream of the centre, and two symmetrical vortices form (b) which grow progressively and are shed at $R_e = 100 − 150$.

When speed continues to increase, so-called Karman vortices form alternately to either side of the cylinder (c). This state is maintained up to $R_e = 2500$, above which number the vortices diffuse and turbulence forms a broad eddying wake, the point of separation being 80° from the axis that is parallel to the direction of flow (d).

When $R_e = 300\,000 − 500\,000$, the whole of the boundary layer is turbulent, and the point of separation moves further downstream than the centre, to about 120° (e). At the critical Reynolds number R_{cr}, laminar separation changes to turbulent separation, and is accompanied by a sharp fall in the drag coefficient.

Given a shroud 4 mm in diameter, and a 4 m/s wind, the Reynolds number will be

$$R_e × 0.004/0.000\,014\,5 = 1103,$$

and flow will be as at (c) with Karman vortices; the value of C_t will be 0.95, as shown in the curve in fig. II.13. In the same conditions a mast 100 mm in

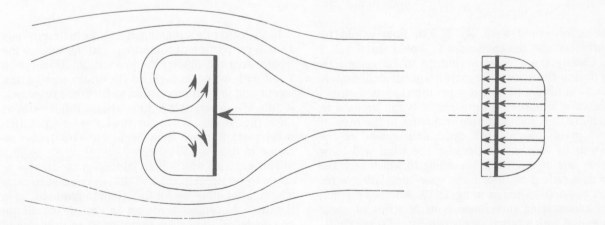

Figure II.17 *When flow is perpendicular to a flat plate, separation occurs at the circumference. The mean*

coefficient of pressure on the face of a disc is 0.83 whereas on the back it is only minus 0.29.

41

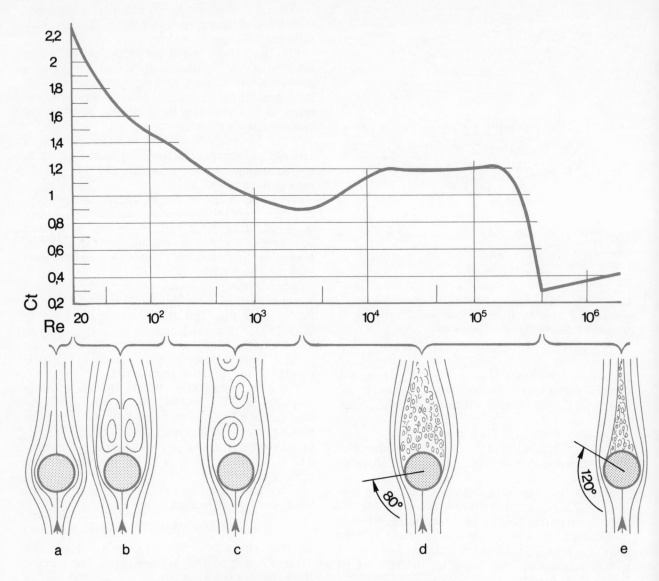

Figure II.18 *Variation in the drag coefficient of a cylinder of infinite length as a function of Reynolds number, with corresponding types of flow.*

diameter would have R_e 27 600, flow would be turbulent and the coefficient C_t would equal 1.2.

Clearly there is an advantage to be gained by reducing the critical Reynolds number deliberately so as to obtain turbulent separation, particularly in the case of masts. Various methods can be used to achieve this, such as fitting thin wires to the mast at two points roughly 130° apart and upwind of the points of separation. Because the wind will blow from one or other side according to which tack the boat is sailing on, four turbulence-stimulating wires are required, fitted as in fig. II.19. Another method of encouraging turbulence is to fit strips of some material with a raised zigzag pattern, or small studs.

It is very rare for rigs and most masts to reach the critical Reynolds number, and air drag is consequently great, as will be seen in Chapter VI.A1.

In the case of a streamlined foil, form drag is only a small proportion of total drag, and the smaller the frontal area the smaller the proportion. Thus, given a foil with a thickness/chord (t/c) ratio of 1/16, the increase in drag in proportion to frictional resistance is only 8%, whereas it is 30% when a foil is twice as thick (fig. II.20). When the thickness of a parallel-sided plate is more than negligible (1/30), the increase in drag is 150%.

This explains why it is so important for all appendages to be streamlined and thin in relation to their length, after allowing for the strength required, as in the case of a centreboard or a fin keel. It should not be concluded, however, that a cross-section should always be flattened to the maximum. For example, the best thickness/chord ratio for a streamlined strut of some particular section is about 1/3.3, and C_t will

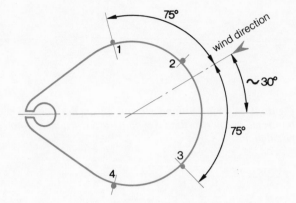

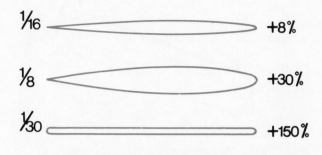

Figure II.19 *Stimulators fitted to a mast to encourage turbulent separation of flow. On port tack wires 1 and 3 act as stimulators, and on starboard tack wires 2 and 4.*

Figure II.20 *Increase in total drag due to form drag for a thin foil, a thick foil and a flat plate.*

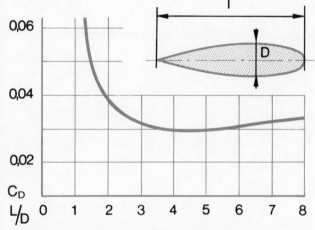

Figure II.21 *Variation in the total drag of a body of rotation of given volume. The optimum length/diameter ratio is at about 4.5.*

then be as little as 0.048, whereas at a ratio of 1/10 it would be 0.1. In this case, though, it is frictional resistance that increases.

When a fairing is to envelop an object with a certain frontal area, the best length/diameter, l/D, ratio is about 2.5 and C_t will equal 0.05.

Similarly, if a body of rotation, like a bulb of ballast for example, is considered, it is volume V that is important. The C_t for a reference area equal to $V^{2/3}$ is optimum when l/D = approximately 4.5, D being the diameter of the body (fig. II.21).

When a body is properly streamlined, it is virtually unaffected by the different variations in flow that have been described for a cylinder. The boundary layers on either side rejoin to form a wake which spreads out in the ambient medium, the breadth of the disturbed area increasing progressively while, at the same time, the difference between wake speed and speed outside the wake diminishes (fig. II.22), the first as $\sqrt{x}$ and the second as $1/\sqrt{x}$. Study of the wake enables frictional resistance and, on occasion, separation drag to be calculated.

4 Creation of a lift force

So far we have only considered immersed cylindrical or streamlined bodies placed parallel to the direction of flow of the fluid. The resultant of all the forces to which they were subject was therfore also parallel to the direction of flow, and corresponded to resistance or drag. We must now look at what happens when a body is placed differently, and we will take a flat plate set in the fluid at an angle to the direction of flow, the angle being called the angle of incidence or the angle of attack (fig. II.23). The surface facing the streamlines is the lower face or surface, and the opposite surface is the back or upper surface. The front upstream edge is the leading edge, and the rear edge is the trailing edge, while the straight line that connects these two extremities is the chord, the length of which is l.

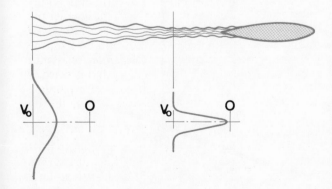

Figure II.22 *How the wake develops and how speed varies within the wake.*

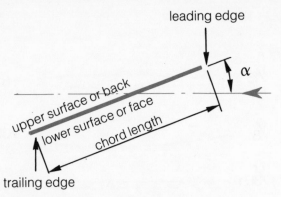

Figure II.23   *The parts of a lift-producing section.*

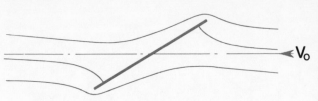

Figure II.24   *Flow around a lift-producing flat plate immersed in a perfect fluid is symmetrical when there is no circulation.*

When studying the streamlines in a perfect fluid, the dividing streamline is seen either side of the plate again, ending at the body at a point of zero velocity or stagnation point and reappearing at the rear stagnation point; fluid flow divides either side of this line. Speed and pressure differences can be deduced because the path of the streamlines is known exactly.

In the basic diagram of potential flow (fig. II.24), when fluid meets a flat plate inclined at an angle of incidence, the pattern of the streamlines is symmetrical either side of the dividing streamline where flow is brought to rest at the stagnation points, which are situated upstream on the face and downstream on the back of the plate.

This does not correspond with reality, however, because the downstream stagnation point is actually positioned near the trailing edge, and the dividing streamline is virtually an extension of the flat plate. To satisfy this condition, which is named after the two great aerodynamicists Kutta and Zhukovsky, the velocity field round the plate is modified by circulation T around the body, the speed of circulation being added at the back of the plate where it acts in the same direction as flow, but deducted on the face where it acts in the opposite direction (fig. II.25).

Flow is therefore no longer symmetrical, and the reduction in speed on the front face causes pressure to rise, whereas pressure drops at the back where speed is increased. The difference in pressure between the two faces of the body gives rise to a force that acts perpendicularly to the direction of flow, namely lift, the value of which is $L = \rho T V_o$.

When the electric analogy process is used, the Kutta-Zhukovsky condition, with the dividing streamline an elongation of the profile section being studied, is obtained by varying the current to the resistor between the two edges and connected to the profile (fig. II.26).

It is known that in practice the analogy is complicated by other phenomena connected with friction and turbulence in the boundary layer, all of which are manifested as a modification of lift, L, and by the appearance of a resistance or drag D, acting in

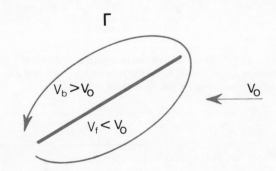

Figure II.25   *Circulation around a lift-producing flat plate.*

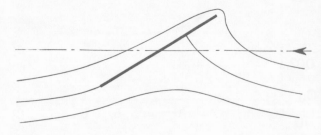

Figure II.26   *Modification of flow around a lift-producing section immersed in a perfect fluid when circulation is incorporated.*

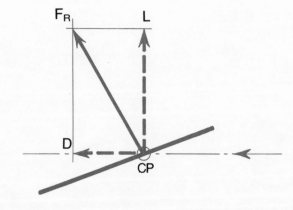

Figure II.27   *Lift L, modified by the viscosity of the fluid, and drag D associated with it, are the components of the resultant force F_R.*

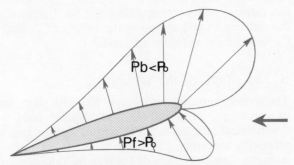

Figure II.28 *The reduction in pressure $P_o - P_b$ on the back is greater than the increase in pressure $P_f - P_o$ on the face.*

the direction of motion. F_R is the force resulting from lift L and drag D, the point of application being the centre of pressure, CP (fig. II.27).

It is also possible to measure the values of the differences in the pressures that are normal to the surface on the upper and lower faces of the plate or foil immersed in the fluid, and this enables us to verify that, whereas pressure on the upstream face P_f is greater than ambient pressure p_a, it is lower on the back p_b. Equally we find (fig. II.28) that the reduction in pressure on the back, $P_o - P_b$, is greater than the equivalent increase in pressure on the face, $P_f - P_o$, and that the greatest pressure differences occur near the nose of the body.

It is now understandable why the ability of a foil to develop a reasonable resultant force depends most on the quality of the flow near the nose and over the back; the resultant force is, after all, made up of the sum of these pressure differences.

In order to compare the measured performance of different sections, these forces are expressed as coefficients which, like all the forces considered up to now, are defined by Newton's formula

$$F = q \times A \times C.$$

C_L and C_D are the coefficients of lift and drag.

The polar curve of fig. II.29 shows the value of C_D plotted as a function of C_L at various angles of incidence. The direction and the value of the resultant total force can be read directly from this diagram, together with the maximum lift to drag ratio of the section being studied. The optimum lift-to-drag ratio, which is the angle at which this section performs best, is shown on the polar diagram by the tangent line from origin O to the polar curve. The values of C_L and C_D can be shown in other ways, but we will see later that there are very many advantages to this method.

The shape of the polar diagram also reveals how flow over the foil changes as the angle of incidence

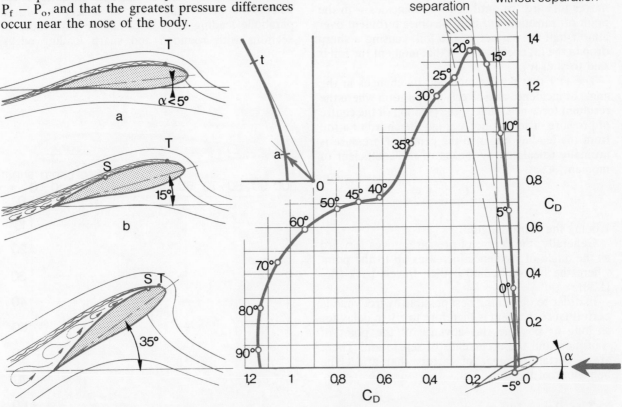

Figure II.29 *Polar curve of an asymmetric section, and the corresponding development of flow over its back. The values of the coefficients C_L and C_D are plotted to the same scale for every angle of incidence. Thus the value of Oa and the angle of the resultant can be found directly for any angle of incidence. The Maximum C_L/C_D ratio is shown by the tangent, t, from 0 to the curve. A polar curve should always indicate the aspect ratio of the foil (here it is infinite) and the Reynolds number (here $R_e = 42 \times 10^4$).*

alters. The position of the transition point where laminar flow over the forward part of the foil changes to turbulent flow further aft, and the occurrence of separation of the turbulent layer, can be seen clearly on the polar curve.

As we have already seen, transition from laminar flow to turbulent flow does not occur at a single point but extends over a zone, which may be more or less extensive, but which can amount to as much as 20% of the length of the foil downstream of the theoretical point of transition.

In our example, up to an angle of 5° where the lift-to-drag ratio is maximum, the point of transition, T, travels forward gradually from one-third to one-tenth of the length of the foil (a). In this part of the polar curve, lift is proportional to the angle of incidence: $C_{L\alpha} \propto C_{AR}(\alpha - \alpha_o)$, where C_{AR} is the coefficient of aspect ratio, α the angle of incidence and α_o the angle of incidence at which $C_L = 0$ (for a symmetrical profile $\alpha_o = 0$).

Drag is proportional to the square of lift:

$$C_{D\alpha} = C_{Do} + \frac{C_L^2}{\pi AR},$$

AR being aspect ratio and C_{Do} the coefficient of drag at which $C_L = 0$. The boundary layer starts to separate from the rear of the foil at an angle of incidence of over 5°, and the point of separation moves forward (b) until at 19° it coincides with the point of transition and flow becomes turbulent over almost half the surface of the foil, causing a sharp drop in the lift coefficient. At that moment the foil is said to stall (c).

The fact that flow is modified by changes in the angle of incidence also affects the position where the resultant force acts, that is, the position of the centre of pressure. The distance x along the chord of a foil from the leading edges to the centre of pressure is normally calculated by means of the coefficient of moment, C_m:

$$x = \frac{-C_m \times 1}{C_L},$$

1 being the chord length.

Generally, the centre of pressure moves forward as the angle of incidence increases up to the point where the foil stalls, and it then travels back (fig. II.30).

In order to obtain the best possible hydrodynamic performance, the aim is therefore to try to delay for as long as possible this advance of the point of transition and the occurrence of separation. There are a certain number of factors that affect the behaviour of the foil.

a The Reynolds number

Because the values of the forces developed on the surface of the foil are essentially a function of the quality of flow, the lower the Reynolds number the better they will be and, consequently, the further downstream will the transition point be. Essentially the differences will appear in the value of C_L, while C_D will remain virtually constant.

b The shape of the section

The section or profile may simply be a thin plate, flat or cambered, or a thicker body which could be symmetrical or asymmetrical, and of varying curvature with maximum thickness nearer to or further from the leading edge. Whatever its thickness, it is essentially the curvature of a thick profile that governs how much lift can be obtained. The greater the curvature, the greater will lift be, always provided that the critical Reynolds number at which separation of the boundary layer occurs is not exceeded. Fig. II.31 shows clearly how much more efficient a cambered plate is than a flat plate.

Nor is thickness responsible only for a direct increase in lift; because the pressure gradient along the foil is improved, the point of separation travels further downstream and the angle at which the profile will stall is greater. Fig. II.32 compares a flat thin plate and a thick streamlined section.

The shape of the leading edge has a very important role to play with regard to the pressures developed along the foil, as can be seen in fig. II.33, where the lift-to-drag ratio of a section with a parabolic leading edge is compared with those of sections with rounded and sharp leading edges.

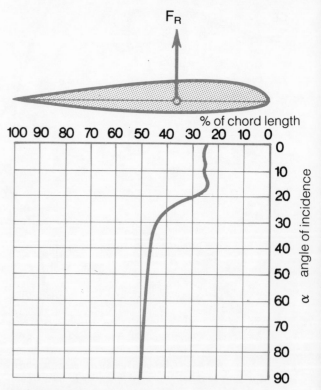

Figure II.30 *How the position of the centre of pressure varies with the angle of incidence.*

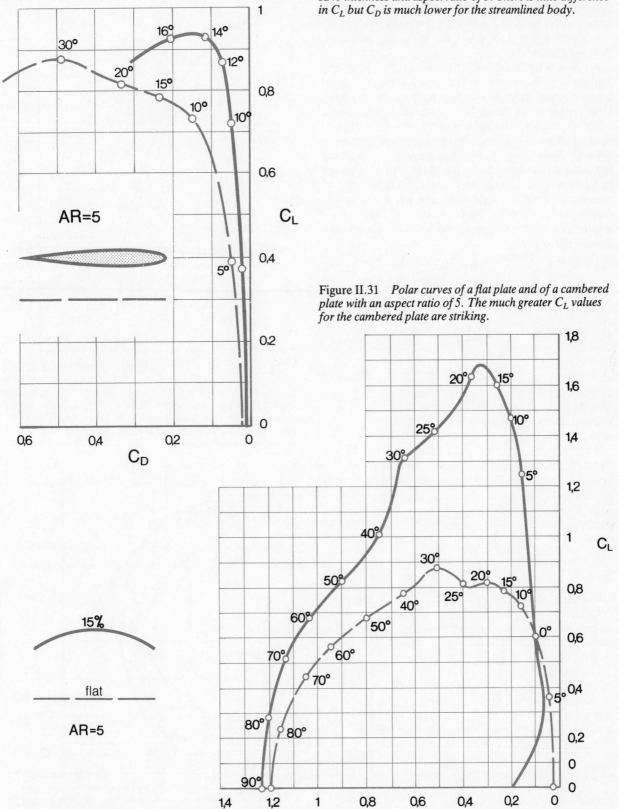

Figure II.32   *Comparison of the polar curves of a plane surface of zero thickness and of a streamlined body with 12% thickness and aspect ratio of 5. There is little difference in C_L but C_D is much lower for the streamlined body.*

Figure II.31   *Polar curves of a flat plate and of a cambered plate with an aspect ratio of 5. The much greater C_L values for the cambered plate are striking.*

There is no doubt that the transition point is kept furthest from the nose when the leading edge is parabolic, whereas with the rounded nose separation occurs at its tangent point with the body of the foil; the sharp-nosed foil stalls as soon as incidence increases above 0.

Profiles with maximum thickness very near the trailing edge have been tested with a view to obtaining the maximum advantage from laminar flow. Excellent results have been obtained with these laminar profiles, particularly at small angles of incidence (up to 3–4°), and the improvement increases with thickness (fig. II.34), but they are extremely sensitive to turbulence in the fluid and to surface roughness (fig. II.35); they are therefore only of interest in certain conditions, i.e. when the sea is calm, the Reynolds number is low and, consequently, speed is slow and limited forces are developed.

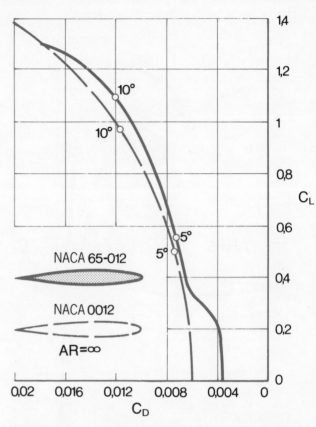

Figure II.34 *A laminar foil, NACA 65$_1$ – 012, compared to an ordinary foil, NACA 0012 with a thickness of 12% and aspect ratio infinite. The laminar foil is considerably superior at small angles of incidence.*

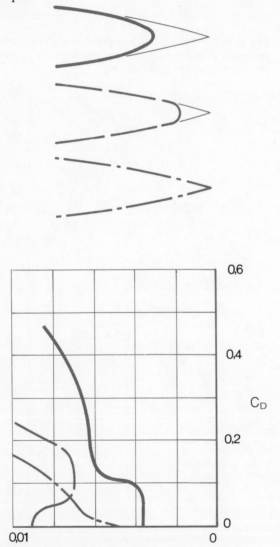

Figure II.33 *Greatly enlarged polar curves for the same foil with three different leading edges, the first being parabolic, the second rounded and the third sharp.*

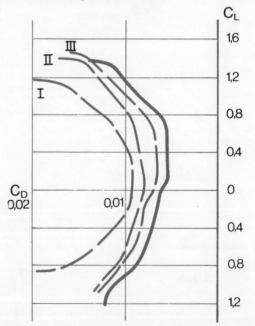

Figure II.35 *Changes in the polar curves of a laminar profile when a rough strip with a l/k ratio of 3400 is fitted at the leading edge (I), 0.2 l — along the length l (II) and 0.3 l (III), given $R_e = 26 \times 10^6$, by comparison with a polished profile.*

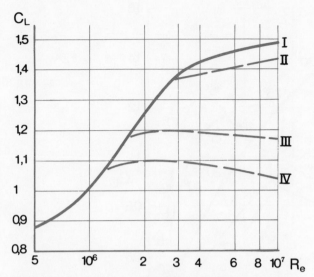

Figure II.36   *Reduction of the lift coefficient as a function of roughness. I is a chromed surface, II polished by hand, III carborundum l/k = 2 × 10⁴ and IV l/k = 3 × 10³.*

c Roughness

As we know, the effect of roughness is to increase frictional resistance, and therefore drag, but a further effect is to cause the point of transition to travel further forward, and this further reduces the value of C_L. The graphs in fig. II.36 compare the results obtained when a foil has a smooth surface, I, with those of the same foil covered with larger and larger grains of carborundum, II, III, IV.

The effect of roughness is also greater when it occurs at a relatively important part of the foil. Thus the polar curves of fig. II.37 are the result of a rough strip on the back of a foil, I at the trailing edge, II in the middle and III at the leading edge; the drop in performance is particularly marked in the last case.

It is clear to what degree the quality of the surface will affect the efficiency of a keel or of a centreboard because, not only is there an increase in frictional resistance when the surface is rough but, more important still, the efficiency with which leeway is opposed is affected adversely.

d Aspect ratio

Aspect ratio greatly affects the performance of a lift-producing foil. Given a foil with a chord of constant length, aspect ratio is the span/chord ratio, S/c, but if the chord is not constant, the equivalent formula S^2/A may be used, A being the surface area. For example, a centreboard with parallel leading and trailing edges, 1.20 m in depth and 0.40 m wide, will have an aspect ratio of $1.2^2/0.48 = 3$. The aspect ratio of another of elliptical planform but the same length and area is the same, $1.2^2/0.48 = 3$, but its maximum chord will be greater than that of the former (fig. II.38).

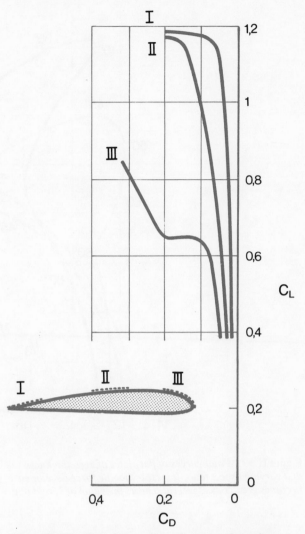

Figure II.37   *The adverse affect of an area of roughness is more marked when it is close to the leading edge of a foil.*

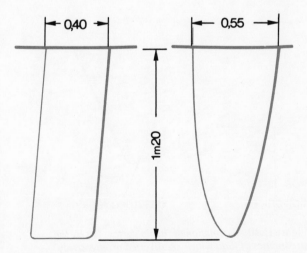

Figure II.38   *Two centreboards of differing shape, but with the same aspect ratio and length.*

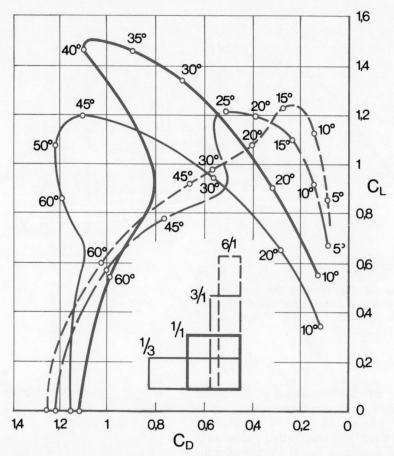

Figure II.39 *Polar curves of flat plates of zero thickness and varying aspect ratio. It is clear that the force developed becomes greater as aspect ratio nears the value of 1, and that the lift-to-drag ratio is improved as aspect ratio becomes higher, but that the angle of incidence at which separation occurs becomes smaller as aspect ratio becomes lower.*

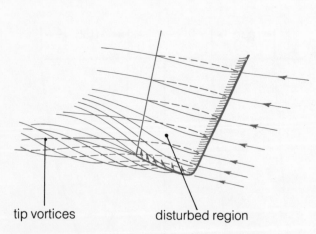

tip vortices   disturbed region

Figure II.40 *Formation of the tip vortex, fed by the streamlines of fluid which are diverted progressively towards the tip on the upstream side and away from the tip on the downstream side.*

The aspect ratio should not be confused with the length-to-breadth ratio; they are the same only when the foil is a rectangle or parallelogram.

In fig. II.39, the polar curves show the difference between foils of varying aspect ratio. It can be seen that the maximum lift-to-drag ratio is obtained when aspect ratio is highest, but on the other hand the greatest force is developed when the aspect ratio is 1, although this is unfortunately at too great an angle of incidence to be useful.

Lift, and therefore drag at a given incidence angle, are proportional to a coefficient

$$C_{AR} = \frac{0.11}{1 + 2/AR},$$

AR being aspect ratio.

Why does aspect ratio affect the performance of a foil? We know that pressure differs on either side of the body. At the tip of the foil, the fluid on the side where pressure is higher tries to pass to the opposite side where pressure is lower by flowing round the margin. An eddy or tip vortex is produced (fig. II.40), in itself causing a major increase in resistance, namely induced drag; additionally, however, a sheet of fluid is drawn by the tip vortex from both sides of the foil, and this causes a reduction in pressure difference; the result is that the lift coefficient of the foil is also reduced.

The value of the lift lost is constant because it depends entirely on the shape of the body and on the section of its extremities, regardless of the actual length of the body; therefore the loss, when taken as a percentage of lift, will decrease as the length of the foil increases.

If a foil is freely immersed in the fluid, as are the wings of an aircraft, a tip vortex will be produced at either end, but if the foil is attached to an object, like a centreboard beneath the hull of a dinghy, a tip vortex can only develop at one end, and the effective aspect ratio will therefore be double that of the geometric aspect ratio. We will see later how this can be of benefit in some particular cases.

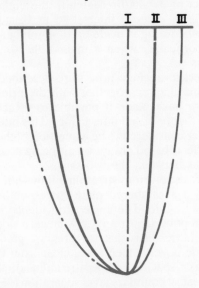

Figure II.41 *Various elliptical planforms: I with a straight leading edge; II asymmetric ellipse; III symmetrical ellipse. These shapes reduce the size of the tip vortex to the minimum.*

e The planform

Prandtl proved that induced drag is minimum when the variation of circulations and pressures over the entire foil from its root to its tip are elliptical. It follows that the chord lengths of a particular foil must also be elliptical, in other words the planform could be a semi-ellipse, or one edge could be straight and the other a quarter of an ellipse (mainsail) or, as is common with centreboards, two quarters of an ellipse (fig. II.41). In practice, however, these shapes should sometimes be adapted on account of variations of certain parameters, such as local speed, incidence etc.

The fact that the RAF's Spitfires of 1940 were so much more manoeuvrable than the German Messerschmidt 109s that they won the Battle of Britain in spite of having less powerful engines has been attributed to the elliptical shape of their wings. A spot of aerodynamic astuteness may perhaps have changed the course of history!

An elliptical shape is not always possible, however, and the question then is, which is the best shape for the tip.

Two separate studies failed to prove that either of the most common forms, 1 and 2 in fig. II.42, has a definite advantage; both provide a certain increase in the effective aspect ratio. Shapes 3 and 4, on the other hand, appear to suffer from the fact that the effective aspect ratio is reduced and, with that, the angle of incidence and the C_D are both increased for the same value of C_L.

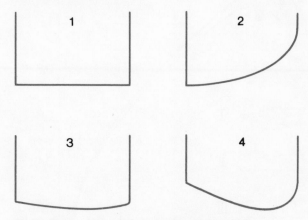

Figure II.42 *Some differently shaped tips of lift-producing foils. Shapes 1 and 2 are preferable to 3 and 4.*

f Tip shapes

Tip vortices are formed as a result of the passage of fluid from the face of a foil (high pressure) to the back (low pressure), but this effect could be reduced by putting an obstacle in their path. The most obvious is an end plate, fitted perpendicularly to the foil at its tip (fig. II.43). If the root of the foil is attached to something similar to an end plate, the effective aspect ratio AR_e obtained by providing an end plate for the tip is

$$AR_e \times 0.59 \text{ h/s or } AR_e \times 0.55 \text{ A}_p/\text{A},$$

depending on whether it is the height, h, of the plate or its surface area A_p that is being considered.

The effect is similar when, for example, a bulb is fitted beneath a fin keel, provided that it is quite distinct from the latter, as in fig. II.44 showing *Pen Duick III*'s bulb keel. Alternatively, an effective shape for the tip can be chosen; this will be more efficient if it terminates in a 'V' than if it is square or semicircular (fig. II.45). It appears that, even with no bulb, a pointed edge at the tip has a favourable effect.

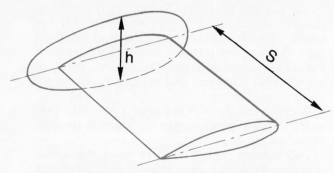

Figure II.43 *A perpendicular plate, placed at the tip of a lift-producing body, increases its effective aspect ratio.*

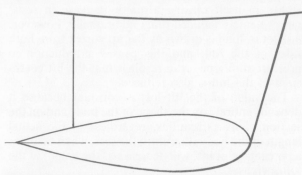

Figure II.44 *Pen Duick III's fin keel with its streamlined bulb. The effective aspect ratio is increased by the presence of the bulb.*

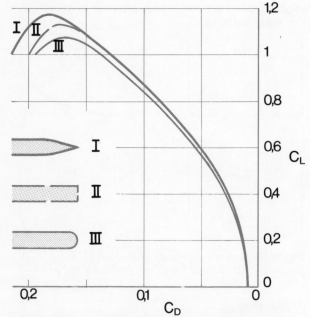

Figure II.45 *Polar diagrams comparing different sections for the tips of lift-producing foils. When optimum performance is required, it is always shape I that is adopted.*

g Combination of two foils

The way in which two foils combine and interact was the subject of detailed research in the biplane era, and this is of especial interest to us because it is relevant when a rig is made up of a number of sails and, in particular, when a mainsail/headsail combination is set.

The electric analogy procedure described at the start of this chapter, together with the principle of circulation, have made it possible to establish the definitive theory of sail interacting. This interaction is no longer considered to be a question of the slot or venturi effect, based always on air being accelerated as it passes between the two sails.

First, let us return to streamline flow with circulation around a cambered plate corresponding to a mainsail set alone. The angle of incidence is 13.7°. Stagnation point is just on the windward side of the sail, and the result is that the pressure gradient on the lee side is very steep (as is clear from the very much closer spacing of the streamlines); this will probably cause boundary layer separation (fig. II.46).

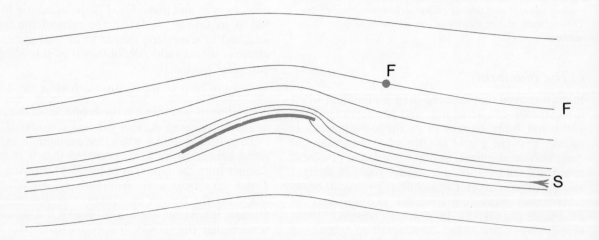

Figure II.46 *Streamlines over a mainsail set alone at an angle of incidence of 13.7°.*

The position of the forestay would be at point F, and it is the distance from this point to the dividing streamline leading to the stagnation point that indicates the value of the quantity of air that passes between point F and the mainsail.

Now let us look at the headsail alone (fig. II.47). This is set at a lower angle of incidence of 4.4°, and the stagnation point is situated right at the leading edge; the pressure gradient on the leeward side of the sail is therefore less steep, and in consequence there will be no separation.

If we now take the two sails together, we can see from the shapes of the streamlines that there are major modifications to flow (fig. II.48). Firstly, the stagnation point on the mainsail has been moved forward, and the streamline now leads to the front of the mast. The pressure gradient on the lee side is considerably slacker, and its peak is further downwind. Although the value of lift is reduced, there is no risk of separation, and there is absolutely no doubt that it is better to be certain of actually having lift, even if of reduced value, rather than having a high lift value in theory only, knowing that it is almost bound to be reduced to zero by boundary layer separation.

The streamlines to windward of the mainsail are greatly deflected; in particular the streamline that corresponds to point F shifts well to leeward of the headsail. Line S', which leads to the stagnation point of the headsail, is much nearer to line S, and in consequence less air passes between the two sails, the remainder being deflected to the leeward side of the headsail. The streamlines spread out in the area between the two sails, showing that velocity is reduced here. This can also be explained by the fact that the direction of circulation around the mainsail is opposed to that around the headsail in this area where they meet (fig. II.49).

The air passing between the two sails only regains its velocity when downwind of the headsail, and it is then moving no faster than when the mainsail is set alone.

Because air flowing over the lee side of the headsail must be moving at the same speed as the air passing between the two sails at the moment when they rejoin, its speed increases and pressure is reduced correspondingly. *The force that the headsail develops is therefore increased by the presence of the mainsail.*

Thus, rather than the headsail improving the mainsail's performance, it is the mainsail that improves the performance of the headsail by deflecting the approaching air so that the angle of incidence is more favourable, and by accelerating flow over the lee side of the sail. So far as circulation is concerned, the two sails should not be taken separately but viewed as a whole.

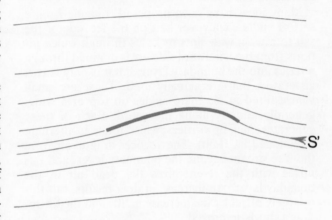

Figure II.47 *Streamlines over a headsail set alone at an angle of incidence of 4.4°.*

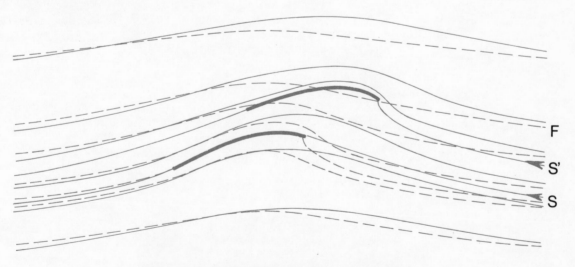

Figure II.48 *Streamlines over a mainsail and headsail combination (the broken lines indicate the streamlines of the mainsail alone).*

Of course the sail is being considered here in two dimensions only (its horizontal section), and other factors will affect flow. In the case of a real sail, flow will be modified by, among other things, variations in its breadth and the relationship of this breadth and the mast diameter; by the presence of the boundary layer, the thickness of which is too great to be ignored; and by the phenomenon of separation. However, these factors do not introduce any fundamental changes.

h Delaying separation

We have seen that loss of lift is caused essentially by the separation of the boundary layer, and it therefore seems worth while to delay the occurrence of separation. The friction that results when air flows over a foil is the basic cause of separation, and the object is therefore either to reduce friction or to accelerate the boundary layer.

Many ideas have been proposed, ranging from a sort of endless conveyor belt on the lee side of the sail to a wing with slots or holes through which air flows from the windward side, or is pumped through nozzles into the boundary layer, but it is only vortex generators that are actually used. These are small vanes, fitted at alternate angles on top of a wing, generally midway along the chord. Each of these generates small tip vortices, which rotate in alternate directions (fig. II.50). The vortices drag in air from the free stream beyond the boundary layer, and this mixes with the re-energizes the dead air in the bounday layer. An increase in drag results, but this is largely offset by the increase in lift, and the lift-to-drag ratio is improved.

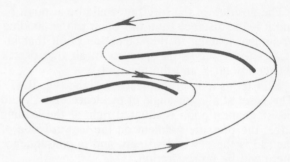

Figure II.49 *Circulation when both mainsail and headsail are set.*

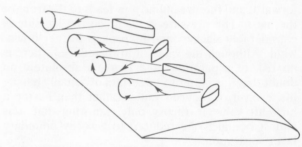

Figure II.50 *Vortex generators.*

III
Equilibrium of a Sailing Boat

A boat that is floating on water, motionless, is in equilibrium; the forces of weight, W, the resultant of which is applied at the centre of gravity, CG, is opposed by the hydrostatic force of buoyancy, B, applied at the centre of buoyancy, CB (fig. III.1). The forces have to be of the same value if the boat is to be in equilibrium, that is to say, the weight of the water displaced must be equal to the weight of the boat, and the two centres CG and CB must be vertically one above the other so that their lines of action are in the same plane.

When an exterior force is applied, the boat will move but the state of equilibrium just described will be disturbed. We will suppose, to start with, that this force F_R is in the vertical fore-and-aft plane, above and parallel to the waterplane. This corresponds roughly to running before the wind.

A Equilibrium in a following wind

In such conditions, all the forces act in the vertical fore-and-aft plane. The boat is subject to driving force F_R and is moved forward. Water opposes this motion with resistance R. As soon as resistance has become equal to driving force speed will be constant (fig. III.2).

However, the two forces F_R and R are separated vertically by a considerable distance, z, because the former acts in the air and the latter in the water. Forces F_R and R therefore form a couple which tends to make the boat tilt forward. As she does so, the centre of buoyancy shifts forward a certain distance, x, and the couple formed by the forces of gravity W and of buoyancy B will shift so that it is in equilibrium with the former couple. $F_R \times z$ will then equal $B \times x$.

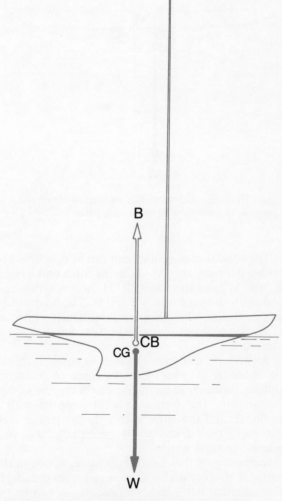

Figure III.1 *The forces of gravity and buoyancy in equilibrium when the boat is stationary.*

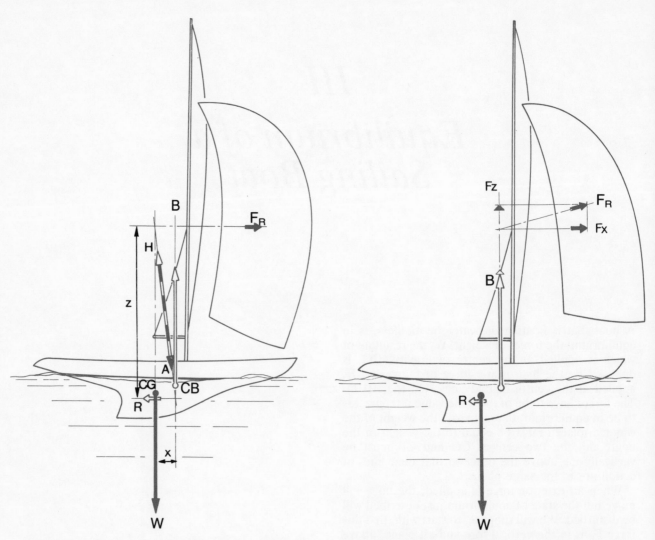

Figure III.2 *Equilibrium when making way in response to a propulsive force parallel to the waterplane.*

Figure III.3 *Change of equilibrium when the driving force is directed upwards. The force of buoyancy is decreased by the value of the vertical component.*

The condition of equilibrium can be confirmed by taking the resultant, A, of driving force and weight, F_R and W, and the resultant, H, of the hydrostatic and hydrodynamic forces B and R. The boat will be in equilibrium when these two resultants, which are of equal value but opposite in direction, act in the same line.

As we have just seen, this state of equilibrium can be obtained as a result of the force of buoyancy shifting forward; alternatively weight may be shifted further aft. The former is what happens with a keelboat, and the latter with a dinghy whose crew can move their body weight, which is a large proportion of total weight.

Suppose now that this driving force, although still acting in the fore-and-aft line, is no longer parallel to the waterline but is inclined upwards, as can be the case when a spinnaker is set (fig. III.3). F_R will then be composed of two forces, F_x which is horizontal

and F_z which is vertical. The same couple is formed as before by F_x and R, but there remains the vertical component F_z, acting in the same direction as buoyancy.

The sum of the vertical forces cannot change because it must remain equal to weight W, therefore B is reduced so that $W = B + F_z$. The reduction of B is by virtue of the fact that, because the hull will be less deeply immersed, the weight of the water displaced will also be reduced. Consequently, given unchanged resistance, there will be an increase in speed.

An alternative possibility is that driving force shifts to one side of the fore-and-aft line by a distance y, but stays parallel to the centreline, say of a una- or cat-rigged boat.

A horizontal couple is then formed, composed of the two forces F_R and R, the value being $F_R \times y$. To balance the action of this couple, another horizontal

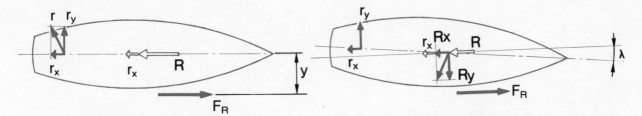

Figure III.4 *The action of putting the helm over to compensate for the effect of the driving force acting to one side of the centreline causes resistance r_x to appear; this is deducted from the force available for propelling the hull.*

Figure III.5 *In order to balance the transverse force of the helm (r_y), the hull has to take up a certain angle of incidence λ in order to develop a lateral force R_y, which is equal and opposite in direction to r_y; this causes additional resistance R_x, which also has to be deducted from the force available for propelling the hull.*

couple is required, of equal value but acting in the opposite direction. Initially the temptation is to achieve this by altering the helm. Putting the tiller over develops a force r, which can be broken down into two forces, r_y being transverse and r_x longitudinal (fig. III.4). Because $r_x + R$ must remain equal to F_R, R will be reduced and, inevitably, speed as well; this is the first harmful result of using the helm.

In order to form a longitudinal couple, there must be a second force that is equal and opposite in direction to the transverse force r_y that results from helm action, and this can only be provided by the hull which swings round so that a certain angle, λ, is formed between her fore-and-aft line and her direction of motion (fig. III.5). Unfortunately this transverse force R_y will be accompanied by longitudinal drag R_x which again reduces the value of R and consequently further reduces speed. The second damaging effect of using the helm is that drag results from the hull swinging round to one side of the direction of motion.

In the vertical plane, however, the two forces r_y and R_y are usually at different heights, r_y being higher than R_y because of the greater depth of the fin keel (fig. III.6), and the result is a couple in the vertical/transverse plane which tends to make the boat heel in the opposite direction to that in which the driving force F_R has shifted. Heeling causes the lines of action of forces W and B to separate, forming a couple which balances the couple r_y and R_y. The unfortunate result of heeling is additional drag, generated on account of the asymmetrical shape of the hull.

Happily, all this can be avoided by making the boat heel the opposite way so that the line of action of the driving force is in the same vertical plane as that of resistance; there is then no need to resort to using the helm (fig. III.7).

In practice, the asymmetry of the hull resulting from deliberately making the boat heel has a similar action to the helm, and equilibrium will generally be achieved without its being necessary to bring driving force back quite as far as the same vertical plane as

resistance (fig. III.8). The amount of resistance resulting from asymmetry will, in any case, be less than the sum of the additional resistances arising from helm action.

Driving force can act in any direction. The four basic forces can then only remain in equilibrium as a result of shifting their lines of action in all planes.

This brings us to conditions that correspond to all points of sailing other than running dead before the wind, and to close-hauled sailing in particular.

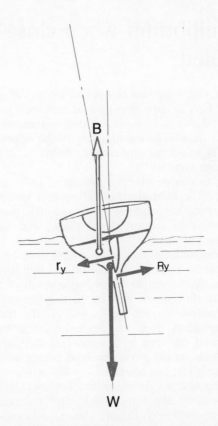

Figure III.6 *The difference in height between the transverse forces developed by the hull and the helm form a couple which increases the angle of heel.*

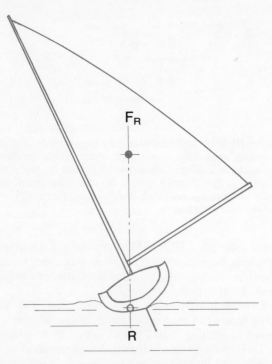

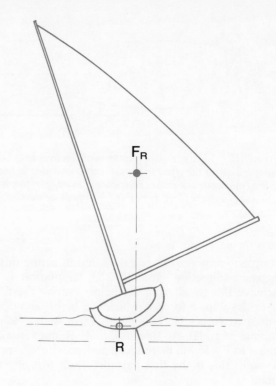

Figure III.7   *In order to avoid interference from the helm, the boat is made to heel to windward so as to bring driving force back into the same vertical plane as hull resistance.*

B Equilibrium when close-hauled

Here again there are two couples of forces, W and B, R and F. The direction of F is now obliquely forward, and also to leeward and downwards, while R is always parallel to F and acting in the opposite direction; W and B must, of course, always act in the vertical plane (fig. III.9).

In order to analyse the equilibrium of these four forces, we have to study their projection in three planes: vertical/longitudinal (fore-and-aft) plane, vertical/transverse (athwartships) plane, and horizontal plane (fig. III.10).

In the longitudinal plane, the couple formed by the components F_R and R of the sail and hull forces is balanced by the couple formed as a result of the longitudinal shift of W and B. In the transverse plane the couple formed by F_H and F_S, the transverse components of F and R, is balanced by a couple caused this time by a transverse shift of W and B, which results from the boat taking up an angle of heel. The two couples F_R − R and F_H − F_S are inclining couples (pitching and heeling), which are opposed by the longitudinal and transverse righting couples B − W. In both planes, just as when running, the lines of action of B and W can be moved by shifting one, or the other, or even both forces.

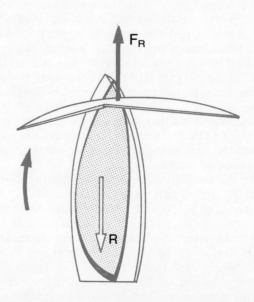

Figure III.8   *However, the asymmetry of the hull when the boat is heeled creates a couple that is opposite in direction to that due to the lateral shift of driving force. If the two couples are to remain in equilibrium, driving force should not be brought quite as far back as parallel to the centreline.*

Only two forces appear in the horizontal plane, F_T and R_T, components of F_R and R; if the boat is directionally stable, these two forces are directly opposed to each other and no couple is formed. Because W and B only act vertically, they have no effect in this plane.

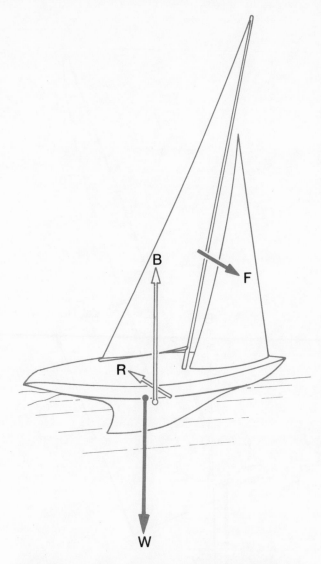

Figure III.9 *When close-hauled, equilibrium depends always on two couples, the first being the forces developed by the sails, F, and the hull, R, and the second being weight W and buoyancy B.*

The sail and hull forces can now be broken down into forces that are parallel and perpendicular to the course (fig. III.11). In the horizontal plane F_H is composed of F_x, representing driving force, and F_y, the force that tends to make the boat move sideways. Respectively they are opposed by R_x, which is the total resistance to forward motion, and R_y, the force that is developed by the lateral plane and resists leeway.

In the transverse plane F_H and F_S give us not only components F_y and R_y but the vertical components F_z and R_z, and the latter are found again in the longitudinal plane.

We can deduce from the fact that the transverse couples F_H and z and W × y are equal that, as z is constant, the value of F_H and, therefore, that of its component F_x which drives the boat forward, will be

directly linked to that of the righting couple W × y. Thus the first factor governing the performance of a sailing boat is her stability.

We also know that, in order to develop lift and a force F_S which will balance F_H, the whole of the immersed hull with keel or centreboard has to meet the water at a certain angle of attack: the leeway angle, λ. The second factor governing the performance of a boat working to windward will therefore be the ability of the lateral plane to develop lift, R_y, efficiently — that is, at as small as possible leeway angle λ, and with the minimum of resistance to forward motion R_x. The latter is indicated by the hydrodynamic drag angle ε_H between R_T and the perpendicular to the course.

How well a sailing boat performs when close-hauled is summarized by her Vmg (speed made good to windward, fig. III.12). Given the same ratio of V_T/V_S, Vmg = $V_S \cos \gamma$ will increase proportionately as γ, and therefore β, decrease.

The aim then is to reduce angle β, which the apparent wind makes with the course, as much as possible, and the sails must be trimmed so that the angle α, which the total force F_T developed by the sails makes with the apparent wind, should also be as small as possible. Given the same value of F_T, driving force would thus be greater and leeway effect smaller. This is linked to the aerodynamic characteristics of the sails, and to the aerodynamic drag angle, ε, between F_T and the perpendicular to the apparent wind.

To sum up, the three basic factors on which close-hauled performance depend are firstly stability, secondly the efficiency of the lateral plane, and thirdly that of the sails, as indicated by the sum of the drag angles $\varepsilon_H + \varepsilon_A$, which equals β.

The skipper's responsibility, so far as the lateral plane is concerned, is relatively obvious; it is essentially a matter of keeping the hull clean — but it is much more complex when it comes to the sails, because having a good suit of sails is not enough. Care is needed to avoid anything that could increase drag and, from that point of view, crew comfort or protection conflict with performance. Dodgers round the cockpit and a hood over the companion certainly make for comfort, while netting between the lifelines forward makes the handling of headsails easier, and rollers and baggywrinkle on the shrouds protect sheets and sails from chafe, but their use will inevitably be paid for by increased windage and poorer performance when close-hauled.

Many such items affect efficiency doubly, not only in the ways just mentioned but also when their weight and their position affect stability. A radar aerial on the mast, for example, or self-steering gear at the stern, mean an increase in weight, but their positions also reduce stability and affect seakeeping.

Every decision to install a new item on board that was not foreseen at the design stage must therefore be taken with the greatest care and deliberation. In

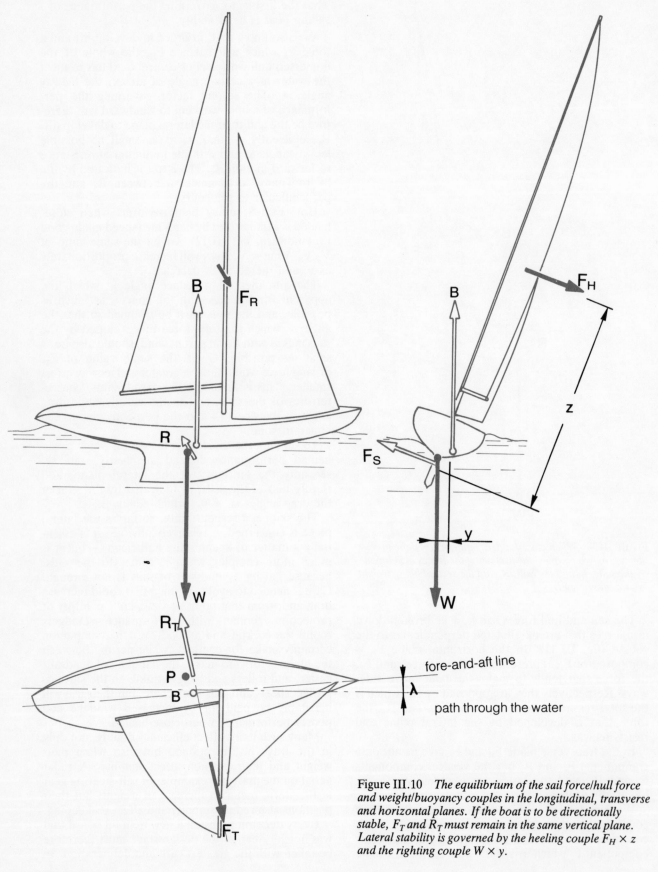

B

F_R

R

W

R_T

P

B

fore-and-aft line

λ

path through the water

F_T

B

F_H

z

F_S

y

W

Figure III.10 *The equilibrium of the sail force/hull force and weight/buoyancy couples in the longitudinal, transverse and horizontal planes. If the boat is to be directionally stable, F_T and R_T must remain in the same vertical plane. Lateral stability is governed by the heeling couple $F_H \times z$ and the righting couple $W \times y$.*

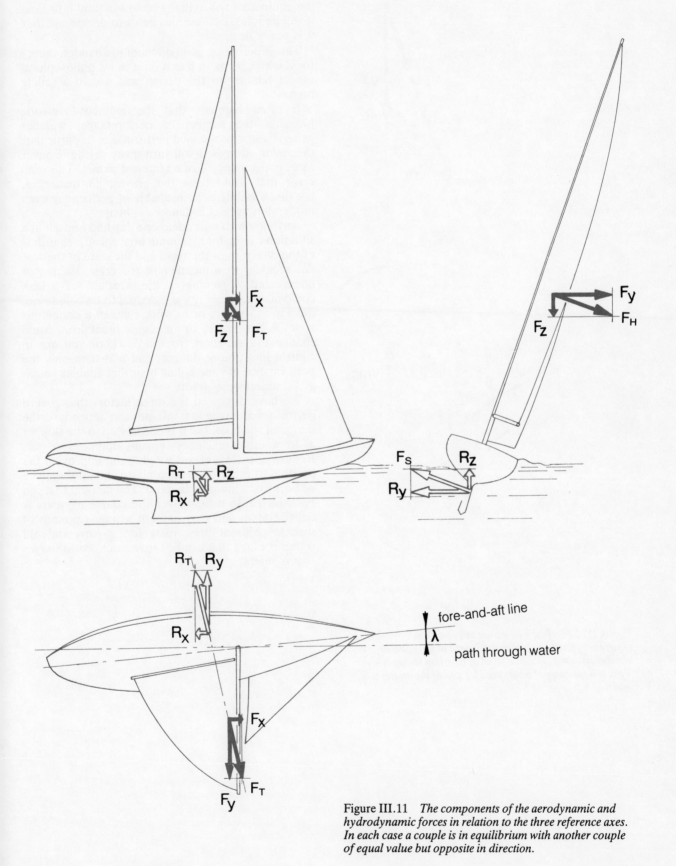

Figure III.11 *The components of the aerodynamic and hydrodynamic forces in relation to the three reference axes. In each case a couple is in equilibrium with another couple of equal value but opposite in direction.*

63

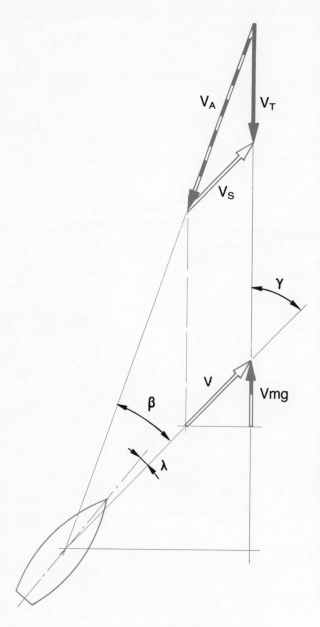

Figure III.12 *How well a boat sails on a close-hauled course is defined by the value of speed made good to windward, Vmg, in a true wind of a certain strength V_T. Vmg is a function of boat speed V_S and of the angles β and γ.*

particular it is wise to consider how much of the time the equipment will actually be in use (and how long it will lie idle), because this helps to decide whether it is really necessary.

This is perhaps a good moment to abandon theory for a while, so as to touch on a more philosophical aspect relating to the design and use of a sailing boat.

It often happens that the moment someone broaches the subject of performance, whether generally or close-hauled performance in particular, the sailor addressed will turn away saying 'I never race, performance is of no interest to me.' This is an error that could have the gravest consequences, because a sailing boat incapable of performing even moderately well is a dangerous boat.

Anybody who sails could one day find himself in a situation calling for maximum boat speed, regardless of the direction of the wind and the state of the sea. An accident to a member of the crew, sudden or unexpected worsening of the weather, or a leak could all mean that it was essential to be able to run quickly to shelter, or to work clear of a dangerous zone. A flat battery or an engine breakdown could change the situation from one where you are in control into one of danger, and it is then only the performance of your sailing boat that enables you to avoid unwelcome drama.

We have discussed the three factors that govern performance; in the first instance this depends on the design of the boat, but it is entirely up to the skipper as to whether efficiency remains optimum or not. Removing useless excess weight, and improving the position of other objects on board should therefore be borne continuously in mind. The amount that can be loaded into a boat over the course of years is unbelievable, and may amount to many pounds of shackles without pins, rusty frying pans and old rotten cordage that can be thrown out. *Performance means safety!*

IV
Stability

We have just seen that the first factor that affects a sailing boat's performance is her transverse stability, because it is this that governs how much driving force she can accept. Longitudinal stability also plays a part, firstly because a change in trim affects the performance of the sails and alters the lateral plane and, secondly, because in certain instances it acts as a safety factor.

In fact, the mechanics of stability are exactly the same, regardless of the direction of action of the disturbing force that causes the phenomena connected with stability. However, because a boat's length is so much greater than her beam, her reactions are much more evident in the transverse plane, and that is why we shall go more deeply into the question of transverse stability.

It is only the stability of a boat at rest that we shall consider, because the modifications which can be caused by waves due to forward motion, or by pressure distribution, call for a much more complex analysis and are second order.

The term stability is used in this chapter in two senses: as a general term describing the ability of a boat to resist heeling in response to an external force; and, more precisely, to describe the state of equilibrium when all the forces and the moments to which the boat is subject are zero.

A Transverse stability

If we take an empty bottle or a jamjar and place it on the water (fig. IV.1), we can spin it round and round; it will not oppose this movement at all, and will stay just as it is left. It turns round its axis of rotation, 0, on which is also found its centre of gravity. The centre of the immersed volume, CB, stays permanently in the same position, vertically below the centre of gravity, CG. Equilibrium is stable, but because the two forces of buoyancy B and weight or gravity G are unable to separate, no couple can be formed to oppose rotation. Motion will be checked only by friction in the boundary layer.

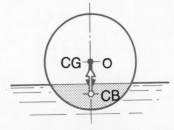

Figure IV.1   *A cylinder floating on the water has zero stability; whatever its position, the forces of weight and of buoyancy on the same axis are equal and opposite and their centres stay one above the other; equilibrium is neutral.*

1 Stability due to weight

If we now pour some plaster or cement into the bottle while it is lying flat and let it harden, the centre of gravity CG will be moved away from 0 (fig. IV.2a) when the bottle is turned. Now, when the bottle is put in the water, we can no longer make it spin round as we wish because the centre of gravity swings around 0, shifting to one side so that it is no longer vertically above the centre of the immersed volume which, itself, does not move (fig. IV.2b). The righting couple W × y which is formed tends to return the bottle to its initial position. Because the bottle is cylindrical, its shape has played no part in forming the righting couple, and stability is due only to the ballast that was added. This is stability due to weight.

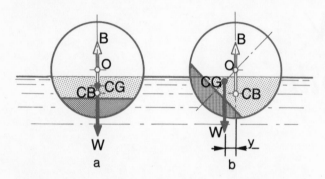

Figure IV.2 *Purely on account of the fact that its centre of gravity shifts, the same cylinder with ballast has stability due to weight.*

2 Stability due to form

Now let us take a wooden plank or a piece of foam plastic that is rectangular in section. As in the case of the bottle, the centre of gravity CG is immediately above the geometric centre of the immersed section, CB (fig. IV.3a). When vertical pressure is applied to one side, the plank will tilt but, unlike the bottle in

fig. IV.1, it will return immediately to its initial position as soon as pressure is removed. This is because, although the centre of gravity has not shifted, the centre of the immersed volume has moved towards the side on which pressure was exerted, so forming a righting couple B × y.

It is only the shape of the section that is responsible for this couple being formed, and this stability is therefore said to be due to shape or form.

3. Total stability

We will now consider what happens when a sailing boat with a normal section heels in response to the wind — but one point has to be made clear at the start. In the case of the plank, force F acting on one side had to be balanced by an equal increase in buoyancy.

On the other hand we saw in Chapter III, fig. III.11, that in the case of a sailing boat the vertical components of the forces forming the heeling and righting couples are in equilibrium. Consequently heeling will not (in this case) cause the boat to become more deeply immersed, and displacement will therefore not be increased. If the volumes of the underwater bodies corresponding to different heeling angles do not change, they are called iso-carenes (equal underwater bodies), and similarly the corresponding waterlines are called the isocarene waterlines. If the section of the underwater body is constant through its length, the shape and volume of the underwater body will not vary with the heeling angle, but this is not the case with a complicated shape like that of a sailing boat, the fore-and-aft trim of which is altered when the boat heels. This point affects the final calculations relating to statical stability, but can be ignored here in this discussion of the theory.

Note that we are assuming that these changes in heeling angle are made without speed being involved. In paragraph 11 below, we will see the effect that speed has.

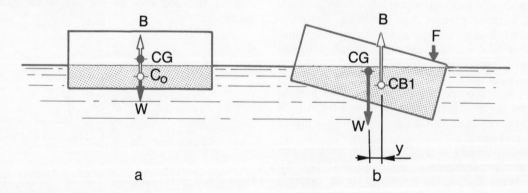

Figure IV.3 *The block of foam floating on the water has stability due to shape when a force F alters the position in which it floats. This time it is the centre of buoyancy alone that shifts.*

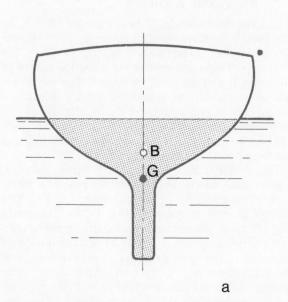

a

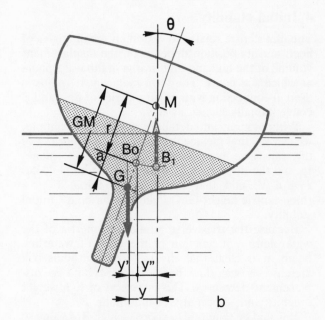

b

Figure IV.4 *A sailing boat that is heeling has both stability due to weight, because her centre of gravity, G, shifts, and stability due to shape because her centre of buoyancy, B, moves. The alteration of the position of the centre of* buoyancy at a small angle of heel is along the circumference of a circle, the instantaneous centre of which is the metacentre, M.

Fig. IV.4a shows the section of a heavily ballasted sailing boat, with her initial centre of gravity below the centre of buoyancy. At a small angle of heel, θ, (of about one degree) the section rotates round point M, which is at the intersection of the vertical through the original centre of buoyancy, B_0, when the boat is lying upright and the vertical through the new centre of buoyancy, B_1, (fig. IV.4b). This instantaneous centre of rotation is called the metacentre, and its importance in the study of stability was first brought to light by the Frenchman Pierre Bouguer in his *Traité du navire* which appeared in 1746. The distance between the centre of gravity, G, and the metacentre, M, is called the metacentric height $\overline{GM}$, and r is the metacentric radius (or BM, see below) of the circle of rotation of the centre of buoyancy around the instantaneous centre M. Righting couple $G \times y = G \times \overline{GM} \sin \theta$.

However, y is actually the sum of y', resulting from the lateral shift of the position of the centre of gravity G by comparison with the vertical through the initial centre of buoyancy B_o, and y'', resulting from the shift of B_o to B_1; therefore

$$G \times y = G(y' + y'') = Gy' + Gy''$$

or

$$G \times \overline{GM} \sin \theta = G \times a \sin \theta + G \times r \sin \theta.$$

$G \times a \sin \theta$ relates to stability due to weight, and $G \times r \sin \theta$ to stability due to form.

$$\overline{GM} \sin \theta = a \sin \theta + r \sin \theta$$

is therefore the total righting lever.

In the majority of cases, the centre of gravity is found above the original centre of buoyancy: a, therefore, is deducted rather than added. Metacentric height is also called r-a, although $\overline{GM}$ is more commonly used (fig. IV.5).

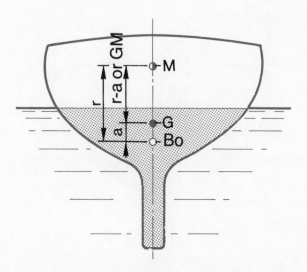

Figure IV.5 *Metacentric height GM or r − a is the distance on the axis between the centre of gravity and the metacentre, and indicates the boat's stability at the small angle of heel being considered.*

4 Initial stability

The metacentre relates to extremely small angles of heel, and its position depends on the displacement volume of the hull and on the area of the waterplane at which she floats. The term metacentric radius is used in connection with greater angles of heel and is conventionally known as BM.

Without going into details by working an example, we can say that metacentric radius is the quotient of the transverse moment of inertia of the waterplane, I_x, and the displacement volume of the hull, ∇, i.e. $r = I_x/\nabla$, and that the value of initial r – a (metacentric height $\overline{GM}$) indicates the boat's initial stability.

Because the transverse moment of inertia of the waterplane is a function of the cube of waterline beam, it is clear that the metacentric radius will increase as waterline beam increases and as displacement decreases. This is typical of lightweight dinghies and, especially, of multihulls.

It would be tempting to choose a high BM value so as to obtain maximum stability at those angles where it is most beneficial for performance, but this should not be overdone because it would result in the boat having an unpleasant motion in a cross sea, with a very short period of roll and very jerky movements. We will return to this point in Chapter VIII.

Because the moment of inertia increases to the power of 4, while volume only increases as the cube, metacentric height should increase linearly. In fact, however, the length/beam ratio decreases with size, but the metacentric height varies much more slowly and values can be taken as ranging from 0.90 m for a boat with a waterline length of 5 m to 1 m or 1.20 m at 15 m.

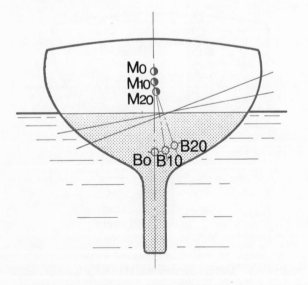

Figure IV.6 *As the centre of buoyancy shifts, the metacentre follows its own path.*

5 B, M, F and Z curves

When the boat's angle of heel changes from θ_n to one that is infinitessimally greater θ_{n+1}, its section pivots about a new metacentre M_n (fig. IV.6). As the section performs a complete rotation, the centre of buoyancy B and the metacentre M follow paths that can be traced in the transverse plane. Because a sailing boat is symmetrical in shape, the curves will be symmetrical either side of the vertical axis; they will also be closed, that is to say that the starting and finishing points of the curves coincide.

The B curve of buoyancy is generally convex, regular and nearly an ellipse, whereas the metacentric curve M, that of the metacentric radius, may reverse sharply in direction (fig. IV.7). The peaks that interrupt the smooth line of the M curve indicate particular positions, such as the immersion of the edge of the deck or of the superstructure, and the emergence of the fin keel. Apart from these special points, which sometimes need closer study, the remainder of the curves can be drawn by plotting points corresponding to 10–30° changes in the angle of heel.

A line normal to the curve of buoyancy, corresponding to a given angle of heel θ_h, is tangential to the M curve at the corresponding point M_h. B_nM_n is the metacentric radius at angle θ_n.

When the shape of the section is simple, as in fig. IV.7, waterline beam and, consequently, the corresponding moment of inertia and the metacentric radius BM are least at an angle of heel of about 100–110°. A reversal of the metacentric curve corresponds to the angle of heel (fig. IV.8a).

If the shape is more complex, and for example includes a keel or a coachroof, the metacentric radius will increase and decrease in turn, and a reversal of the metacentric curve will occur on each occasion (fig. IV.8b).

In the case of a sailing boat, the metacentric radius BM generally has a maximum value when $\theta = 0$ and 180°, and a minimum value when $\theta =$ about 90°, and the completed curve looks like a curvilinear lozenge, rather similar to an ace of diamonds (fig. IV.8a). However, when the sections are so shaped that waterline beam increases initially as the boat starts to heel, the curved lozenge can become convex in shape.

If the value of BM is maximum not when $\theta = 0$ and 180°, but at an intermediate angle (for example in the case of boats with small waterline beam), the trace will curve the opposite way initially before reversing at an angle of heel that corresponds to maximum BM (fig. IV.9b). This is typical of most boats designed for an IOR Mk III rating, when low initial stability is required so as to reduce the CGF as much as possible. The boat's stability increases as soon as she heels, and this shows how inefficient this method of measuring is when it comes to determining the real value of stability (fig. IV.9).

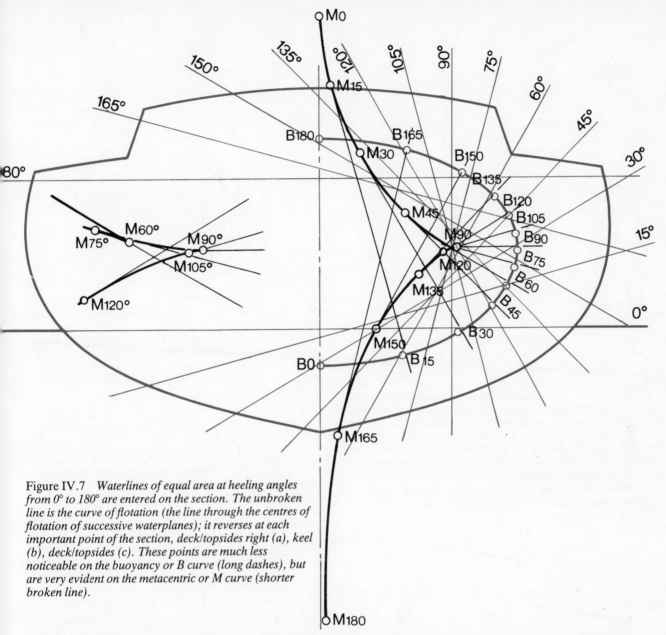

Figure IV.7 *Waterlines of equal area at heeling angles from 0° to 180° are entered on the section. The unbroken line is the curve of flotation (the line through the centres of flotation of successive waterplanes); it reverses at each important point of the section, deck/topsides right (a), keel (b), deck/topsides (c). These points are much less noticeable on the buoyancy or B curve (long dashes), but are very evident on the metacentric or M curve (shorter broken line).*

It is also interesting to trace the Z curve, which is the projection of the foot of the perpendicular from the centre of gravity on to the verticals through the heeled centres of buoyancy; these perpendiculars correspond to righting levers. (Fig. IV.10)

This curve has two interesting characteristics, the first being the point of tangency with the metacentric curve, which indicates very exactly the heeling angle corresponding to the maximum righting couple. The second is the angle of the tangent from point G; this is perpendicular to the tangent which corresponds to the reversal point, and indicates the angle of statical capsize.

6 Curve of statical stability and angle of vanishing stability

The real stability of a boat is best shown by a stability curve, namely a graph which shows the righting arm or righting moment at all angles of heel.
$$\overline{GZ}$$
Either y can be considered alone, or the product of
$$G \times \overline{GZ}$$
$G \times y$ which comes to the same thing because G is a constant.

The graph is traced by plotting the abscissae and ordinates that match the angles of heel and the
$$\overline{GZ}$$
values of $G \times y$ (fig. IV.11).

The boat is stable while the curve is rising, and every increase in heeling moment can be matched by an equal increase in righting moment.

At a certain limiting angle of heel, θ_1, righting moment reaches its maximum value, after which it decreases, no longer being able to counter an increase in heeling moment. However, if heeling moment then decreases, the boat will return to her initial position because righting moment is still posi-

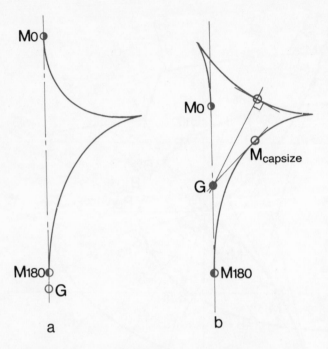

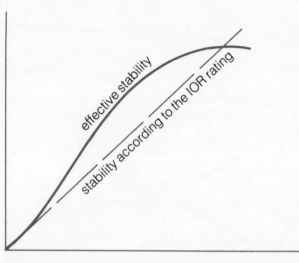

Figure IV.8   *Two typical developed metacentric curves of sections with simple forms, (a) metacentric height decreases from the start, (b) metacentric height increases initially and then decreases. The two positions of the centre of gravity in relation to the metacentric curve are also shown. In (a) G is outside the curve, and righting moment is always positive. In (b) G is inside the curve; righting moment is maximum where a line from G is perpendicular to the M curve (M maximum), and nil where the line from G is tangential to the curve, $M_{capsize}$.*

Figure IV.9   *When a boat has a narrow waterplane, like those designed for an IOR rating, the curvature at the start of the stability curve indicates that initial stability is poor; this gives a false idea of actual stability at heeling angles up to 30°.*

Figure IV.10   *Every normal from the buoyancy curve is tangential to the metacentric curve at the point corresponding to the metacentre. In order to calculate righting moment, either y $\overline{GZ}$ or $\overline{GM}$ sin θ can be considered.*

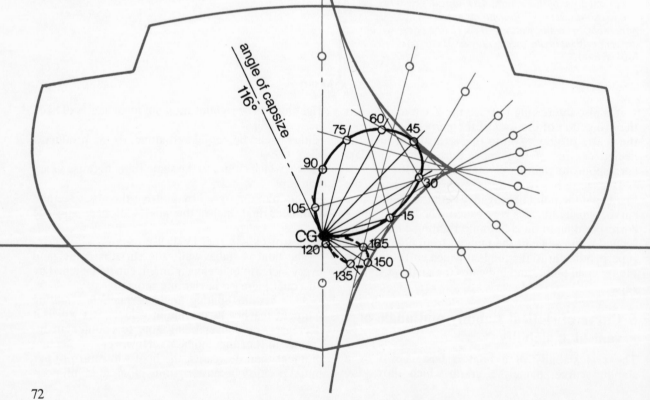

tive. On the other hand, if heeling moment continues to increase the boat will capsize.

When the angle of heel continues to increase, there comes a point at which the centre of buoyancy and the centre of gravity are again in the same vertical plane; this is the angle of vanishing statical stability, θ_2, at which there is no lever arm or righting moment.

If this angle occurs at 180° of heel, the boat is said to be self-righting because she will always return to an even keel when the heeling force ceases to act — but this is not always the case, and if the angle of vanishing stability θ_2 is under 180° there will be a considerable zone where the boat has inverse stability, which will automatically turn her to float keel upwards. This often happens with lightweight dinghies, and in particular with multihulls; the latter are extremely difficult to right after they have turned turtle.

Stability here should not be confused with stable equilibrium, by which is meant that an object that has been displaced from its original state of equilibrium will either return to it (stable equilibrium) or will not do so (unstable equilibrium). This idea is linked to the fact that equilibrium is stable when the centre of gravity is lower than it would be in any other position nearby, a condition that is realized in the case of a boat when metacentric height is positive, $r - a > 0$, that is to say when the centre of gravity is beneath the metacentre. This is why the equilibrium of a ballasted boat with a low centre of gravity is stable at 0° of heel and unstable at 180°, whereas that of a dinghy with a higher centre of gravity is stable not only at 0° but at 180° (fig. IV.12).

The value of the heeling moments can also be plotted on the statical stability curve. A moment that

is constant regardless of the angle of heel would be shown by a straight line M_c, parallel to the axis of the abscissa (fig. IV.13), whereas a curve indicates that heeling moment varies, for example as it does when heeling couple diminishes at a greater angle of heel because the area of sail projected to the wind becomes progressively smaller.

A graph of permissible maximum heeling moments M_v can be traced, and this will be tangential to the stability curve. The point of tangency can be seen to correspond to an angle of heel θ_3, which is slightly greater than θ_1, and the angle of maximum righting moment is therefore slightly greater.

If we now plot a curve of heeling moments, M_v, that are less than maximum heeling moments, the curve will cut the stability curve at the two points C1 and C2 in fig. IV.26. The part of the curve between C1 and C2 indicates the boat's reserve stability when she is subjected to a heeling moment corresponding to the values of C1 and C2.

7 Factors which affect the stability curve

It is often difficult to establish to what degree stability of shape and stability of weight are affected when one particular parameter is altered, but we will try to isolate a few essential principles by giving examples.

First of all we will consider two sections that have the same wetted area, the same draught and the same freeboard, but different beam. The centre of gravity of the less beamy boat will be slightly lower because less of her weight will be concentrated high up. In spite of this it is evident from fig. IV.14 that, up to about 90° of heel, her righting moment is inferior to that of the beamier boat. This confirms

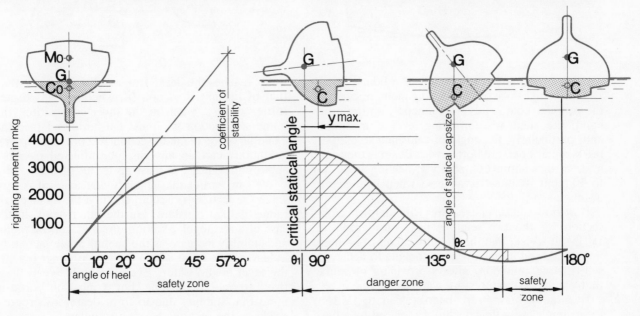

Figure IV.11   *Typical stability curve, based on the values of righting couples up to 180°.*

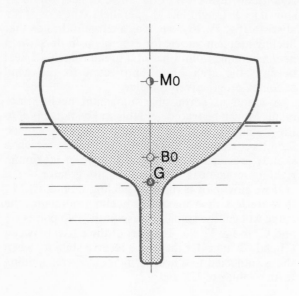

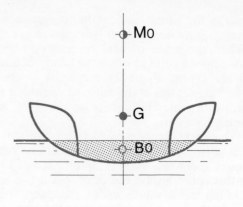

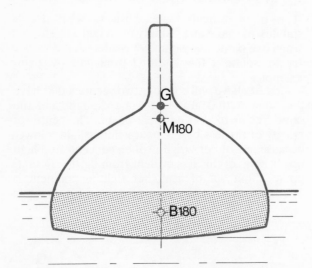

Figure IV.12 *The ballasted boat is unstable at 180° because her centre of gravity is above her metacentre, whereas the centreboard dinghy is stable when upside down, her metacentre being above her centre of gravity.*

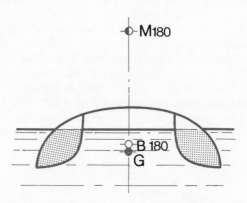

that initial stability is a function of a boat's beam, and the initial slope of the righting moment curve of the beamier boat is therefore steeper; on the other hand, the angle when righting lever is maximum and, particularly, the angle of vanishing stability of the beamier boat, are both lower. Beam is therefore a factor that improves stability at heeling angles up to 30°, but its effect is adverse when it comes to ultimate safety.

If we now add superstructures with identical cross-sections to the two sections just considered (fig. IV.15), it is clear that the stability curves of both are improved, and it may even be possible to achieve a self-righting condition, always providing of course that the superstructures are watertight.

Even an increase in freeboard (as in fig.IV.16b) for example, with the coachroof replaced by a flush deck) will improve stability at all angles greater than 30°, up to the point where she has heeled so far that

water reaches the deck. Her stability is greater than that of the initial section (a) when she has turned turtle because, when in the inverted position, the immersed section is almost flat-bottomed (see the example of the plank in section A.2 of this chapter).

Stability can, in any case, be affected by more subtle differences, at least up to 30° of heel.

We saw earlier that stability due to form is zero when the section is circular, and that the metacentric radius is then constant. On the other hand, in the case of a rectangular section, the metacentric radius and stability increase as the heeling angle increases, at least to the point where the upper corner reaches the level of the water. Every shape between these two extremes is possible, but it must be borne in mind that stability due to form decreases progressively as the sections become rounder.

We will now compare two boats with the same basic section and the same waterline beam and draft,

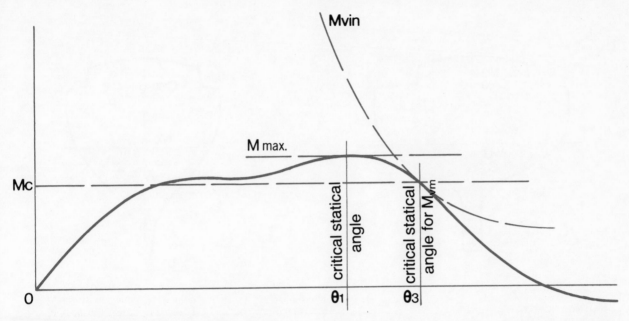

Figure IV.13   *Constant heeling moment M_c or a variable heeling moment M_{vm} plotted on the stability curve; both* *balance righting moment at the angle of maximum righting moment.*

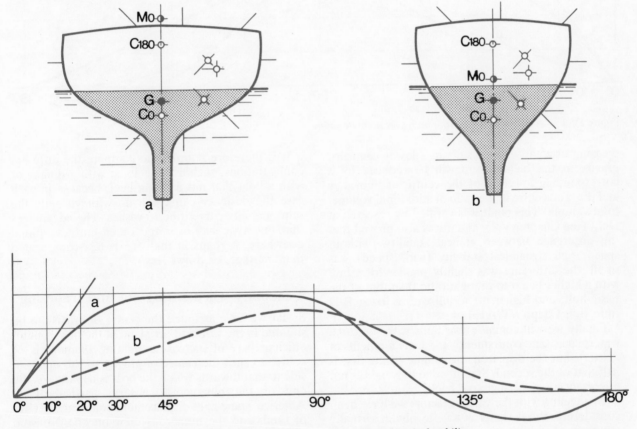

Figure IV.14   *The effect that waterline beam has on the shape of the curve of statical stability.*

one of which has a long thick keel and the other a fin keel with a bulb, the ballast weight being the same in both cases (fig. IV.17). We will assume that the centre of gravity is the same in both boats but that the centre of buoyancy of the bulb keel boat is higher, as is the metacentre. Initial stability will be greater, as will stability at all heeling angles.

It is therefore important not to place volume low down when designing a section, and this is why, given a boat with a thick keel, the effect of in-

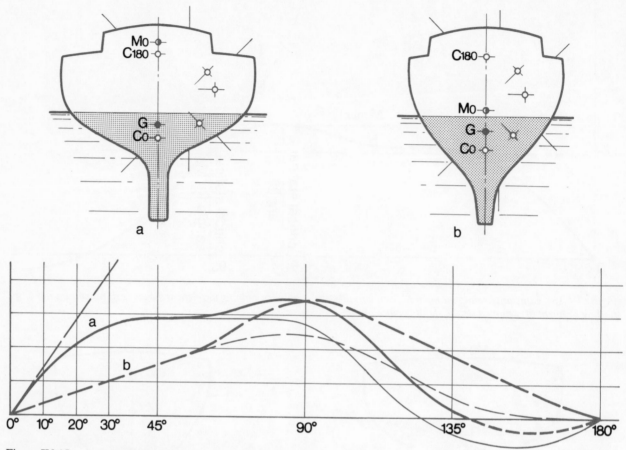

Figure IV.15 *A watertight coachroof increases ultimate safety.*

creasing draught which results in a lower centre of gravity in the ballast ratio will be reduced by a corresponding lowering of the centre of buoyancy and the metacentre in the ratio of additional volume/total volume. This point was verified by research at Delft (see Chapter V.3), and it was also proved that the difference between statical stability (without speed) and dynamical stability (with speed) was small; the difference was slightly smaller for a hull with a higher beam-to-draught ratio than that of the basic hull, and higher for a hull with a lower B/D ratio (see Chapter V.A1a).

Finally we will compare two hulls with the same waterplanes (and consequently the same moments of inertia), but the displacement volume of the first is half that of the second. Stability due to weight is not important at small angles of heel.

By juggling with the various factors we have been considering, the designer is able to obtain virtually any form of stability curve that he requires. He can increase initial stability by reducing weight; beam affects initial stability too, as well as stability at angles up to about 30°; by increasing freeboard he delays the angle of vanishing stability; and he can reduce stability in an inverted position by altering the volume of the superstructure.

It is therefore pointless to compare the different configurations, such as a keelboat with a dinghy or with a boat that has a lifting keel, because in each case the designer can come up with virtually the same stability curve if he so wishes. The advantages that one type has over the other must be found elsewhere, perhaps in that one is less complicated than another, or draws less.

8 Stability when sitting out and trapezing

So far we have assumed the centre of gravity to be situated in the fore-and-aft plane of the boat, but an efficient way of increasing righting moment is of course to shift the centre of gravity to the opposite side to that towards which the boat is heeling. At the end of the nineteenth century, particularly in America, some light displacement boats carried bags of sand, and the numerous crew on board passed them from one side to the other every time the boats went about; the term 'sandbaggers' stems from this.

This practice was forbidden by the early rules of yacht racing and today only live ballast weight, that of the crew, can be moved. Crew weight can be increased when necessary, for example by wearing soaking sweaters, but this practice is also restricted

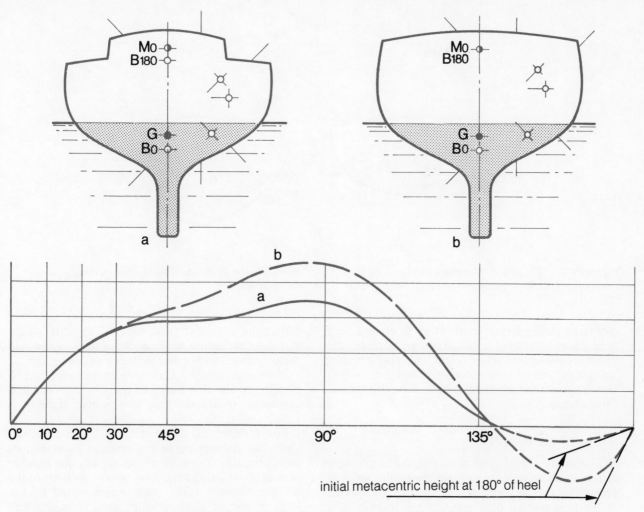

Figure IV.16   *The stability curve of the hull with a flush deck shows that its stability is greater than that of the hull with a coachroof. Every increase in volume high up* *increases stability at large angles of heel. On the other hand, initial stability in the inverted position is also greater.*

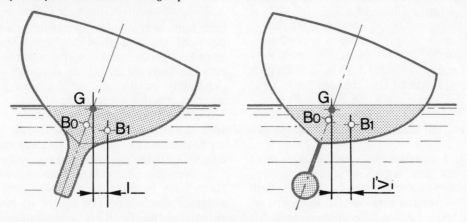

Figure IV.17   *Any decrease in volume low down causes stability to increase.*

by IYRU rules. Initially the crew can sit to windward, then he can sit out and lean back to windward as far as possible with his feet wedged under toe-straps, and then he can hang the whole weight of his body outboard on the end of a trapeze wire, with his feet braced against the gunwale. The additional stability due to weight resulting from this considerably increases the boat's righting moment (fig. IV.19).

Although increasing stability by shifting crew weight to windward is indispensable in the case of lightweight dinghies, it can also be useful when it

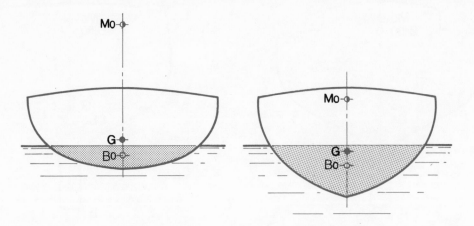

Figure IV.18 *The light displacement hull has a higher metacentre and consequently greater initial stability than* *another hull with the same waterplane area but greater displacement.*

comes to racing larger boats. High freeboard with tumblehome is then a disadvantage because the effect is to raise the crew's weight and bring it nearer amidships, and these are considerations that have to be set against the advantages of high freeboard and tumblehome.

9 Multihull stability

The stability characteristics of multihulls are very different, their stability virtually being due only to form. This can be very easily understood by looking at the fundamental differences in the stability of a classic keelboat and that of a racing catamaran.

The righting moment curves of two well-known boats, the *Dragon* and the *Hellcat*, are compared in fig. IV.20. Their main dimensions are:

	Dragon	Hellcat
Overall length	8.90 m	7.62 m
Waterline length	6 m	6.90 m
Maximum beam	1.96 m	4.25 m
Displacement, ready to sail	2185 kg	400 kg
Maximum sail area	26.60 m²	29 m²

As can be seen, sail area and waterline length are comparable.

Although the *Dragon* weighs over five times more than the *Hellcat*, the latter's maximum righting couple is similar when it is assumed that, in both boats, the crew stand or sit as far outboard as possible. The result of this difference in weight is that the *Dragon* is hard put to exceed 6 knots, whereas the *Hellcat* can sail at over 20 knots.

We find, too, that the *Hellcat* is most stable at an angle of heel of about 6°, whereas in the *Dragon*'s case maximum righting couple is at about 40°. The *Dragon*'s stability remains virtually constant thereafter until her heeling angle is about 55° when, being an open boat, she will fill and sink. Were she given a

watertight coachroof and cockpit, stability would stay near maximum to about 90° of heel, and would then diminish to become negative at about 135°.

If we superposed a heeling moment curve corresponding to the first hump of the *Dragon*'s stability curve, we would see that her reserve stability is good.

For catamarans the pattern is quite different. Once the stability curve has reached its maximum value, righting couple decreases rapidly and reaches zero at about 70° of heel. The curve stays short of the heeling moment curve (this is aggravated by the large degree of windage that results from one hull being in the air) and consequently there is no reserve stability. The helmsman has to keep his boat balanced continually close to the angle of heel where righting moment is maximum. The equilibrium of multihulls is normally stable when they are in two positions: the first when they are at about 0° on an even keel (in the case of a trimaran this depends on how the floats are arranged); the other at about 180°, depending on the size of the superstructure and whether it is fully watertight.

Various attempts have been made to remedy the lack of reserve stability in multihulls, and all these try to increase the angle of vanishing stability, particularly by using the trimaran configuration.

In every case, the centre of buoyancy of the two or three hulls is taken as that of all the submerged volumes combined. The centre of buoyancy of a catamaran (fig. IV.21) is generally midway between the two hulls when the boat is at an angle of heel of 0°. Initial righting moment will be very high because, owing to the distance between the hulls, the total moment of inertia of the two waterplanes in relation to the fore-and-aft line is very large. When the boat starts to heel, the combined centre of buoyancy will shift towards the leeward centre of buoyancy in the inverse ratio of the immersed volume of the two

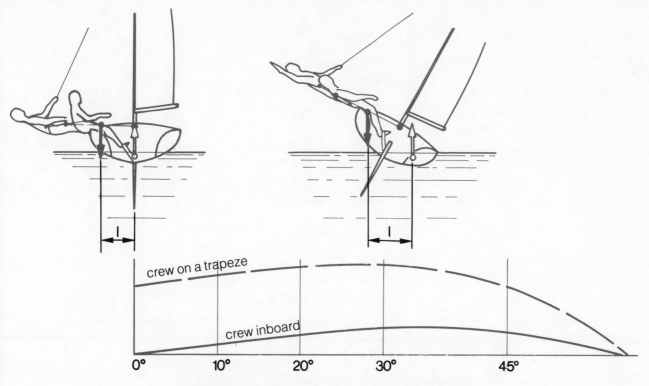

Figure IV.19 *Stability curves for a sailing dinghy with the crew inboard and with the crew on a trapeze; it is very clear that the trapeze has a major effect.*

hulls. At the very instant when the windward hull has just been lifted clear of the water, the combined centre of buoyancy will coincide with that of the leeward hull. Righting moment will then be maximum and, thereafter, will decrease roughly as a function of the sine of the angle of heel.

In the case of a trimaran, conditions are the same when she is on an even keel, and initial stability is the sum of the moments of inertia of the central hull and of the two floats in relation to the fore-and-aft line. The shape of the stability curve, however, will differ in accordance with the volume and height of the floats either side. If the volume of the floats is greater than total displacement (fig. IV.22), conditions are the same as for the catamaran when righting moment is maximum, but the corresponding angle of heel is slightly greater because the distance between the float and the central hull is not so great as the distance between the two hulls of the catamaran. Thereafter the shape of the curve is similar to that of the catamaran.

On the other hand, if the volume of the float is slightly less than total displacement (fig. IV.23), the float will become submerged and the mast will touch the water when the boat has heeled barely more than 90°. If the floats are so fitted that the centre of buoyancy of the floats combined is above the centre of gravity, positive righting moment can be maintained up to 90° of heel. However, because the floats will not be immersed when the trimaran is on an even keel, initial stability will be that of the central hull alone. As can be imagined, this arrangement is extremely sensitive to any anticipated alteration of displacement due to loads taken on board.

Attempts have also been made to improve the safety of catamarans by fitting ballast. Michael Henderson has designed and built two catamarans with ballasted fin keels, *Golden Miller* and *Misty Miller*, both with masthead floats. It is interesting to compare the stability curve of *Golden Miller* (fig. IV.24) with the curve in fig. IV.21. There is no doubt, though, that this solution means that much of the advantage of a catamaran configuration is lost, at least so far as the design of the hull is concerned, due to the increase in wetted area and displacement.

10 Stability on an inclined surface

So far we have been considering stability in relation to a horizontal water surface, but the sea is covered in waves, and the great Atlantic rollers normally slope at about 7°, and can sometimes be a great deal steeper than that.

A boat sailing in a beam sea will therefore sometimes find herself floating in water that slopes the same way as she is heeling. It is immediately obvious (fig. IV.25) that in these conditions the result of a shift of the centre of buoyancy from C_1 to C_2 is a considerable reduction in righting moment.

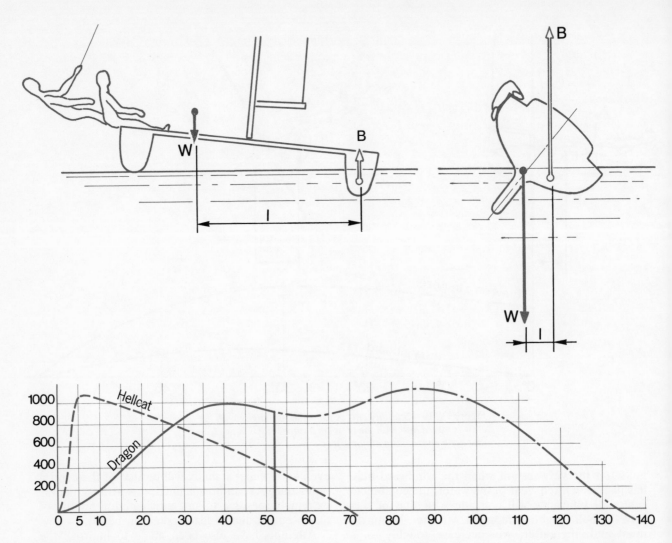

Figure IV.20   *The* Hellcat *catamaran and the* Dragon *have the same maximum righting couple, but the former* owes her stability to her form and the latter to her weight.

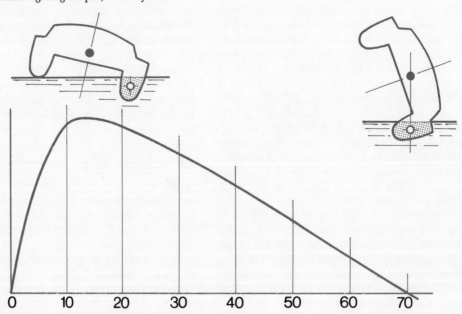

Figure IV.21   *Stability curve typical of a cruising catamaran.*

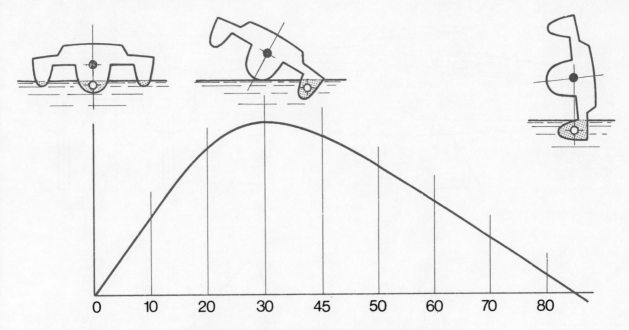

Figure IV.22 *Stability curve typical of a trimaran when the volume of one of the floats is at least equal to the craft's entire displacement.*

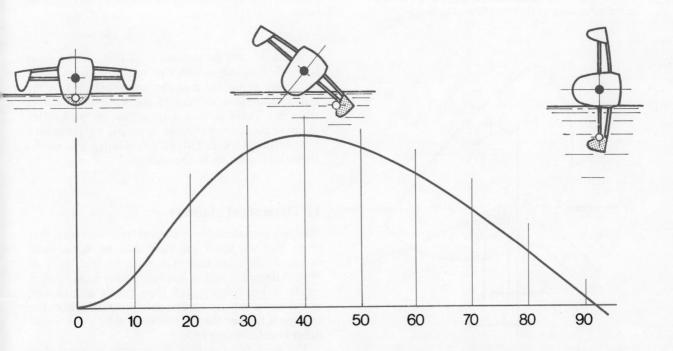

Figure IV.23 *Stability curve typical of a trimaran when the volume of each float is less than the total displacement of the boat; the float is positioned high so that righting couple remains positive at 90° of heel.*

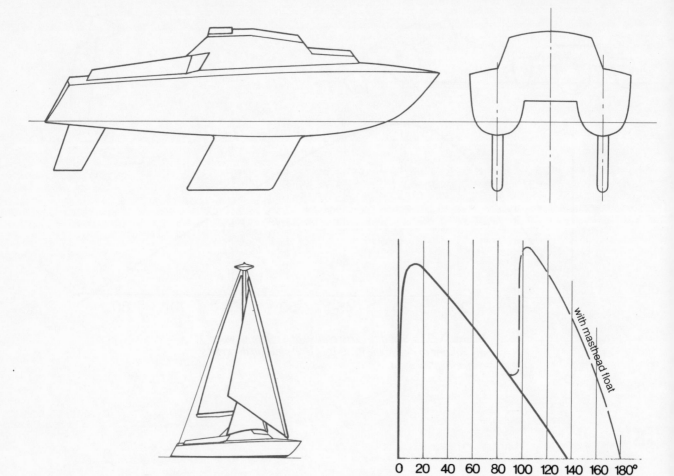

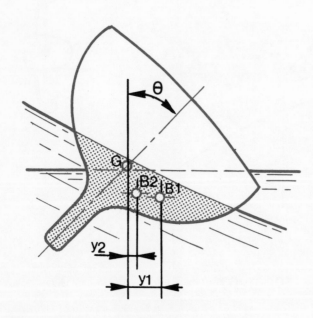

Figure IV.24   *M. Henderson's compromise with his ballasted catamaran* Golden Miller. *The major*

contribution to safety made by the masthead float should be noted.

Figure IV.25   *The stability of a boat can be reduced dangerously on the sloping face or back of a wave.*

It should also be remembered that, at the same time, the angular velocity of water particles varies according to depth, and the immersed part of the hull is therefore subject to an additional heeling moment. There is also a reduction of the heeling moment due to variation of apparent weight caused by centrifugal force. This variation is negative on the crests and positive in the troughs.[3]

11 Dynamical stability

We have considered only statical stability so far, that is to say we have assumed that no speed was involved when the boat was made to heel. It is all very different when a heeling moment is applied suddenly because the hull then moves at a certain speed and stores up kinetic energy which makes the boat heel further than the angle at which she would otherwise have stopped.

The work of a couple is equal to the product of its moment and the angle of rotation effected. In fig. IV.26 the curve of statical stability and the heeling

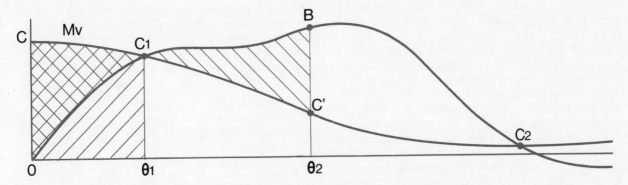

Figure IV.26   *Characteristic elements of dynamical stability for a heeling couple with initial value C.*

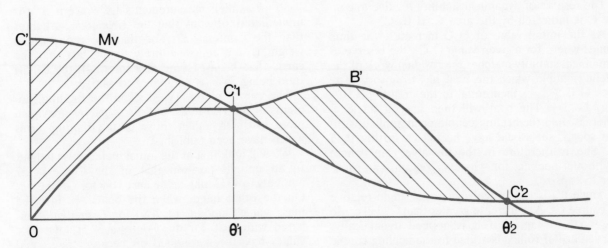

Figure IV.27   *Critical dynamical stability occurs when the heeling couple is increased to a value such that the work of the heeling couple is equal to the work of the righting*   *couple. Area $C'_1 B' C'_2 C'_1$ indicates the reserve stability for heeling couple C'.*

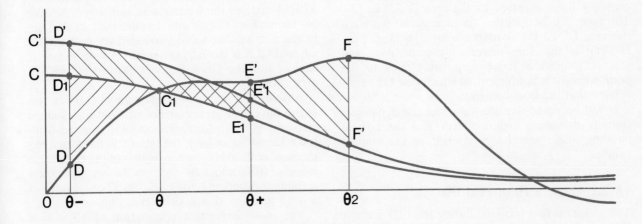

Figure IV.28   *The effect that rolling has on dynamical stability.*

moment curve M_v are shown; the work of the heeling couple that causes the boat to take up a heeling angle of θ_1 is represented graphically by the area O C C_1 θ_1.

While the hull is heeling over progressively to angle θ_1, the work of resistance corresponding to righting moment is represented by the area O C_1 θ_1. The remaining work, represented by the area O C C_1 contained between the two curves, has to be absorbed and the area C_1 B C', which is equal to O C C_1, represents the work still to be done; the boat therefore heels as far as θ_2. If the heeling force then remains steady, the boat will return towards angle θ_1. If the fluids were perfect, the boat would not stop oscillating between O and θ_2, but in reality the amplitude of each oscillation is reduced progressively as the work is absorbed by the media in which she oscillates.

The reserve of dynamical stability relative to couple C is indicated by the area C_1 B C_2 C'.

As the initial value of O C increases, the time comes when, for a given value O C', the reserve of dynamical stability matches the residual work of the heeling couple which the boat has to absorb. The area O C ' C'_1 is then equal to the area C'_1 B' C'_2 (fig. IV.27). The boat will then heel at angle θ_2 whereas, had the heeling couple been applied without speed, she would have heeled no further than θ_1. She is therefore in the unstable zone where additional heeling, for whatever reason, can cause her to capsize.

Angle θ'_1 is the critical dynamical angle relative to couple C'. Any increase greater than C' will cause the boat to capsize if it is applied dynamically, particularly if rolling is added to the heeling couple (fig. IV.28).

Suppose that a sailing boat subject to a heeling moment C is at an angle of heel θ, and that she rolls either side of θ from θ_+ to θ_-. The work done is then represented by the areas D D_1 C_1 and C_1 E' E_1. When heeling moment in a gust rises to C', the curve of heeling moments is raised at the instant where rolling takes the boat to θ_+. The work of the heeling couple will be increased by the area D' D_1 E_1 E'_1. The boat will heel further to an angle of θ_2, when the area E'_1 E' F F' equals the area D_1 D' E'_1 E_1. Heeling is therefore increased considerably, and reserve stability is reduced, possibly even to the point where it is insufficient, in which case the result will be that the boat capsizes.

It will be noted that the values of the dynamical stability maximum righting lever and the corresponding angle are always inferior to the statical values.

12 Experience from real life

The accidents that occurred during the 1979 Fastnet Race, and the research carried out afterwards for the R.O.R.C. enquiry by the Wolfson Unit at South-ampton University comparing two IOR Class V yachts, have provided interesting information on the factors relating to stability. One yacht was a Contessa 32 designed by David Sadler in 1969, and the other a 1978 Ron Holland Half Tonner, *Grimalkin*, sister ship to the very successful *Silver Jubilee*.

	Contessa 32	*Grimalkin*
Overall length	9.65 m	9.14 m
Waterline length	7.16 m	7.54 m
Maximum beam	2.93 m	3.12 m
Draught	1.75 m	1.72 m
Displacement	4586 kg	3774 kg
Ballast	2042 kg	1356 kg
Ballast ratio	44.5 per cent	36 per cent
Sail area	37.79 m²	37.64 m²

Fig. IV.29 shows the midship sections of the two boats superimposed.

So far as their measurements are concerned, it is immediately obvious that the *Grimalkin* is lighter than the Contessa 32, and that the reduction in weight is due almost entirely to the fact that she carries less ballast (some of it internal), the ballast ratio being 36% as compared to 44.5%.

The curves of fig. IV.30 show the righting moments of the two hulls, and these curves are much more instructive than those of the righting arms which have been published.

We will look first at the initial metacentric height. In an upright position that of the Contessa 32 amounts to 4333 mkg, as against 3198 for *Grimalkin*. On the other hand, when the boats are inverted these values amount to 7280 for *Grimalkin* compared with 1030 for the Contessa 32. (Note: The values have been rounded off because they could only be determined from the tangents to the published curves, but they are nevertheless sufficiently significant for conclusions to be drawn.) The initial stability of the latter is therefore considerably worse when inverted than when lying upright, whereas *Grimalkin* has very much greater initial stability when inverted than when on an even keel.

Maximum righting moment is also very different, at 3214 mkg for the Contessa 32 and only 1852 mkg for *Grimalkin*. Taking into account the fact that the product of sail area and vertical distance between CE and CLR is virtually the same for both yachts, it is clear that the *Grimalkin* will have to reduce sail area sooner.

A point that is very noticeable about these curves is the difference in the angles of vanishing statical stability, 117° for *Grimalkin* and 157° for the Contessa 32. At 90° of heel, the latter still has a righting moment of 2870 mkg, whereas that of the *Grimalkin* is only 1050 mkg. In fact, so far as dynamical stability is concerned, the Contessa 32 could support a wind pressure that is three times higher.

The most interesting comparison of all is that relating to the ratios of the enclosed areas up to the capsizing angle and from the capsizing angle up to

84

180°. Knowing that these areas represent the work required to make the yacht capsize and, when she is inverted, to allow her to return to her normal upright position, the following table can be drawn up:

	Before capsize	After capsize	Ratio
Contessa 32	4530*	30	151/1
Grimalkin	2125	695	3.06/1
Ratio	2.13/1	1/23.17	

*non-dimensional values

The comparison between the ratios of work before and after capsizing are particularly remarkable. Wind and sea together would have to provide 50 times as much effort to right the *Grimalkin* as to right a Contessa 32. If the differences in initial stability at 180° are included as well, it is easy to understand that it could take several minutes before the former is righted. Taking the three factors, ratio of the areas of righting moments before and after capsizing, initial metacentric heights at 0° and 180°, and the angles of vanishing stability, it is relatively easy to state the limits beyond which a yacht is no longer safe.

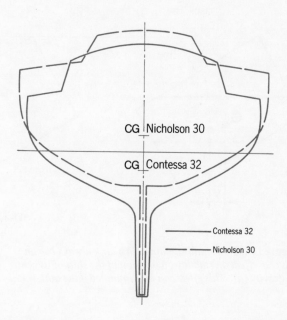

Figure IV.29 *The midship sections of the Contessa 32 and* Grimalkin *compared.*

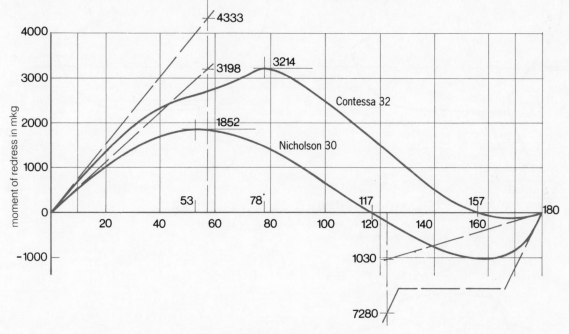

Figure IV.30 *Righting moment curves of the Contessa 32 and* Grimalkin.

The author would fix these at about 15 for the ratio of the areas, equality for initial metacentric height, and 140° for the angle of vanishing stability, but that is just a quick approximation which should be checked with statistical research into a large number of yachts, classifying them according to the type of sailing involved, such as ocean passages, offshore racing, coastal cruising and so on. In a

recent report at the Chesapeake Bay symposium,[4] it was found that the angle of vanishing stability for current racing yachts (1981) was 125°.

It will be noted that we have not included maximum righting moment, and this is because its major role is as a factor of performance and of comfort (angle of heel, need to reduce sail area later or sooner) rather than as a safety factor.

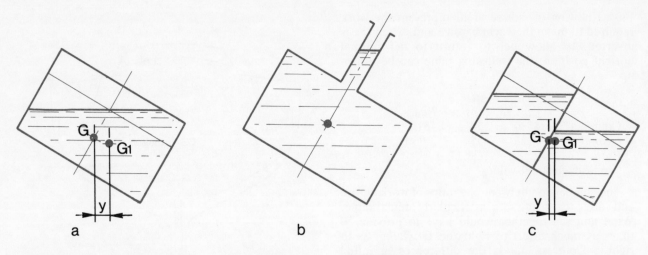

Figure IV.31 *Liquid contained in a tank always has an adverse effect on stability on account of the shift of its centre of gravity (a). This effect can be eliminated if the tank is full* *(b), or at least reduced if the container is divided into several compartments by longitudinal baffles (c).*

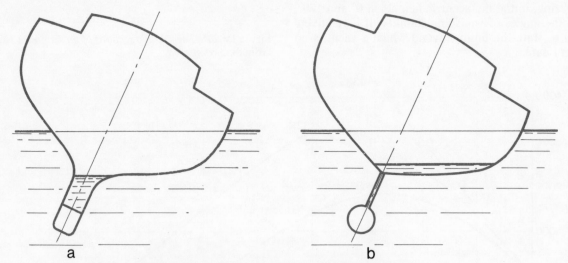

Figure IV.32 *One advantage of a hollow keel is that a certain amount of any water that may be shipped is contained inside it.*

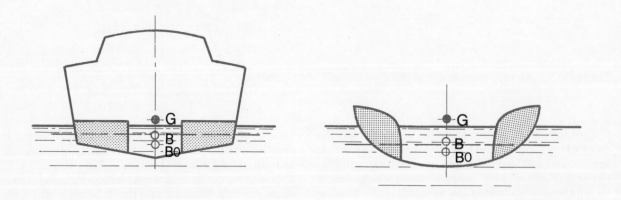

Figure IV.33 *The centre of buoyancy of a hull swamped with water becomes the centre of buoyancy of the immersed* *part of its buoyant volume. Seen here are a cabin boat and an open sailing dinghy.*

The influence of the coachroof, marked by the hump in the curve above 50°, should be noted however because all openings (ventilators, cowls, hatches) obviously should be watertight if this is to contribute to safety.

It only remains to see why there are these major differences between the two boats. First there is the position of the centre of gravity, which is 23 cm below the waterline of the Contessa 32 and 20 cm above it in the *Grimalkin*, and then there is the ratio between freeboard and maximum depth — FMD/CMD in the IOR measurement. (Jeremy Rogers, in a 1980 paper on stability problems, provides the following formula for determining the position of the centre of gravity in relation to the waterline, based on IOR measurements to calculate SV.

$$G = FMD - \left\{ CMD \left[\frac{(0.03L \times BWL^3 \times 64) - (54 \times RM)}{DSPL} + 0.6\ CMDI \right] \right\},$$

G being positive above the waterline and negative below the waterline. All the measurements are in the foot-pound-second system. It should be noted, however, that in the examples above the values obtained are considerably lower than those given by the Wolfson Unit, which were the result of a stability test.)

Breadth at the deck also affects stability and, especially, the ratio between beam at the waterline and maximum beam (BWL/B MAX). Finally there is the positive contribution of the superstructure (smaller in *Grimalkin*, 1.25 as against 2.2 m³) and the negative effect of the cockpit and the sharply raked transom.

13 Effect of free surface of liquids

The volume of free liquids within the boat consists of that contained in tanks (water, fuel) and any water taken on board as a result of a leak or damage.

The effect will differ considerably depending on whether the liquid is in a tank that is full or empty. If the fluid is in a container, the shift of its centre of gravity will be slight but always unfavourable (fig. IV.31) because it always travels towards the direction in which the boat is heeling, causing the general centre of gravity to move proportionately in the same direction and, consequently, producing a reduction in righting couple (a). The fuller the tank, the less the centre of gravity will shift, the least when it is filled to the cap (b); its movement is also reduced if the tank has longitudinal baffles that divide the free area into smaller spaces and prevent flow from one side to the other.

There is little difference when the liquid is not in a tank, at least up to a certain angle of heel, provided that the liquid stays contained in the bilges of a sailing boat, for example if she has a hollow fin keel or wineglass-shaped sections (fig. IV.32a). If this is not the case and her section is as in fig. IV.32b, the situation will be very different. A major heeling moment will result from the shift of the weight of the liquid, particularly at heeling angles between 0 and 90°. The thickness of the skin generally being negligible, it can be assumed that the area of the sections affected is reduced by the difference between the free surface of the fluid and the section of the hull itself.

Thus, when considering the ability of a boat to float when it is entirely swamped, the centre of buoyancy will coincide with the centre of the various buoyancy tanks and compartments combined (fig. IV.33). In boats with accommodation, a relatively small proportion of such areas will be above the water, and stability is due essentially to weight, whereas in light dinghies this proportion is much greater and it is stability of form that is important.

Free surfaces of liquids also have a very bad effect on dynamical stability. Because the volume and the free surfaces are separate from the hull itself, their rolling period differs from that of the hull. Their effect will be beneficial at certain times when they are out of phase with the general motion of the boat, but at the times when they are in phase the work of their heeling moment, which is large when the liquid is not confined in a container, is added to the work effected by the general heeling moment, and the critical angle at which dynamical righting moment is greatest is therefore considerably reduced.

14 Unsinkability and stability

Under French legislation, a boat described as unsinkable has to satisfy certain criteria in respect of freeboard and stability (figs. IV.34 and IV.35) when there is direct communication between her interior and exterior, such as planking stove in beneath the waterline or a seacock torn out.

The first condition to be satisfied, unsinkability when on an even keel, calls for flotation compartments and material with a buoyant capacity that at least corresponds to the displacement of the boat, completely fitted out, and with a full crew on board. The buoyant volumes will be immersed just to the level where their capacity is exactly equal to total displacement (fig. IV.36), and all the remaining volume remains above water level.

Where the buoyancy is placed low (actually beneath the centre of gravity), freeboard after being swamped is great, and that is useful. If we now make the boat heel, we see that beyond a certain angle, up to which the shift of the centre of buoyancy compensates for that of the centre of gravity, the boat becomes unstable and capsizes (fig. IV.37).

If stability is to remain positive at a heeling angle of over 90°, the centre of buoyancy must stay above the centre of gravity, and it is therefore necessary to

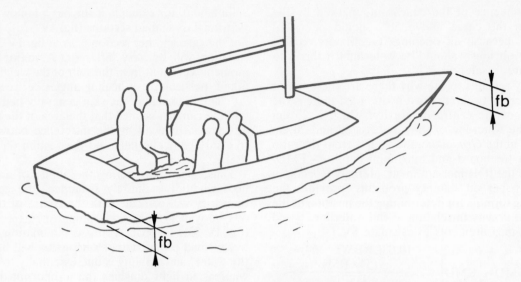

Figure IV.34 *With the crew in the cockpit, the boat's trim should be maintained correctly, and freeboard fb should be adequate at bow and stern.*

Figure IV.35 *When floating at 90°, with the crew hanging on the toerails and lifelines, the boat must still have a tendency to right herself, and should not become immersed more deeply than the mast; she must still be trimmed correctly.*

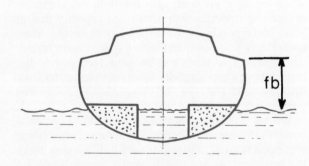

Figure IV.36 *To be able to float in an upright position, the capacity of the buoyant volumes must at least correspond to the displacement of the boat fully fitted out with her crew on board. The lower the buoyant areas are sited, the greater will freeboard be.*

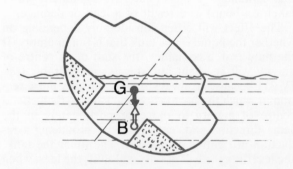

Figure IV.37 *Beyond a certain angle of heel, the centre of buoyancy can no longer shift to counter gravity acting at the centre of gravity, and the boat capsizes. In the figure, the weight of the boat G and buoyancy B are on the same vertical axis; a few more degrees of heel and the moment created by forces G and B will cause the boat to capsize.*

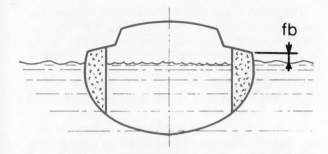

Figure IV.38 *To maintain positive stability at 90°, the buoyancy should be sited higher. In small boats, whose centre of gravity is relatively high, this means that buoyancy needs to be placed directly beneath the deck, and this causes a major reduction in freeboard, fb.*

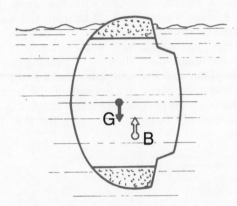

Figure IV.39 *If the buoyancy is placed sufficiently high but its capacity is scarcely greater than displacement, the boat will have a positive righting couple at 90°, but will be almost totally submerged.*

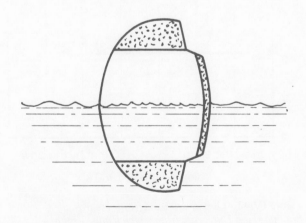

Figure IV.40 *Ideal distribution, combining sufficient minimum freeboard when upright with positive stability and normal immersion when heeled.*

raise the buoyancy as high as possible; in small boats with a relatively high centre of gravity, this leads to buoyancy being sited immediately beneath the deck (fig. IV.38) and to a major reduction in freeboard in the swamped condition. When this boat is heeled to 90°, if the capacity of the buoyant volumes is only slightly greater than the displacement, the boat will be much more deeply immersed; the mast, the bow and the stern will be totally submerged (fig. IV.39). The buoyancy has to be increased greatly now, and in fact capacity needs to be almost double the displacement if water level is not to rise above the boat's vertical plane of symmetry, the fore-and-aft plane. The answer is therefore an arrangement such as in fig. IV.40, which combines adequate minimum freeboard in an upright position with positive stability and normal depth of immersion when heeled at 90°.

The buoyant volume can of course be subdivided into separate sections, the important point being to keep the same centre of buoyancy, and it is essential to distribute the buoyancy along the length of the boat so that correct trim is maintained, with freeboard virtually the same at either end, and good longitudinal stability.

These technical requirements mean that there are certain constraints in the design of the accommodation. Interior beam will be reduced at eye level, and this restricts the apparent interior volume, but the reduction can be small if care is taken to spread the buoyancy fairly evenly from bow to stern. This happens automatically when sandwich construction is used, as for example on the Etap 22.

Given a boat 6 m long, displacing 1 tonne and therefore requiring about 2 m³ of buoyancy, 0.5 m³ can be beneath the deck with an average thickness of 5 cm (2.5 cm at the coachroof and 7.5 cm elsewhere), 1 m³ shaped like a belt 60 cm high and 14 cm thick at the top of the sides, and the remainder distributed in the extremities. This would provide a swamped freeboard of 20 cm. Cabin space will not be reduced too much, and all the interior space will be available for stowage.

The problem inevitably becomes more and more difficult to resolve as the size of the boat increases, and it is virtually impossible to make a boat over 8 m in length unsinkable without having to accept large sacrifices so far as the accommodation is concerned.

When making an accurate calculation of the buoyant volume required, the volume of the material used for hull construction has to be deducted. Although small in the case of metal and GRP hulls, it is large enough not to be ignored when the boat is of wood or of sandwich construction. It is absolutely essential to know the weight and the relative density of the material used if this volume is to be determined.

B Longitudinal stability

The process is exactly the same as for transverse stability.

As we saw in Chapter III, the aerodynamic force exerted on the sails has a longitudinal component, F_x, which corresponds to driving force and causes a longitudinal pitching couple in exactly the same way as the transverse component, F_y, causes the transverse heeling couple. Pitching is countered in the same way too, in that when the boat tilts forward the centre of buoyancy shifts further forward as well, forming a longitudinal righting couple which balances the pitching couple (fig. IV.41).

The change of trim resulting from pitching moment affects resistance, of course, and the sailing boat's directional stability as well, but the consequences are not necessarily harmful, as shown by research carried out on a Dragon at Southampton University,[1] although the differences are very small (fig. IV.42).

The effect of the vertical resultant R_z must also be taken into account; the position of R_z in the longitudinal direction varies very considerably with speed. It can form a positive righting couple which is deducted from the pitching couple, and this is particularly marked in the case of light displacement boats when the effects of dynamic lift become evident.

In every case, the fore-and-aft position of the crew of a light displacement boat is just as important as sitting out transversely.

The same characteristics of hull form have the same effects as in the case of transverse stability and, in particular, the longitudinal moment of inertia of the waterplane has an important effect on longitudinal metacentric height. A waterplane that has full ends (fig. IV.43) will have a greater longitudinal moment of inertia than one with fine ends, and greater fullness forward and aft beneath the waterline increases stability.

However, apart from very small boats, it is very rare for the longitudinal stability of a sailing boat to be inadequate, and the only known cases of pitchpoling (capsizing stem first), even in the case of centreboard dinghies or racing catamarans, are due to accidental causes such as burying the bow in a wave.

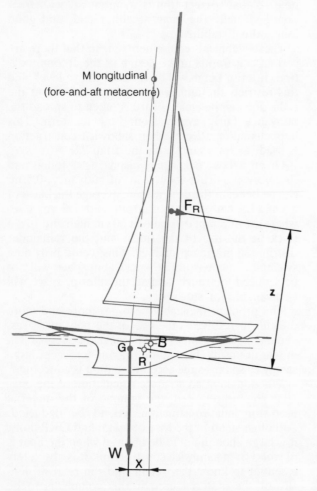

Figure IV.41 *Longitudinal stability, like transverse stability, is obtained when the centre of buoyancy shifts to form a righting couple $W \times x$ which is equal to pitching moment $F_R \times z$.*

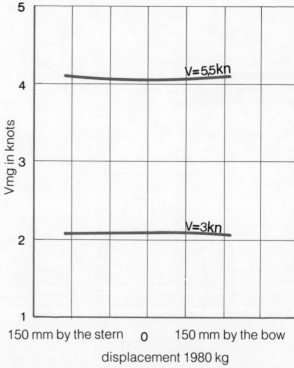

Figure IV.42 *Curves extracted from research at Southampton University from which it appears that a difference in the trim of a Dragon, corresponding to the bow or stern being trimmed down 150 mm, has very little effect on Vmg. The results would certainly have been less favourable if the tests had been carried out in a seaway.*

On the other hand, longitudinal stability is very important when it comes to studying pitching in waves, and although hull form is important because it affects metacentric height, on which the period of pitching depends, and because the volume and balance of the overhangs fore and aft both give rise to and deaden motion simultaneously, it is nevertheless only one of the factors relating to this problem. This will be discussed in more detail in Chapter VIII.

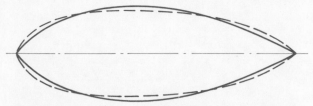

Figure IV.43 *Of these two waterplanes, which are equal in area, the one with the continuous lines has greater transverse stability but less longitudinal stability than the one with broken lines.*

V
Hydrodynamic Forces

As we saw in Chapter III, apart from stability the factors that most affect the speed of a boat and her ability to work to windward are: resistance to forward motion; and the ability to develop as great a lateral force as is possible without increasing resistance beyond a minimum.

First we will study resistance alone, such as is met when sailing in a following wind, and then we shall see what price has to be paid in terms of resistance when the anti-leeway or side force needed for sailing close-hauled is created. Thus we shall be able to draw up the balance sheet of total hull resistance, at the same time considering the effect of dimensional and design details on resistances.

A Resistance when there is no leeway

A hull moving on the surface of water is subject to the same resistances as the totally immersed body we studied in Chapter II, namely frictional resistance, separation, ventilation and, possibly, cavitation, form drag and wake drag. But whereas the variations in pressure along the hull cannot be observed visually in the case of a wholly immersed body, they are, so to speak, liberated at the surface. The interface between air and water is disturbed, and various wave systems are created which, in turn, modify pressure distribution over the hull and cause the appearance of a resistance force; the energy expended on propulsion is equal to the energy needed to overcome the resistances already mentioned, and to maintain these wave systems.

The total resistance which opposes a hull that is moving in calm water can be divided into two main components: frictional resistance which acts tangentially; and pressure resistances normal to the hull,

composed of form drag, separation-ventilation drag and wave-making drag. The phenomena connected with these resistances interact, and additional factors may therefore emerge due, among other things, to the interaction of wave-making and friction, wave-making and separation, separation and friction.

Of all these components of total resistance, frictional resistance can be isolated relatively easily, whereas other resistances, and the interaction of friction with them, are extremely difficult to analyse individually. Practical studies are therefore generally limited to discriminating between theoretical frictional resistance and residual resistance, which is made up of all the other resistances. When studying resistance in a tank, the value of residual resistance is found as the difference between total resistance as measured and frictional resistance as calculated. These resistances do not follow the same law of similitude because frictional resistance varies with the Reynolds number (see Chapter II, p.46) and residual resistance as the square of speed.

It was the Englishman William Froude, the first person to undertake the systematic tank testing that had interested the Swedish naval architect Fredrik Henrik Chapman 100 years earlier, who recognized the need to consider these two resistances separately. Basing his calculations on the laws of similitude of general mechanics, and on his own observations of wave systems raised by models of differing size, Froude stated in his law of comparison in 1868 that the residuary resistance of hulls which are geometrically similar varies as the ratio of the cube of their linear dimensions, while their speeds vary as the square root of their linear dimensions.

This principle was known 36 years earlier to the Frenchman Reech, but he did not make the comparison with resistance.

Froude's Law states that the wave-making resistance coefficients of two geometrically similar hulls of different lengths are the same when moving at the same $V/\sqrt{L}$ value, V being the speed at which they are moving and L being waterline length. $V/\sqrt{L}$ is also termed the speed-to-length ratio, but the dimensionless Froude number F_r is sometimes preferred, $V/\sqrt{gL}$, g being acceleration due to gravity (9.81 cm/s²).

$$F_r = \frac{\text{speed to length ratio}}{3132}.$$

Unfortunately the speed-to-length ratio varies with the units being used. Here we will use metres/second for speeds and metres for length, but $V/\sqrt{L}$ can equally well be found when speed is in knots or feet per second, and length in feet. Conversion factors are as follows:

Speed	Length	x by	Speed/length ratio in
km/h	metre	0.278	m/s and m
knots	metre	0.524	m/s and m
knots	feet	0.93	m/s and m
knots	feet	1.81	knots and m

If we wish to compare the residual resistance of a sailing boat with a waterline length of 9 m, sailing at a speed of 3 m/s, with a model one-tenth of her size, the latter's velocity must be 0.948 m/s because $3/\sqrt{9} = 0.948/\sqrt{0.9}$. Speeds will therefore be in the ratio of the root of the scale $3/0.948 = 3.16 = \sqrt{10}$.

1 Residual resistance

In spite of the problems of analysing the different components of residual resistance quantitatively, the various phenomena that are its cause can be described, at least qualitatively, in particular in regard to form and wave-making drag, and resistance due to separation-ventilation, so as to try to determine what factors will help to reduce resistance.

a Form drag and wave-making resistance

Two different approaches enable hull resistance to be determined, namely measurements and observations made when tank-testing a model, and calculations based on the theory of wave generation.

Without going into the study of waves in detail, which would far exceed the scope of this book, we can select some points that will help to improve our understanding of wave-making.

One of the first contributions to the subject came in 1904 from Lord Kelvin, who showed that the wave pattern created by a pressure point moving on the surface of water is composed of a system of transverse waves roughly at right angles to the path of the point, and a divergent wave system which spreads out from it. The entire pattern is bounded by two straight lines which, in deep water, are each at an

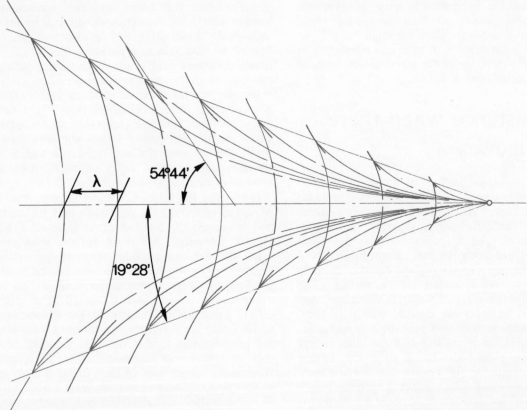

Figure V.1 *Divergent and transverse wave systems formed by a moving pressure point. It is the compounding of the two systems that causes the formation of the small* waves which are seen along the line where they meet. The values given for the angles are valid only in deep water.

angle of 19° 28' to this path (fig. V.1). It is the interference between the two systems that gives the divergent waves their characteristic shape, their average direction being constant at an angle of 54° 44' to the path. The systems move at the same speed as the point, and it is therefore possible to deduce that wavelength between the crests $\lambda = 2\pi V^2/g = 0.64\ V^2$.

With regard to the divergent waves, $2\pi V^2/g$ is the component of velocity parallel to the path, and consequently the actual distance between crests, λ', taken perpendicular to the latter is

$$\lambda' = (2\pi V^2/g)\cos^2 \psi,$$

when ψ is the angle between the perpendicular to the crests and the line of the point's path (fig. V.2).

The height of the wave systems formed (especially that of the transverse waves) will decrease quite quickly as they spread out laterally, because the energy contained in the wave is constant (partly absorbed by viscosity) and has to be distributed over an increasingly greater length. It should also be noted that more energy is absorbed by the transverse waves than by the divergent waves, and the difference becomes greater as speed increases.

Now, in place of a single point, we will consider a simple body with two pointed ends, joined by a parallel middle part, as was used by Wigley when showing that the shape of the wave along the body was the result of five different disturbances of the surface (fig. V.3):

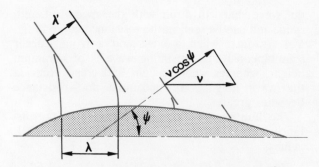

Figure V.2 *Wavelength and velocity of the small waves that result from the compounding of the divergent and transverse waves.*

one symmetrical disturbance corresponding to Bernoulli's theorem (Chapter II.3f) with peaks at bow and stern and a hollow between them;
two wave systems starting with a crest, one at the bow and the other at the stern;
two wave systems starting with a trough, one at each end of the parallel middle body where the angles change.
These five disturbances combine to form a system which becomes regular two wavelengths downstream, and then progressively reduces in height.

The fact that there is interference between the various systems is evident. As wavelength varies with speed, it is easy to understand that because the spacing between the points where the wave systems start is virtually constant, it is the whole profile of

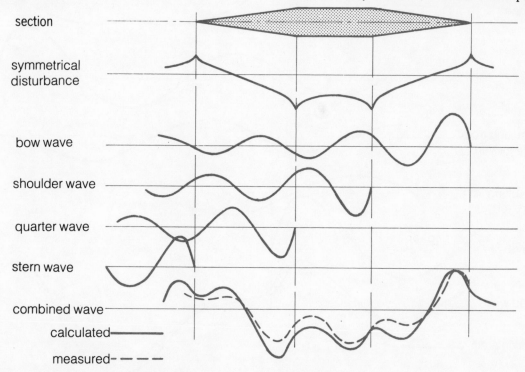

Figure V.3 *Breakdown of the various wave systems created by a body with a parallel middle body and pointed ends, based on Wigley's calculations, and comparison of* the combination of these systems with waves actually observed.

the wave that will differ with the speed-to-length ratio, and can be seen in the resistance curve in fig. V.4. In fact, when a crest and a trough occur simultaneously, the resulting wave is of minimum height, whereas when troughs and crests coincide the wave heights are maximum and resistance becomes greater.

The humps and hollows in the wave-making resistance curve correspond to the following $V/\sqrt{L}$ values:

Humps	0.63		0.74	0.92	1.56
Hollows	0.6	0.68	0.82	1.09	

As a result of their researches, William Froude and his son, R.E. Froude, after him, gave theoretical values (defined by the moment when the crest of the bow wave coincides with or is directly opposed to the trough of the wave formed abaft the quarter) for the humps and hollows of the curve; these values correspond successively to $\sqrt{gZ}/\pi$, $\sqrt{gZ}/\pi^2$, $\sqrt{gZ}/\pi^3$, $\sqrt{gZ}/\pi^4$, etc. Z, the distance between the crest of the bow wave and the trough of the quarter wave, is normally less than the waterline length, LWL.

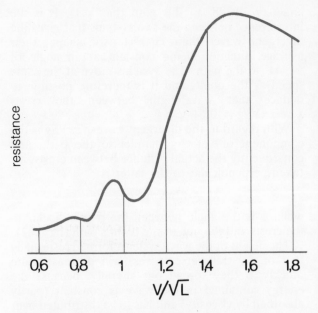

Figure V.4 *Humps in the calculated resistance curve which match the composition of the transverse waves forward and aft.*

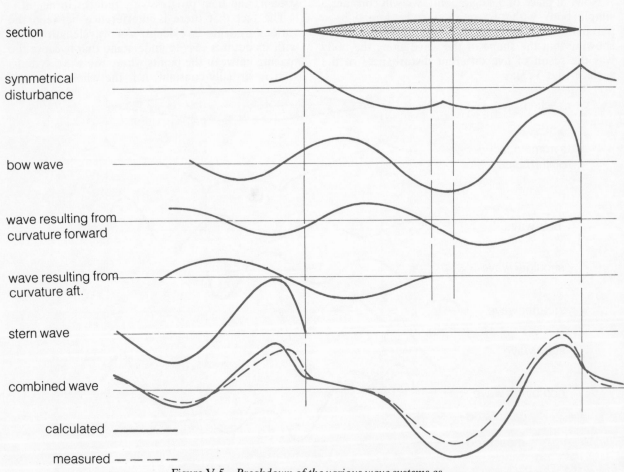

section

symmetrical disturbance

bow wave

wave resulting from curvature forward

wave resulting from curvature aft.

stern wave

combined wave

calculated ———

measured – – – –

(all as in Figure V.3)

Figure V.5 *Breakdown of the various wave systems as calculated by Wigley for a body with two convex extremities connected by a very short parallel middle body*

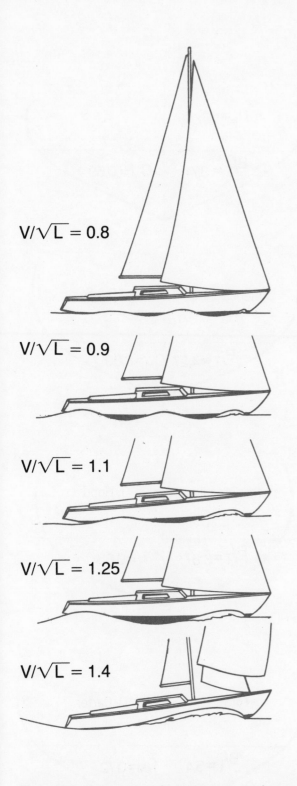

$V/\sqrt{L} = 0.8$

$V/\sqrt{L} = 0.9$

$V/\sqrt{L} = 1.1$

$V/\sqrt{L} = 1.25$

$V/\sqrt{L} = 1.4$

Given a more streamlined shape with two convex parts fore and aft separated by a very short parallel middle body (fig. V.5), we find the five wave components again, but can see that the wave system that begins with a trough at the level of the shoulder no longer starts at a fixed point but near the bow; it is not as high, and merges rapidly with the bow wave. The height of the wave system that starts with a trough at the quarter is also reduced.

In fact, only two wave systems can usually be seen on the water, and these are the waves that are formed at the bow and those formed at the stern, but if there is a particularly abrupt change of curvature a third wave may appear at the quarter.

Then again, the speed-to-length ratio corresponding to the characteristic disturbances of the different wave systems is indicated by the attitude taken up by the boat (fig. V.6), at any rate in the case of a relatively heavy displacement boat. We will see later that there can be a great change in the case of a light boat, when it comes to planing.

The measured resistance curve is also found to be slightly higher than the theoretical curve, the humps and hollows in particular being much weaker and sometimes slightly out of phase (fig. V.7). There are several reasons for this, such as simplifications required for mathematics, stability of flow, the effect of viscosity on wave formation (the effect of waves on the real value of the wetted surface on which frictional resistance calculations are based), and the change in the boat's trim, quite apart from mistakes in the calculations themselves.

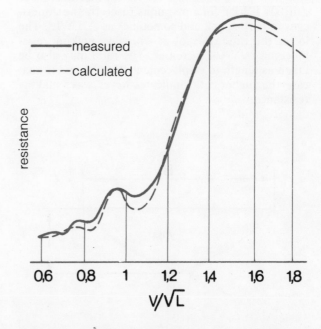

Figure V.6 *Composition of transverse waves at bow and stern as speed increases. When V/√L is over 1.1, the first trough of the transverse bow wave gradually moves aft and superposes itself on the trough of the stern system. The forward trough increases as it moves further aft, the boat sinks deeper and then squats. The boat is then on the verge of planing.*

Figure V.7 *The humps and hollows are less marked in the measured resistance curve than in the calculated curve because various secondary influences are not taken into account when the calculations are made.*

Although much research has gone into the problem of calculating wave-making resistance mathematically, and the contributions made by Reech, Froude father and son, Rankine, Michell, Wigley, Havelock, Weinblum, Guillotin and, more recently, the Japanese Inui (who has closely studied the effect of bulbs) can be applied to the relatively standard shapes of commercial and fighting vessels, there is still a long way to go before the wave-making resistance of a sailing boat's hull can be calculated.

Certain parameters that affect the resistance, at least qualitatively, of the underwater body can be singled out, however, although the shape of this and of the part of the topsides immediately above the waterline are also important.

b Factors affecting wave-making resistance and form drag

These are essentially the displacement-to-length ratio, the shapes of the midship section and of the waterplane, the shape of the curve of areas and the prismatic coefficient.

The displacement to length ratio If we confine ourselves strictly to the problem of wave-making resistance, there is no doubt that, in accordance with Froude's Law, the lighter the boat's displacement the smaller will wave-making resistance be. A decision as to what a boat's displacement will be for a given waterline length depends therefore on other factors, in particular on capacity, stability and seaworthiness. The displacement to length ratio is generally given as $\triangle/(0.1 \text{ LWL})^3$ for metric units or $\triangle/(0.01 \text{ LWL})^3$ for f.p.s. units (used by the Americans in particular), and sometimes as $\triangle/\text{LWL}^3$. The lower the ratio, the lower will wave-making resistance be as $V/\sqrt{L}$ increases. The ratio may also be taken as length to displacement, $L/\sqrt[3]{\triangle}$, and in that case the higher ratio indicates lower wave-making resistance.

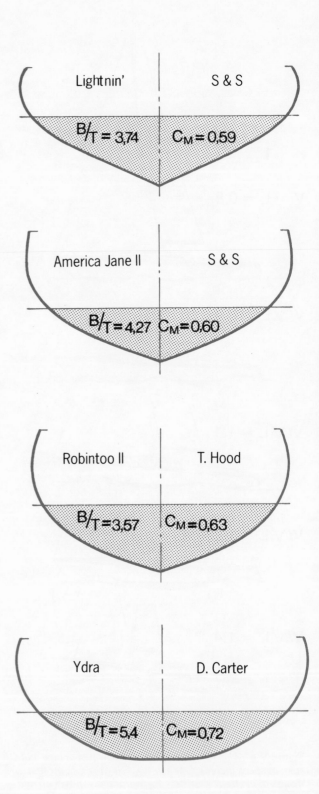

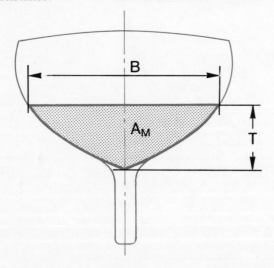

Figure V.8 *Measurements relating to the midship section:* $B = beam$ $T = draught$: $A_M = midship\ section\ area$.

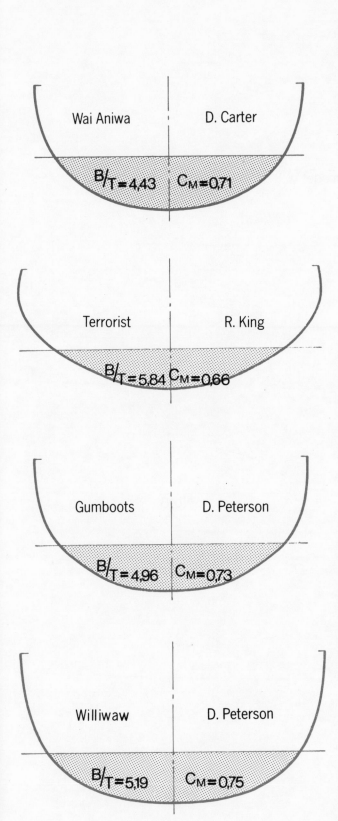

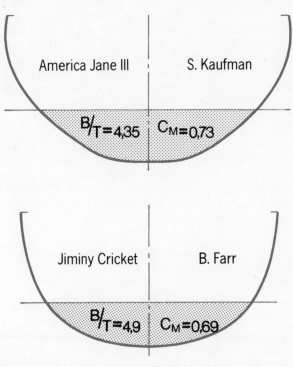

Figure V.9 Some examples of midship sections of One Tonners.

The shape of the midship section This is defined by the beam-to-draft ratio, B/T, and by the midship section coefficient

$$C_M = \frac{A_M}{B \times T},$$

A_M being the area of the immersed midship section. Little has been proved about the effect of the midship section on wave-making resistance, but it does seem that an increase in the B/T ratio results in greater resistance, while the effect of the midship section coefficient on wave-making resistance will be balanced by its effect on the value of the wetted surface, and consequently on frictional resistance. It will be noted, however, that the midship section coefficient and the B/T ratio tend to increase in modern sailing boats; values have changed respectively from 0.55 and 3.2 to 0.75 and 5.2 (fig. V.9), but it is impossible to tell how much of this is due to the IOR and how much to efforts to reduce resistance. It does seem that the higher values of the midship section coefficient (approx. 0.70) and of the B/T ratio (ca 5) are of interest, if only on account of the gain in wetted surface.

The seems to be confirmed by research at the Davidson Laboratory on four shapes developed from a basic hull, beam at the waterline and draught being modified in the ratio of 4:5 and 5:4 giving B/T ratios of 3.27 and 5.1. At higher speeds ($V/\sqrt{L} = 1.2$), the resistance of the deeper sections was slightly

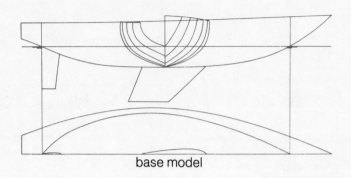

base model

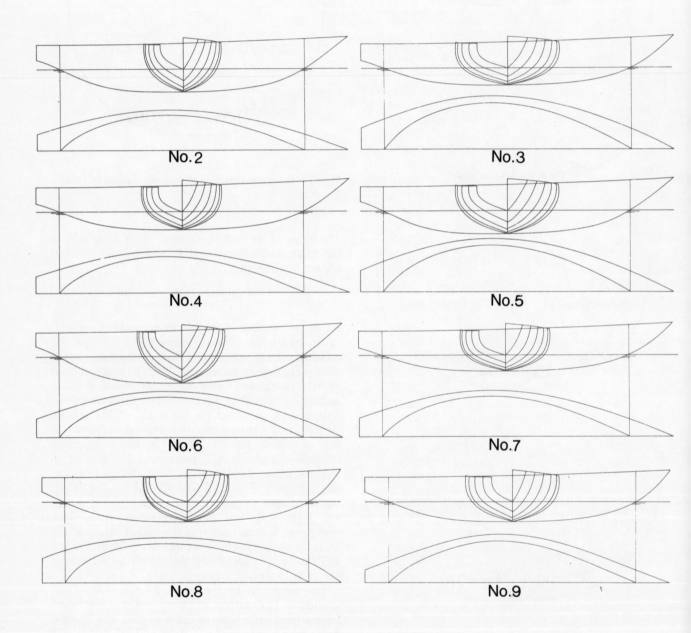

No.2

No.3

No.4

No.5

No.6

No.7

No.8

No.9

Figure V.10   *The nine shapes derived from the Standfast 43
that were studied in the towing tank at Delft.*

TABLE V.I

MAIN DIMENSIONS OF MODELS (METRES)

Number of model	L_{HT}	L_{fl}	B_{MAX}	B_{fl}	T_c	TE	$\triangle_c$	B^2	S_{fl}
1	12.65	10.04	3.67	3.17	0.79	1.94	9.18	1.62	21.8
2	12.65	10.04	3.21	2.76	0.91	2.06	9.18	1.62	19.1
3	12.65	10.06	4.25	3.64	0.68	1.83	9.16	1.63	25.2
4	12.65	10.06	3.32	2.85	0.72	1.87	7.55	1.34	19.8
5	12.65	10.05	4.24	3.64	0.92	2.07	12.10	2.15	25.3
6	12.65	10.00	3.66	3.17	1.06	2.21	12.24	2.16	21.9
7	12.65	10.06	3.68	3.17	0.64	1.79	7.35	1.31	21.8
8	12.65	10.15	3.54	3.05	0.79	1.94	9.18	1.57	22.1
9	12.65	10.07	3.81	3.28	0.79	1.94	9.18	1.68	21.5

TABLE V.II

COEFFICIENTS

Number of model	L_{fl}/B_{fl}	B_{fl}/T_c	C_p	$L_{fl}/\triangle_c^{1/3}$	CC %
1	3.17	3.99	0.568	4.78	− 2.29
2	3.64	3.04	0.569	4.78	− 2.29
3	2.76	5.35	0.565	4.78	− 2.31
4	3.53	3.95	0.564	5.10	− 2.32
5	2.76	3.96	0.574	4.36	− 2.44
6	3.15	2.98	0.568	4.34	− 2.38
7	3.17	4.95	0.562	5.14	− 2.31
8	3.32	3.84	0.585	4.78	− 2.37
9	3.07	4.13	0.546	4.78	− 2.19

higher with the hull both upright and heeled. This has also been confirmed in tests made by Pierre de Saix.

Other more recent tests have been made at Delft with the collaboration of the Massachusetts Institute of Technology in connection with H. Irving Pratt's project for a new offshore racing handicap system, using nine different shapes based on a model with a waterline length of 10 metres, the Standfast 43 designed by F. Maas. Models 1–9 which interest us here have virtually the same centre of buoyancy and the same prismatic coefficient.

As compared to model 1, model 2 is less beamy and has greater draught, while 3 is beamier but draws less. Models 4 and 5 have the same B/T ratio, but 4 displaces less whereas 5 is heavier displacement. Numbers 6 and 7 have the same LWL/BWL ratio, but 6 is heavier and her depth is greater, while 7 is lighter and her depth is less. Model 8 has a higher prismatic coefficient and fuller ends, whereas 9 has a lower prismatic and finer ends (fig. V.10). All had the same ballast keel and rudder. The tables give the measurements and variations in the coefficients and ratios of the models, the scale of which was 1/6.25.

Models 4, 5, 6 and 7 show how important the length/displacement ratio is with regard to resistance; in each case the resistance of the heavier boat is greater, disregarding heeling and making leeway, while resistance is less than that of the base model for a lighter boat, given constant BWL/D and LWL/BWL ratios.

Models 2 and 3 show how small the effect is of the BWL/D ratio, but the larger boat with less depth has a slight advantage at speeds corresponding to $V/\sqrt{L} > 0.9$.

In fact the resistance due to divergent waves increases with the midship section's beam, while resistance due to transverse waves increases with the depth of the section, and more rapidly as boat speed increases.

High values of BWL/D are characteristic of light displacement boats, and it is absolutely essential then that BWL should be large enough to provide adequate stability. Normally C_M decreases as the speed-to-length ratio increases.

The shape of the waterplane This is defined by the coefficient of fineness of the waterplane,

$$C_{WL} = \frac{A_W}{LWL \times BWL},$$

A_W being the waterplane area, and the length-to-beam ratio, LWL/BWL. The angle of entry at the bow and the equivalent angle at the stern must also be considered (fig. V.11).

The LWL/BWL ratio depends largely on the midship section, which determines the value of BWL. The waterplane coefficient, on the other hand, is affected both by the prismatic coefficient which, as

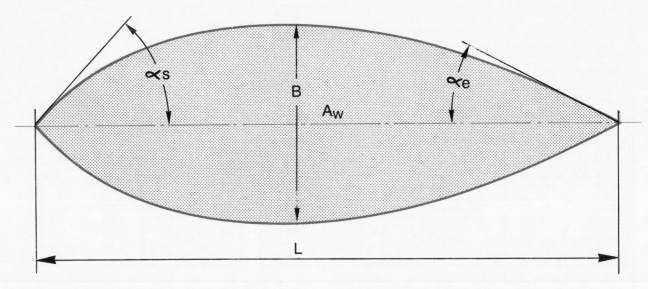

Figure V.11 *Measurements relating to the waterplane. LWL = waterline length, BWL = waterline beam,*

A_W = *area of the waterplane,* α_e = *angle of entry,* α_s = *angle of exit at the stern.*

we shall see, governs the volume of the ends, and by longitudinal stability and the effect that that has on motion in a seaway.

The angles at bow and stern are linked to the speed-to-length ratio; the lower the speed-to-length ratio, the smaller will the angles be except at very low values of $V/\sqrt{L}$.

When $V/\sqrt{L} < 0.5$, the angle of entry can be extremely great, and the bows will then be very full, as is still seen in classic traditional boats such as the *boeier* and other Dutch craft. At such low speeds it is the drag caused by separation aft that is the predominant part of resistance, and this calls for drawn-out shapes and waterlines that are smoothly streamlined (fig. V.12). There is no need to search further for the reason why the 'cod's head and mackerel tail' shape was so successful at a time when the speed of vessels was limited in any case (fig. V.13).

When $V/\sqrt{L}$ is about 1, the part played by wave-making resistance, by comparison with total resistance, increases very rapidly and justifies the use of an angle of entry that is as acute as possible. This will lead to concave waterlines (fig. V.14), but exaggerating the concavity would cause the hull to curve more abruptly at the level of the shoulders, and this would increase the wave system developed there. Slightly concave waterlines aft can be of some advantage, provided that they do not result in excessive curvature at the quarters, which would cause separation or, at least, an increase in the thickness of the boundary layer. This is the type of waterplane that was used for the *America* (fig. V.15).

These shapes result more or less directly from Scott Russell's waveline theory, stated in 1834, that in order to match waterlines as exactly as possible to waves, they should have a sine curve forward and a trochoidal curve aft, the ratio between the lengths of

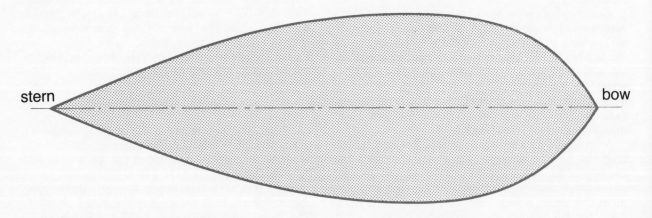

Figure V.12 *Shape of waterplane when V/√L is lower than 0.5.*

102

Figure V.13 *Drawing illustrating the cod's head-mackerel's tail theory, from Mathew Bak* Fragments of Ancient English Shipwrightry, *c.1586.*

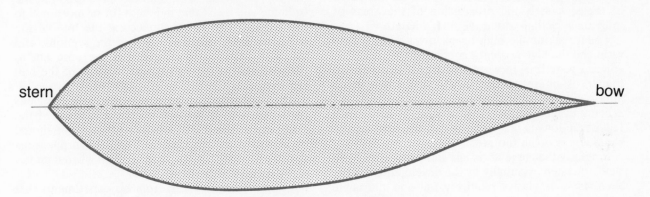

stern

bow

Figure V.14 *Shape of waterplane when V/√L is near 1.*

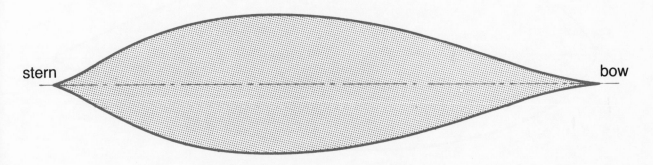

stern

bow

Figure V.15 *Waterplane of the schooner* America.

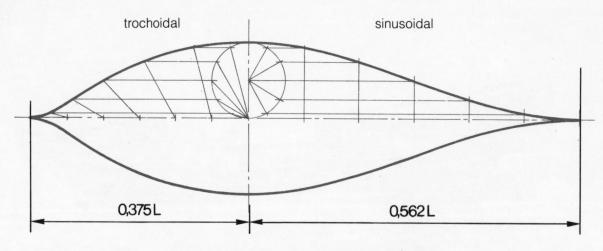

trochoidal   sinusoidal

0,375 L   0,562 L

Figure V.16   *Waterplane shape according to Scott Russell,*
the bow being a sinusoidal curve and the stern trochoidal;
the lengths are in the ratio of 0.562/0.375.

the two parts being 0.562/0.375 (fig. V.16). This theory, which was perhaps valid at a period when hulls were narrow and deep and displacement was heavy, is not of interest today. Colin Archer, the Norwegian naval architect of Scots descent, adapted it and, in 1877, advanced his wave-form theory, demonstrating with models of various shapes, that it was not the waterlines of hulls of more usual proportions that should be curved like waves, but the curve of areas, namely the progression of the areas of individual sections along the boat's length.

Today, taking the high beam-to-waterline length ratio and the high prismatic coefficient into account, concave waterlines forward, which in any case are no longer of interest when $V/\sqrt{L} > 1$, have been almost entirely abandoned for yachts because, on account of measurements for ratings, the result with few exceptions is that the angle at the level of the shoulders is much too great.

Similarly the curve aft is fair and convex, its form being dictated essentially by the development of the sections; it is always relatively full and the angle wide to provide good lift (fig. V.17).

In every case, however, the determining factors are those that are linked to the curve of areas, and this must be defined. A horizontal line is divided into equally spaced parts matching the spacing of the sections on the body plan; at each section a vertical ordinate is drawn, its length being proportional to the underwater area of the section. For example, if the area of section 5 on the body plan is 33 m², the ordinate will be 33 mm in length (or proportional to that value). The curve connecting the tops of the ordinates is the curve of areas of the sections, and the area between this curve and the base line is proportional to the underwater volume of the hull (fig. V.18).

The curve of areas therefore shows how the areas of the sections develop from one extremity of the waterline to the other. Obviously this curve should be perfectly smooth, and the variation in pressures developed along the length of the hull when it moves will depend on its shape.

Colin Archer deduced from his experiments that

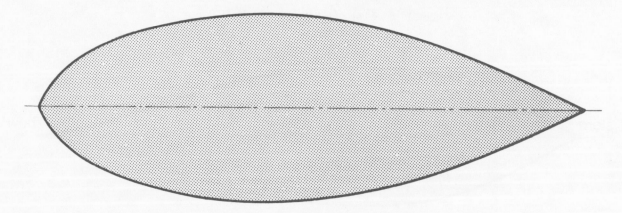

Figure V.17   *Waterplane of a modern sailing yacht (Sagitta 35).*

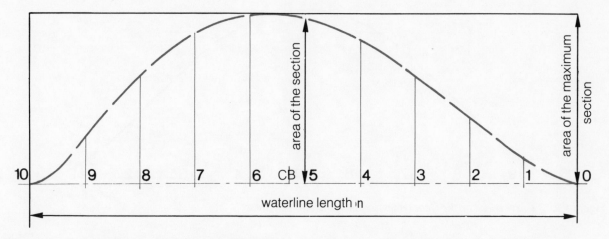

Figure V.18   *Curve of areas. The area beneath the curve indicates the volume of the hull, and the ratio of this area to the circumscribing rectangle is the prismatic coefficient, Cp.*

The longitudinal position of the centre of buoyancy coincides with that of the centre of gravity.

the shape of the curve of areas should be sinusoidal forward and trochoidal aft, but he does not appear to have defined precisely the proportion of the two parts, nor always to have put his own theory into practice (fig. V.19).

It should be noted that the coefficient of the area contained beneath the sine curve is 0.5, while the area under the trochoid varies with the ratio of the diameter of the circle to length, but is always greater than 0.5.

Less importance is attached today to the curve of areas itself; instead two of its characteristics are considered, namely the prismatic coefficient and the position of the section where beam is maximum or of the centre of gravity of the area. Although these are certainly two decisive factors to which we will return, variation of pressures around the hull is nevertheless governed mainly by the shape of the curve of areas.

The author's own studies lead him to consider that it should be possible to get good results from exploring the field of statistical curves, like the Gauss rules (fig. V.20).

Whatever shape is chosen, it is clear that the point where waves form at the shoulders and the quarters will depend on where the curve changes direction forward and aft; consequently the shorter the concave part of the curve, the greater will the distance between the waves be, and that means that both maximum transverse wavelength and speed can be greater.

The prismatic coefficient   This is the ratio of the immersed volume of the hull to that of a prism, the length of which is the same as waterline length, and the area of the section the same as that of the maximum wetted section of the hull (fig. V.21). This is shown graphically as the ratio of the area of the curve of areas to the circumscribing rectangle. Its value is

$$C_P = \frac{\Delta}{\text{LWL} \times A_M},$$

A_M being the area of the immersed maximum section. The prismatic is closely linked to the $V/\sqrt{L}$ selected for the vessel, and its curve is shown in fig. V.22.

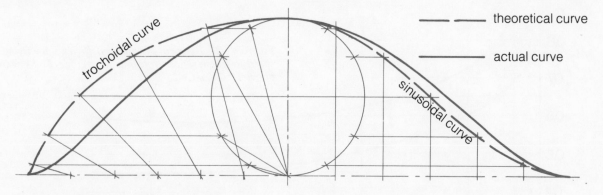

theoretical curve

actual curve

Figure V.19   *Curve of areas based on the Colin Archer theory. The difference between this and the actual curve of*   *one of his boats, the RS 22, is quite considerable.*

105

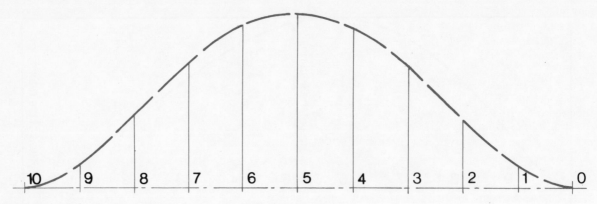

Figure V.20   *Curve based on the Gauss rules, applied to a curve of areas.*

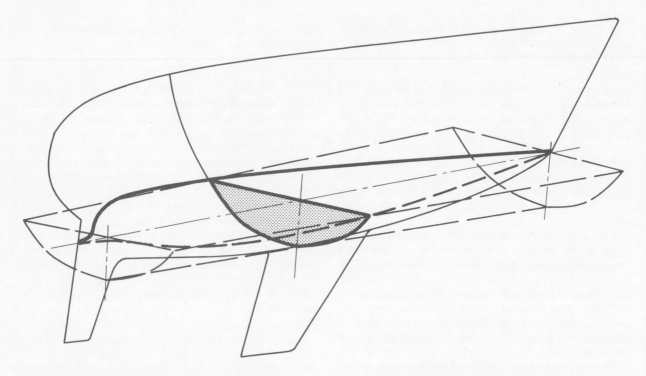

Figure V.21   *The prismatic coefficient C_p is the ratio between the immersed volume of the hull and the volume of*   *a prism of the same length as the waterline and a cross-section area equal to that of the largest section.*

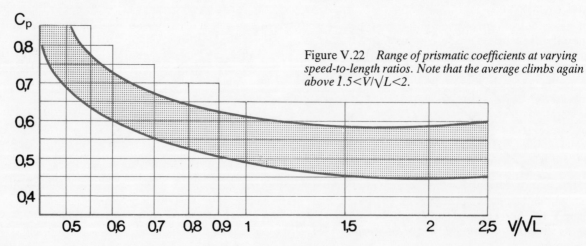

Figure V.22   *Range of prismatic coefficients at varying speed-to-length ratios. Note that the average climbs again above $1.5 < V/\sqrt{L} < 2$.*

Although a speed-to-length ratio can be selected for a vessel driven by mechanical power, this is not the case with a sailing boat, the speed of which is utterly variable because it depends on the force of the wind.

Values of prismatic coefficients for sailing boats are always relatively low, particularly if the area of the section includes that of the ballast keel. They are lower still in the case of a hard chine boat (especially one with a single chine), and may easily be under 0.45. This may be one reason why hard chine boats are inferior at slow speeds. Values for round bilge boats are normally between 0.50 and 0.58. Since the IOR was introduced there has been a very marked tendency for the prismatic coefficient to increase due to the adoption of U-shaped sections forward, and more convex longitudinals aft which may involve blisters or a bustle. It appears that the optimum value is somewhere around 0.55, this value being calculated without taking the ballast keel into account — at least for those boats where it is clearly distinct from the hull. It should be noted that on the graph in fig. V.22 this corresponds to the maximum range of speed that a sailing boat can achieve.

This is confirmed in the thesis by Pierre de Saix, where three hulls of the same origin but with prismatic coefficients of 0.48, 0.53 and 0.61 are compared (fig. V.23). When on an even keel, model 1 is superior to 3 only at speeds below 6.3 knots, model 2 is superior to both up to 7.4 knots, and thereafter model 3 is best. If the result is considered in terms of Vmg, model 2 (C_P = 0.53) is best at most ranges of wind speed.

Similar results were found with the studies of the nine models at Delft (tables V.I–III), the form with the lowest prismatic coefficient (0.546) showing a very slight advantage between $V/\sqrt{L}$ = 0.8 and $V/\sqrt{L}$ = 1. At higher speed-to-length ratios, the boat with the prismatic coefficient of 0.585 has the advantage.

The value of the prismatic coefficient actually to be used should be determined by statistical calculation of the normal mean speed expected, based on the type of sailing or racing planned, or on anticipated wind and sea conditions. Thus a boat that will be sailed in light airs for the most part, as is generally the case on inland waters, should have a lower prismatic coefficient than one designed for offshore sailing in windy regions. Such calculations can be based on an analysis either of the weather experienced during previous racing seasons, or of the winds that can be expected as shown in the Pilot Charts, but this is a tedious process. It may be that a few naval architects have researched this subject for their own purposes but, if so, no one has divulged the results he has obtained.

The fore-and-aft position of the centre of buoyancy, as shown by the centre of gravity of the curve of areas, has also changed over the years. It appears that its influence on resistance has not been studied

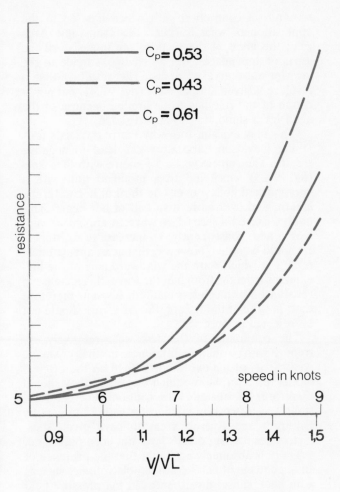

Figure V.23 *The resistance curves for three hulls of the same family with different prismatic coefficients.*

in the case of sailing boats, and that it has been rather a passing fashion.

It can be said, however, that although at slower speeds ($V/\sqrt{L}$ < 0.5) the centre of buoyancy is forward of amidships, it will shift abaft amidships when $V/\sqrt{L}$ > 1. This shift can be achieved automatically with a light centreboard dinghy by shifting weight to alter trim, but it is more difficult to do so in ballasted boats. Currently the centre of buoyancy of such a hull without a ballast keel is roughly 3–4% abaft amidships. It is always important that the maximum section should be far enough aft, and nearer the stern than the ballast keel so that it can develop side force to counter leeway without interference.

Whether the sections of the keel should be included in the curve of areas is often questioned. Although the answer can be yes in the case of a long keel that is not really distinct from the hull itself (very heavy displacement boats of the Colin Archer type, or an almost parallel-sided fin keel of the ballasted-centreboard type), it is more difficult to give a ruling for short, deep fin keels.

This configuration could, however, be compared to that of the wing and fuselage of an aircraft, research in connection with which has led to the application of what is called the Transsonic Area rule; the areas of the sections are inclusive of the areas of appendages, but no change is made to the law for the curve of areas. The result is that a fuselage is given a wasp waist (fig. V.24), but application of the rule has to be limited because of the need for a smoothly developed shape.

This may explain, too, why Pierre de Saix's tests at the Davidson Laboratory can lead to negative results. The subject was a 5.5-metre with long keel (fig. V.25) which led to a modified hull with a very marked hollow over one-third of her waterline length, and over more than half of her beam. This hollow caused a secondary wave to appear at mid-length and, consequently, an increase in resistance. It should be noted, however, that at an angle of heel of 20°, at which point the windward part of the hull emerges from the trough of the wave, this increase in resistance was much less marked. It seems therefore that, in spite of this failure, the Area rule should not be rejected at once.

The conditions of this test were relatively extreme, with a major difference in the prismatic coefficients of the two models (0.48 on the original model, 0.52 on the modified one), and they should therefore be treated with caution. Furthermore, some recent work in connection with 12-metres by Elvstrøm and Kjærulf seem to have given satisfactory results, but details have not been published.

There is absolutely no doubt that the presence of an appendage of fairly considerable volume, such as a fin keel, causes disturbances in the pressure field around the hull, but it is equally certain that it can only be integrated with the total volume to the point where it does not cause so much distortion of shape

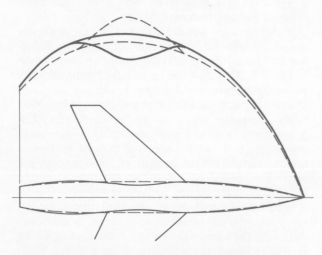

Figure V.24 *The transsonic area rule applied to an aircraft designed for supersonic speeds, the initial shape being shown by the broken line, and the waist effect that results from the rule by the continuous line. The coefficient of drag can differ as much as 25% (from Aérodynamique expérimentale by P. Rebuffet).*

that severe disturbances occur in the boundary layer (see Chapter II.3e, p. 37) and in the pressure field. The fairing joining the fin keel to the hull can also affect the separation point.

It seems that partial integration is possible within the reasonable limits imposed by deformation of shape and the generation of a secondary wave. The flat area found on some current boats at the root of the ballast keel is mainly due to the depth measurements at the midship section for an IOR rating, but it happens to match these ideas, and may then be doubly advantageous.

The bulb A device that has been in use for some years now on commercial vessels to reduce wave-making resistance. It is an appendage beneath the surface of the water which protrudes forward of the stem or aft from the stern, with the object of creating a wave system of the same amplitude as, but opposite in effect to, the bow and stern waves. Interference between the two systems considerably reduces the resultant wave systems and, theoretically, causes a substantial decrease in wave-making resistance (fig. V.26).

The most interesting research into the effects of bulbs is that of Professor Inui, in Japan. It appears that the position and shape of the bulb are closely linked to the hull form and the speed-to-length ratio. The latter point is hard to resolve in the case of a sailing boat because the requirement is for minimum resistance at a great range of speeds, and the increase in wetted area may be a disadvantage at lower speeds. On the other hand, the volume of the extremities fore and aft is increased by the need to fair in the bulbs and this, plus their own volume, results in a beneficial increase in the prismatic coefficient. The behaviour of the bulbs in rough water must also be considered; it is known that in commercial vessels the bulb has a good effect on pitching, which it damps, but what will happen when it emerges from the water on account of the much greater variations in a sailing boat's trim? Furthermore the position with regard to an IOR rating if designers start to use bulbs in practice is not yet clear.

Bill Luders, the great 5.5-metre specialist who was deeply involved in tuning the 12-metre *Weatherly* in 1962 and who designed and built *American Eagle* for the America's Cup elimination trials in 1964, had already envisaged in 1966 that there was a possibility of giving sailing boats bulbs. Elvstrøm and Kjærulf took up this idea for the French 12-metre, but this never saw the light of day and they then applied it to a fifty-fifty built in Denmark by Nelson Marine, the Nelson/Elvstrøm 38 (fig.V.27)).

The two young Belgian naval architects, D. Charles and W.D. Salomon, have carried out research in connection with a Quarter-Tonner at the University of Liège; this has two bulbs, one forward and one aft. It will certainly be very interesting to know the results of these researches, and it is

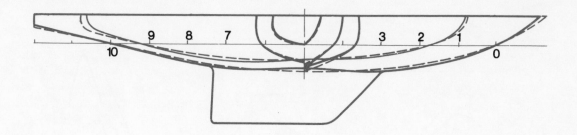

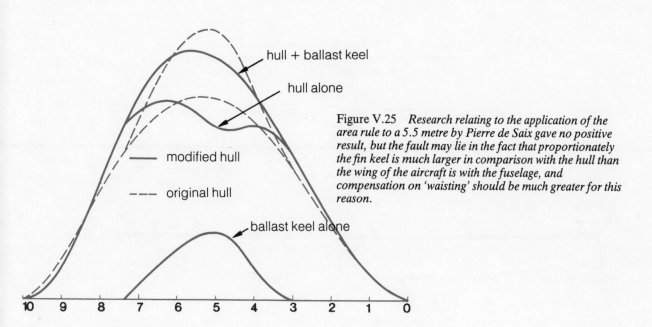

hull + ballast keel

hull alone

modified hull

--- original hull

ballast keel alone

Figure V.25 *Research relating to the application of the area rule to a 5.5 metre by Pierre de Saix gave no positive result, but the fault may lie in the fact that proportionately the fin keel is much larger in comparison with the hull than the wing of the aircraft is with the fuselage, and compensation on 'waisting' should be much greater for this reason.*

difficult to forecast how the technique of bulbs for yachts will evolve when aesthetic and functional (difficulties over anchoring) considerations are taken into account, quite apart from the question as to how they might be penalized in racing rules (fig.V.28).

c Resistance due to separation-ventilation

The fiasco in the America's Cup elimination trials in 1974 of the American 12-metre *Mariner*, designed by Britton Chance Jr, revealed the effects of this type of resistance as it affects sailing boats. Basing his ideas on observations of the phenomenon described in Chapter II. 3e, p.37, the American designer cut the stern of the boat off short so that the hull would have an effective length that exceeded the length of a normal hull, as measured for the rating (fig. V.29). *Mariner*'s mediocre performance, although probably not due solely to this idea, showed how tricky it is to adventure into such marginal realms where tank-testing is unable to provide accurate information.

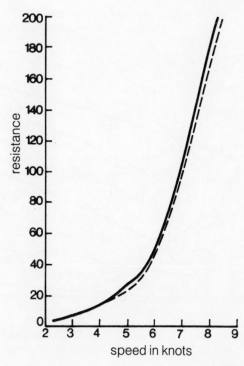

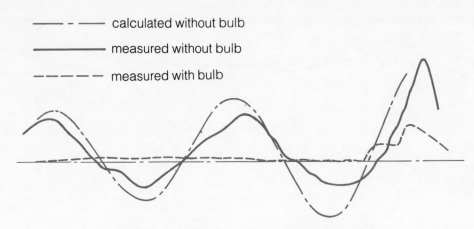

calculated without bulb
measured without bulb
measured with bulb

Figure V.26 *Comparison between the shape of waves calculated and measured on a hull with no bulb, and those measured on the keel with a bulb.*

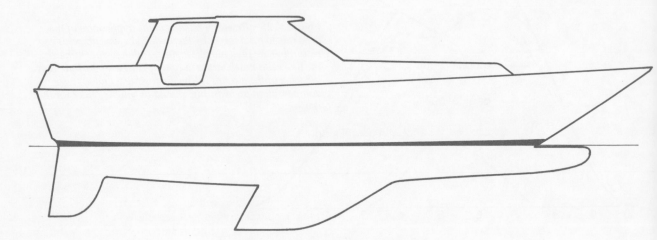

Figure V.27 *The Nelson/Elvstrøm 38, the first series-produced sailing boat with a bulb at the stem.*

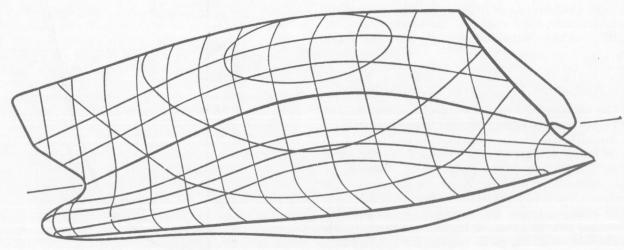

Figure V.28 *Perspective view of the Quarter Tonner by D. Charles and W. D. Salomon, studied at the University of Liège.*

110

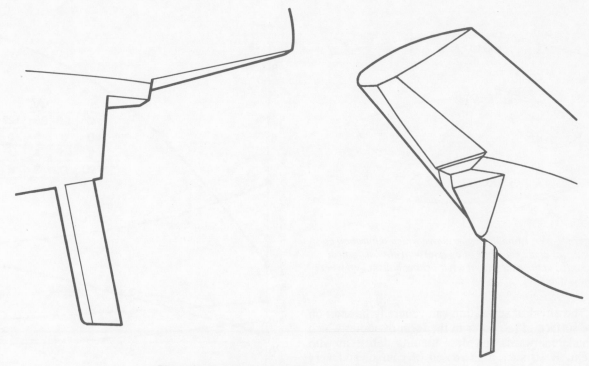

Figure V.29 *Two views of the stern of the 12-metre Mariner. The chopped off underwater body is with a view to benefiting from the measurement of waterline length aft.*

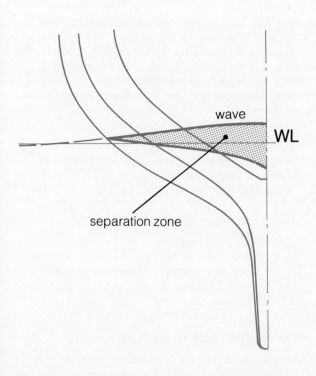

Figure V.30 *Separation zone at the stern of a sailing boat.*

Let us remind outselves briefly that the following main characteristics affect separation: pressure gradient round the hull, character of flow (and consequently surface roughness); speed of water and hull and hydrostatic pressure in the zone concerned; and hull form.

The occurrence of separation depends directly on the slope of the area presented to the pressure gradient along the streamlines. It appears that, in the case of a sailing boat, the zone affected by separation is essentially a relatively wide but not very deep part of the afterbody (fig. V.30). At this point steamline flow is almost horizontal, and it has been found that separation occurs at an angle of over 13–15° (fig. V.31). At a greater depth, due to the increase in hydrostatic pressure, the angle increases progressively by about 2° for every metre of depth.

Discontinuities can occur in the contour of the waterplane of a hard chine hull where the chines emerge forward and aft. The angle of the shoulder of the curve here should not be less than 165°. This means that there is a definite advantage to having a design with several chines, rather than a single chine hull.

When flow acts mainly in a vertical or diagonal direction, as is the case when the stern is beamy and flat or has a very pronounced bustle, the critical angle is over 22°.

111

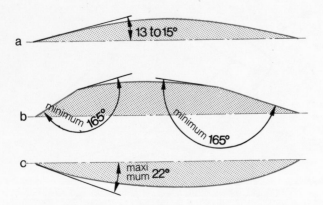

Figure V.31 *Limiting angles above which separation can occur: (a) at the waterline of a vessel with almost vertical sides; (b) at the waterline of a hard chine hull; (c) aft where flow is diagonal.*

The effect of separation can generally be seen on the surface of the water in the form of eddies which circulate inwards and drag floating debris in with them. Resistance is increased of course, and very often there is a considerable reduction in the efficiency of the rudder at a certain angle either side of amidships. This was a fault found mainly in the American 12-metres of 1970, as well as in the earliest boats with bustles, at much the same period.

2 Frictional resistance

We have already looked at the question of friction in some detail in Chapter II.3d, and the effects are the same, whether the body is completely immersed or floating on the surface. However, both the size of the areas affected, and the speed of flow over these areas, are modified by the formation of waves, and there can be further aggravation when the effects of heeling and leeway are also included.

A technical note from the University of Southampton makes this point. Given leeway of 5°, heeling angle 20° and a speed-to-length ratio of 1.15, wetted area is 3.5% greater than static wetted area (fig. V.32).

3 Total resistance

Having looked in turn at each of the various resistances that oppose the forward motion of a hull, it is time to consider the proportions of their effects at various speeds. The curves of fig. V.33 show the proportions of frictional resistance and of residual resistance as a function of the speed-to-length ratio for a relatively heavy displacement, traditional type of sailing boat with a waterline length of 10 m ($L/\sqrt[3]{\Delta} = 4.2$). Above $V/\sqrt{L} = 1$, it is residual resistance that plays the major role, and it increases towards a value that, in practice, reaches a limit at

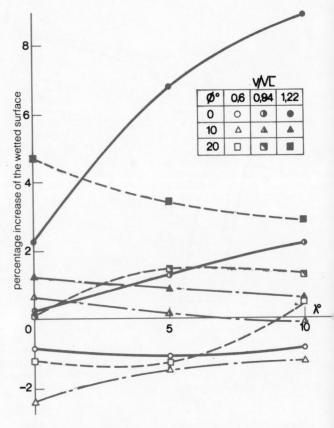

Figure V.32 *Variation of the wetted surface as a function of the angle of heel, and of leeway and of speed.*

about $V/\sqrt{L} = 1.25$; this corresponds to the last attitude of the boat in fig. V.6.

Figure V.34 shows the values of the various coefficients of resistance, and draws attention in particular to the importantance of form drag.

The following are the formulae relating to total resistance:

Total resistance, $R_T = R_f + R_r$
Friction resistance $R_f = C_f \times \rho/2 \times A \times V^2$
Residual resistance $R_r = R_W + R_F$
Wave-making resistance $R_W = C_W \times$
$$\rho/2 \times \Delta/L \times V^2$$
Form drag $R_F = C_F \times \rho/2 \times A_M \times V^2$

ρ = density of water
Δ displacement in m³
A_M = area of maximum immersed section
A = wetted surface
L LWL in m

4 Resistance due to heeling

As soon as the sailing boat heels, the symmetry of her form vanishes and, in consequence, flow becomes asymmetric, the pressure field around the hull

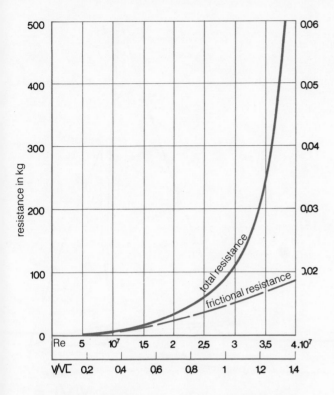

Figure V.33 *Resistance curve in kg of a classic sailing boat with a waterline length of 10 m.*

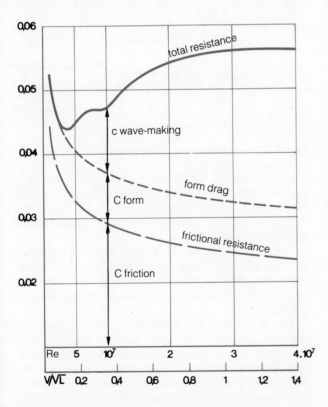

Figure V.34 *The part played respectively by friction, form and wave-making resistance as components of total resistance.*

is disturbed, and form drag increases. Although heeling occurs by itself very frequently when a boat is on a run, because she will so often start to roll on this point of sailing, its influence on resistance has rarely been studied. Juan Baader gives the following values showing how resistance when heeled is increased by comparison with resistance when she is on an even keel.

It is clear that this increase is considerable once the boat is heeling at a greater angle, and apart from being detrimental to the performance of a sailing boat in other ways, rolling has an adverse effect on resistance.

The increase in resistance is due essentially to the asymmetry of the hull, and consequently the more closely the shape of the section approximates to an arc of a circle, the less asymmetric will the hull be when heeled; in addition, narrow sections that draw more are preferable to those that are beamier and shallower.

B Planing

When a sailing boat reaches a speed-to-length ratio of about 1.25, we have seen firstly that the increase in resistance is such that it is virtually impossible for her to exceed this speed and, secondly, that the trim has altered considerably, her attitude being somewhat down by the stern, as in fig. V.35.

When the hull exceeds a speed-to-length ratio of about 1.5, the trough of the bow wave coincides with that of the stern wave and, if speed continues to rise, the hull settles into a sort of 'bed' in the water; the water is thrust out to either side and then reunites aft of the transom, piling up sometimes to a considerable height. The streamlines leave the transom in a direction almost parallel to the fore-and-aft line.

The hull can then be considered to have a fictitious length matching that of the 'bed' she makes (fig. V.36). At this moment, the angle of trim of the bottom of the hull is such that it meets the surface of the water at an angle of incidence which generates lift.

Provided that there is adequate propulsive force and, in particular, provided that the boat is light enough, dynamic lift will enable the hull to raise itself as speed increases further, and when the speed-to-length ratio is greater than about 1.5, the boat will start to plane, skimming over the surface rather than forcing her way through the water. Being less deeply immersed, the decrease in wetted area causes a major reduction in frictional and wave-making resistance and form drag. On the other hand, the smaller waterplane area reduces longitudinal and lateral stability, although dynamic lift can help to counter this latter effect.

1 Theory of planing

It could be tempting first to compare the phenomena that arise when a plane surface meets the surface of water at a positive angle of incidence with that of an aerodynamic foil, but this would be to forget the fact that the foil is entirely immersed in the fluid, and lift results mainly from low pressure on the back. So far as planing is concerned, we are interested only in pressures on the face.

Fig. V.37 shows the pattern of the flow of a perfect fluid over a flat plane surface of infinite breadth; flow meets the surface at an angle of incidence, i. Although the major part of flow beneath the plane surface is directed towards the trailing edge, a thin layer of water is deflected towards the leading edge; the streamline separating the two, the dividing streamline, leads to the stagnation point. In the case of a boat, the layer that is deflected forward is water, seen as spray and directed forward towards the bow.

At stagnation point the speed of the fluid becomes zero, and pressure there will be maximum,

$$\text{i.e. } \tfrac{1}{2} \times \rho \times V^2,$$

while at the trailing edge speed equals V and pressure is zero. Pressures on the body are as indicated by the curve in fig. V.38, and the resultant of pressure, F, acts perpendicular to the surface of the plane.

If we assume that the water does not move, but that the body is moving towards the right at a speed V, the velocities imparted to the molecules of water at the front and the rear of the plane can be determined. At the front, the spray will be deflected forward at a velocity equal to 2V cos i/2, while at the rear the velocity of the deflection downwards will be equal to 2V sin i/2. Thus the energy lost will be equal to $\tfrac{1}{2} \times \rho \times \delta \times V(2V \cos i/2)^2$, and the work done by normal force F is equal to $F \times V \times \sin i$.

Because the energy input and losses are equal, $F \times V \sin i = \tfrac{1}{2} \times \rho \times \delta \; V(2V \cos i/2)^2$, and therefore

$$F = \rho \times \delta \times V^2 \times \frac{2 \cos i/2}{\sin i} = \rho \times \delta \times V^2 \cot i/2.$$

The quantity of spray thrown out by a hull is therefore one indication of how well her underwater body performs.

Force F developed by dynamic lift is composed of the vertical lift force, L, transmitted to the hull and of resistance R. The respective values of these two forces will of course vary with the angle of incidence. For any given displacement, resistance will be minimum at a certain angle of incidence, and that will be the optimum angle (fig. V.39) Juan Baader has used two extremely interesting graphs, taken from

$V/\sqrt{L} = 2$

$V/\sqrt{L} = 3$

Figure V.35 *Attitude of a sailing dinghy planing.*

Sottorf's work in Hamburg; the first, which we have just looked at, makes it possible to determine certain basic values, while the second (fig. V.40) shows the optimum angle of incidence and the coefficient of minimum resistance.

Thus, for a flat plate 1 m wide, carrying a load of 750 kg and propelled at a speed of 20 m/s, the optimum angle of incidence will be 4.7° and the coefficient of resistance 0.095, that is a resistance of 7.1 kg.

This is not the only resistance to be overcome by the hull, however, because there is the frictional resistance that results when it slides over the water, and this is a function of the wetted surface and the coefficient of friction. Although the wetted surface decreases as speed increases, because i increases frictional resistance will increase, although less rapidly than in the case of a displacement hull, as can be seen in fig. V.41.

114

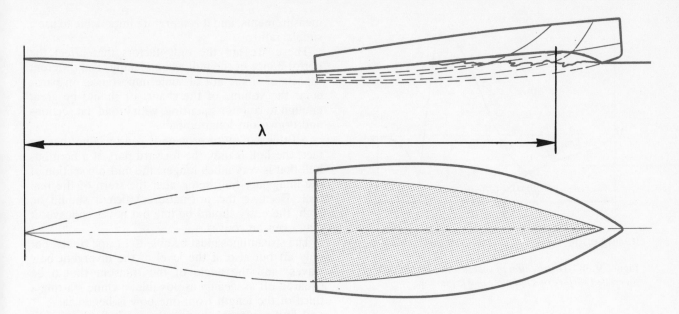

Figure V.36 *A planing hull can be taken as being made up of the front part of a hull of fictitious length equal to that of* the 'bed' which she forms in the water.

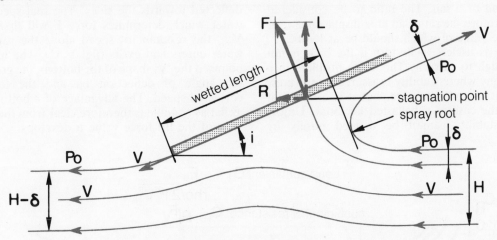

Figure V.37 *Part of the flow circulating beneath a planing body is turned forwards towards the direction in which the body is moving.*

2 Factors which affect planing performance

Planing is affected by two types of factors, those that are linked to the dimensions of the boat herself, and those relating to the shape of her wetted area.

The measurement to be considered first is, of course, weight or, to be more exact, the load applied per unit of lifting area. Because it is very difficult to state the value of the area affected when planing, it is generally taken as being equal to the area of the waterplane, A_W, and the load is given as the ratio Δ/A_W. This area is rarely included with hull measurements, however, and the displacement to length ratio is then used in the form $\Delta(LWL/100)^3$. Table V.III below gives some examples. The maximum permissible value for $\Delta/(LWL/100)^3$ is about 50.

If a hull is to be able to exceed the speed limit imposed by the length of its waterline, it must first of all be able to sail at hull speed; its waterline length must therefore be adequate for its displacement. Waterline length can be introduced in the first ratio in the table as a denominator, and the ratio then becomes $\Delta/A_W \times LWL$. It is easy to see that a boat could have a reasonable Δ/A_W ratio, but the area might have been obtained at the expense of length by making breadth extreme and such a boat would find it difficult to exceed hull speed due to her inadequate length.

The other important measurement is sail area, which directly governs the driving force that is

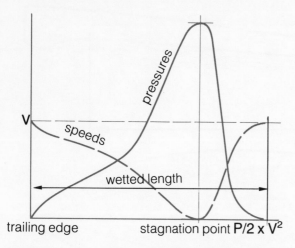

V

speeds

pressures

wetted length

trailing edge   stagnation point $P/2 \times V^2$

Figure V.38   *Distribution of speeds and pressures along the wetted surface of a flat plate that is planing.*

measurements, and it is therefore impossible to use a simple ratio.

These are not the only factors that affect the performance of the hull when planing, and different aspects of shape are of some importance. In particular the volume of the shape aft should be great enough to counter squatting, with broad flat sections and drawn out longitudinals.

All this is easy to provide if you imagine that, in fact, the hull is only the forward part of a fictitious hull that is very much longer, the midship section of the imaginary hull being near the stern of the real hull. Because the prismatic coefficient should be high, the entry should be fine but never concave; it may even be convex.

The streamlines must be able to escape freely, not only aft but also at the level of the divergent bow waves, and the angle of the transom should be squared off as cleanly as possible; a chine starting a third of the length from one bow is beneficial.

A hull very rarely has an absolutely flat bottom; it is usually a 'V' shape which may be more or less pronounced. Spray is not then thrust ahead, but is deflected towards the sides. The real speed of the water which determines force F will therefore be V_{cor}, the resultant of speed along the axes where water enters and exists (fig. V.42). The more pronounced the 'V' shape of the bottom, the greater will the angle of deflection be and the lower the corrected speed. The advantage of a bottom that is as flat as possible is therefore clear from the point of view of the lift force value it develops.

generated; it will serve no useful purpose to provide a light long hull if the boat sets a pocket handkerchief instead of a sail. The ratio to be considered here is therefore the ratio sail area/displacement, or $SA/\Delta^{2/3}$, the value of which should be at least 27.

Sail area is useless in its turn if the boat is not stable enough to carry it. This is no problem in a sailing dinghy where stability is assured by the crew who sit out or use a trapeze, but it is a different matter in the case of a ballasted keelboat. Unfortunately, stability cannot be defined purely by

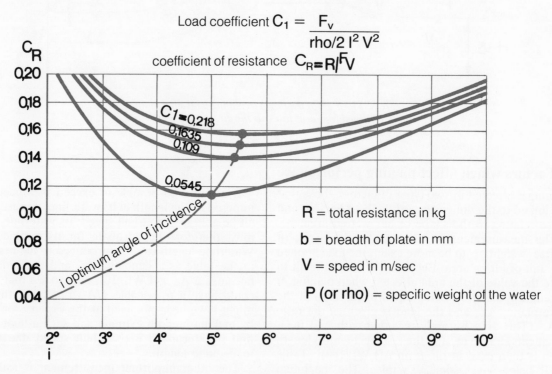

Load coefficient $C_1 = \dfrac{F_v}{rho/2 \; l^2 \; V^2}$

coefficient of resistance $C_R = R/F_V$

C_R

$C_1 = 0.218$
0.1635
0.109

0.0545

i optimum angle of incidence

R = total resistance in kg

b = breadth of plate in mm

V = speed in m/sec

P (or rho) = specific weight of the water

Figure V.39   *Resistance of a flat plate as a function of the angle of incidence and of the load coefficient.*

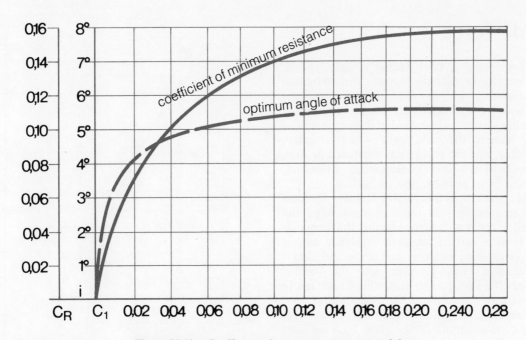

Figure V.40 *Coefficient of minimum resistance and the angle of incidence of a flat plate as a function of the load coefficient.*

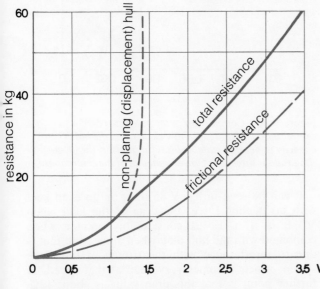

Figure V.41 *Resistance curve of a light sailing dinghy of the 505 type. The dotted line indicates the curve of a non-planing hull.*

Figure V.42 *When the boat has a 'V' bottom, the spray is deflected to either side. The speed to take into account when determining the lift force is composed of the speed of entry and of exit of the water ejected as side spray and forward spray.*

TABLE V.III

	$\triangle/S_{fl}$	$\triangle/(L_{fl}/100)^3$	$\triangle/S_{fl} \times L_{fl}$	$S_v/\triangle^{2/3}$
Laser	0.0545	27	0.0141	28.4
Contender	0.0498	18.5	0.0108	33
International Canoe	0.0503	11.4	0.0097	34
Finn	0.0716	33.9	0.0177	27
505	0.0749	29.55	0.0164	38.8
FD	0.0620	18.65	0.0110	45.4

C Side force

Having considered a boat sailing straight ahead, without heeling or making leeway, corresponding roughly to running with the wind astern, we will now look at how the hydrodynamic forces needed for, and resulting from, close-hauled sailing are developed, namely the side force which counters heeling force, and the additional resistance or drag that arises both as a direct consequence of this and, in ballasted boats at least, due to heeling.

We have already seen (Chapter II.4 and Chapter III.B) that a lifting side force appears when the whole hull of the boat is turned so that the fore-and-aft line is at a certain angle of incidence to her direction of movement. Every part of the hull, that is the underwater body together with the various appendages (fin keel, rudder etc), will all react but in a different way according to their capabilities.

So far as the underwater body itself is concerned, the results are generally rather poor. Flow all over the hull is disturbed and, instead of passing symmetrically to either side of the fore-and-aft line, water tries to flow beneath the hull; the less deep and the flatter the hull, the more easily will it do so. The wave systems will also be disturbed.

It is easy to believe that whenever a relatively small side force is created, a rapid increase in resistance will result, as is shown in fig. V.43.

1 Distribution of side force between underwater body and appendages

The major part of side force is provided by the appendages, that is by the ballast keel or fin keel, together with the rudder assembly.

Pierre de Saix's research at the Davidson laboratory provides very full information on this subject. By studying a hull and ballast keel, both separately and together, he was able to determine not only the part each played individually, but also their effect on each other. The hull studied was that of a classic 5.5-metre built in the 1960s, with the rudder an integral part of the ballast keel (fig. V.44).

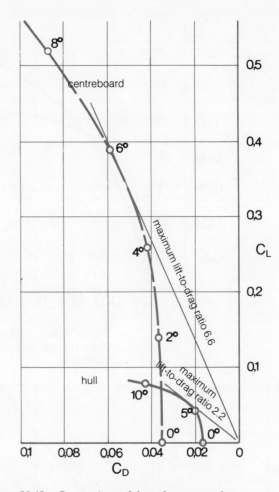

Figure V.43 *Comparison of the polar curves of a centreboard and of a hull show clearly that the hull's capacity to develop suitable lift is far inferior; the lift-to-drag ratio is three times lower than that of the centreboard.*

It can be seen in fig. V.45 that, on an even keel with no heeling force, the drag of the keel when $V/\sqrt{L}$ is over 1.5 is considerably greater when combined with the hull than when alone, and that is due to interference with the trough of the wave system which becomes very deep at that speed. A further point is that this drag value is about 12%

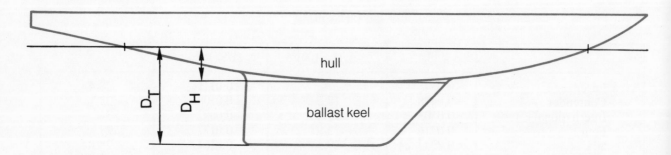

Figure V.44 *The 5.5-metre model that was used for tests at the Stevens Institute*

higher than the value of the difference between the drag of the complete model and that of the hull alone, and this shows that there is interaction between the two.

The results when heeling and making leeway are given in fig. V.46. Angle α is the angle of attack at which the hull meets the water in the plane perpendicular to the plane of symmetry, and not in the horizontal plane; $\alpha = \lambda/\cos\theta$. In actual fact the real angle of attack for the complete model is higher because of the movement of water which, as we have just mentioned, tends to pass beneath the hull. At the level of the ballast keel it can be estimated as equal to $\alpha = \alpha(1 + 2D_D/D_T)$.

This partly explains why the side force developed by the ballast keel when attached to the hull is higher than that produced by the ballast keel alone. Another cause is the increase in the theoretical aspect ratio of the ballast keel due to the presence of the hull, an increase that varies between 1 and 0.69 when the ratio D_H/D_T changes from 1 to 0.5.

It is of course at 0° of heel that side force is greatest and drag least, and it will be noted that side force decreases at an angle of heel above 30°, because that is when the keel emerges in the trough of the wave.

The two appendages to the hull do not 'perform' the same because their aspect ratio is not the same in the lateral plane, and consequently the angle of incidence at which they are most efficient is also different. It is therefore easy to understand the interest there is in altering the orientation of the ballast keel in relation to the hull.

In a centreboard dinghy like the 505, which has a very small wetted area and a very flat bottom, the hull can only develop a significant amount of side force when at a very large angle of incidence, and the cost is great in terms of drag. Furthermore this very large angle of incidence reduces the angle of incidence of the sails to the apparent wind, and that causes a large drop in the performance of the jib/mainsail combination. Viewing the performance of a boat of this type as a whole, it is therefore tempting to eliminate the hull almost entirely from the point of view of resisting leeway, and to leave it to the centreboard alone to develop side force. It would then be envisaged that the positive orientation of the centreboard would be as determined by its own performance.

However, it is not the same for all types of boat. In a racing catamaran, for example, the very large lateral wetted area of the hull and the slenderness of her waterlines make for a very efficient lateral plane, and so there is no question of disregarding this part of the hull's role.

If we plot on a single graph the polar curve of the hull opposite to that of the centreboard, we see as in fig. V.47 that the maximum F_S/R ratios, as indicated by the tangents to the curves, are at an angle of attack of 5° 30' for the centreboard and 6° 30' for the

hull. In this case optimum combined performance will be obtained with the centreboard in a position that is 1° negative.

The difference would be even greater if a centreboard were a curved foil with a much greater F_S/R ratio at a smaller angle of attack, and this shows how difficult it can sometimes be to determine exactly how great an angle of incidence to give to a centreboard. Thus in the case of a bilge keeler with both keels immersed at the same time, it is preferable that the bilge keels should be offset at a positive angle, because otherwise the windward keel would work at too large an angle of incidence, and this would cause a great increase in drag. If the two keels diverged, a vertical component would arise and increase heeling moment.

There have been experiments with adjustable keels for keelboats, but those fitted in 1971 to Dick Carter's New Zealand and German One Tonners, *Wai Aniwa* and *Optimist B*, do not seem to have made a significant contribution because it was not until her keel had been immobilized to comply with a new IOR Mk III rule that *Wai Aniwa* won the One Ton Cup in 1973.

2 Ballast keel performance

It was essentially on account of problems of strength that ballast was for so long carried inside the hulls of sailing boats. The ballast carried by the schooner *America*, for example, was made of molten iron, moulded to the shape of the spaces between her

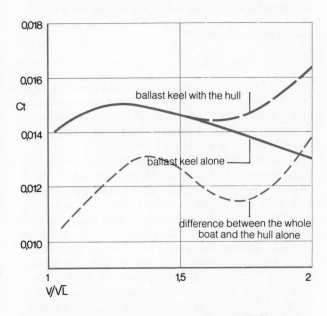

Figure V.45 *How the drag of the ballast keel differs as a function of speed. Although the hull's presence has a less favourable effect at higher speeds, it is evidently beneficial in general because the real drag calculated from the difference between the complete boat and the hull alone is lower than that of the ballast keel alone.*

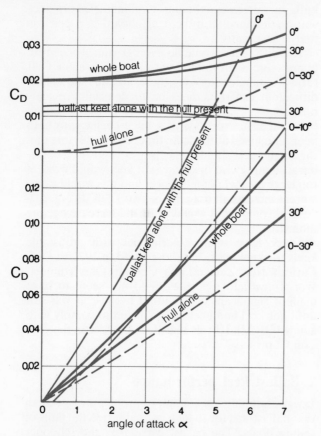

Figure V.46 *Value of lift and drag as a function of the angle of attack and of heeling. Note the extremely damaging effect that heeling has on the efficiency of the ballast keel; to obtain the same value of lift at 30° and at 0° the angle of attack has to be multiplied by 1.5. The presence of the hull inhibits increase in drag.*

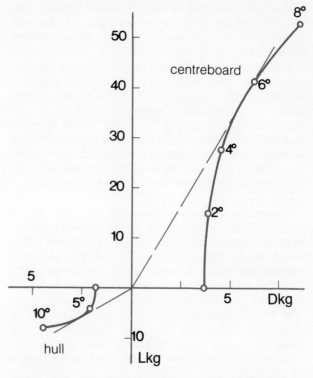

Figure V.47 *When the hull and centreboard polar curves are plotted opposite each other, the maximum lift-to-drag ratio can be seen to be obtained at different angles of attack, and it could be interesting to offset the centreboard slightly.*

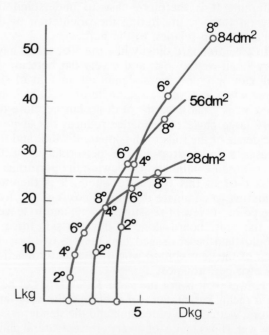

Figure V.48 *Polar curves of forces developed by three centreboards of increasing area. If the lift to be developed is 25 kg, for example, the 56 dm² centreboard will be the best because the drag of the others is greater. It is noticeable that it is preferable to have too much area rather than too little; the effect of the former is to reduce the angle of attack, and that can only help the total drag of the boat.*

frames. For many years, just a small quantity of a boat's ballast was fitted beneath the wooden keel, and it was not until 1876 that the 10-tonner *Florence*, designed and built in America by James Reid & Co, carried all her lead ballast externally.

Gradually the keel became deeper, and it was that great innovator Nathaniel Herreshoff who, on 9 October 1891, launched the first sailing boat with a bulb keel, the *Dilemma*, a small sloop 7.62 m on the waterline; she had a steel ballast keel weighing 400 kg fastened to the hull with angle irons, with a two-ton bulb, shaped like a cigar at the lower end. After 1893, with the *Jubilee* designed by John B. Payne and the *Pilgrim* by the successors of E. Burgess, Steward and Binney, two unsuccessful candidates for the defence of the America's Cup, the independent ballast keel made its appearance on large racing yachts. The consequences of reducing displacement and wetted area, together with the need for more and more ballast, had led development to this ultimate conclusion, and there was no alternative but to admit how important a part the design of the ballast

120

keel played in performance of the lateral plane as a whole.

Performance is linked basically to three factors, the lateral area, the planform and the profile of the sections.

a The lateral area

This should be adequate to provide the side force required with a maximum reduction of the angle of incidence, but it should not, however, be so great as to increase resistance (mainly frictional resistance), which would cancel out the benefit gained.

If we plot on the same graph the polar curves of the actual forces (not the coefficients) developed, as in fig. V.48, we see that only one area will develop a given value of side force for a lower value of drag. Consequently there is only one optimum lateral area for each value of side force required.

We know that this side force is equal (but acts in the opposite direction) to the heeling force developed by the sails, and also that because it is a function of the square of boat speed it varies with the size of the boat and her sails, with the efficiency of the sails, and with speed. The faster the type of boat, for example a racing catamaran, the smaller can the lateral area be. But a boat does not sail at a constant speed and, when going about for example, there can be a very great variation in speed as well as in heeling force. It is therefore interesting to study the relationships that exist between these various elements.

Initially, when the speed of the boat is nil, the ratio of boat speed/wind speed is also nil and, consequently, maximum lateral area is needed to avoid too great an angle of incidence. As soon as the boat starts to make way, her speed increases more quickly than the speed of the apparent wind. The

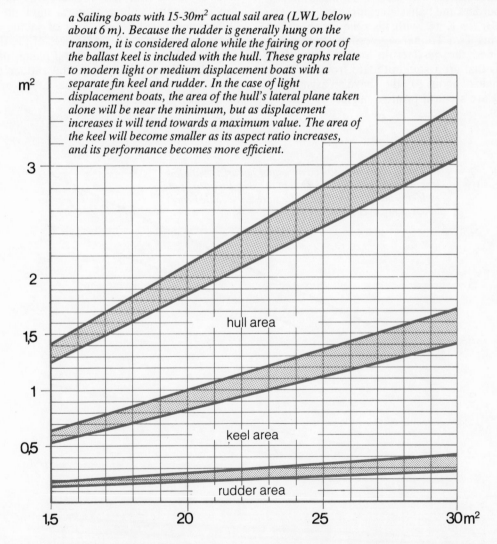

a Sailing boats with 15-30m² actual sail area (LWL below about 6 m). Because the rudder is generally hung on the transom, it is considered alone while the fairing or root of the ballast keel is included with the hull. These graphs relate to modern light or medium displacement boats with a separate fin keel and rudder. In the case of light displacement boats, the area of the hull's lateral plane taken alone will be near the minimum, but as displacement increases it will tend towards a maximum value. The area of the keel will become smaller as its aspect ratio increases, and its performance becomes more efficient.

Figure V.49   *Area of the lateral plane as a function of sail area. Each shaded band indicates the range in relation to the area of the sum of the preceding elements; the first is the rudder alone or the rudder plus a skeg; the second is the previous area plus that of the keel; the third is the total area of the lateral plane.*

ratio boat speed/wind speed is no longer nil, but nearer 1 (or more in the case of a racing multihull or an ice-boat). The side force developed by the centreboard increases very rapidly, and the angle of incidence decreases. When a value corresponding to the centreboard's maximum F_S/R ratio is reached, the lateral area should then be reduced so as to avoid developing useless drag.

If the wind force increases now, boat speed will not increase proportionately, the ratio boat speed/wind speed will drop back towards 0, and heeling force will increase. In order to develop a corresponding hydrodynamic side force while maintaining the maximum F_S/R ratio, an increase in the lateral area is needed.

Of course, on points of sailing other than close-hauled, when side force decreases in relation to driving force, the aim is to reduce the lateral area as much as possible so that drag is kept at a minimum.

It is understandable why there is so much interest in centreboarders and ballasted centreboarders. The American Bruce King, with his One Tonner *Terrorist* and his Two Tonner *Aggressive II*, seems to have obtained the best results so far with lifting bilgeboards that are raked outboard from the vertical at an angle of about 10°; they have an asymmetric profile and are set at a positive angle.

Another element is the rudder, which must also be taken into account in the lateral plan. In small boats it is often a relatively large area, and the question is, should it help to create side force? The answer is clear from what has been said already. When starting to make way, the maximum lateral area is needed and the centreboard should be moved so far forward that the area of the rudder is required to establish equilibrium of heeling force and side force. Then the centreboard will gradually be shifted further aft to eliminate the need for the rudder's contribution and to reduce drag. Only when the boat speed/wind speed ratio drops and an increase in lateral area is required should the rudder again play a part.

Obviously longitudinal equilibrium and lateral stability, which call for different alterations in lateral area, are not being considered at this point.

Assuming that the boat is sufficiently stable to be able to make full use of her sails in optimum conditions, the sail area/lateral area ratio can be determined for different sizes of sailing boat (fig. V.49), as well as the relative sizes of the three basic areas which make up the lateral plane, namely the centreboard or ballast keel, the rudder or rudder and skeg combination, and the lateral area of the hull itself.

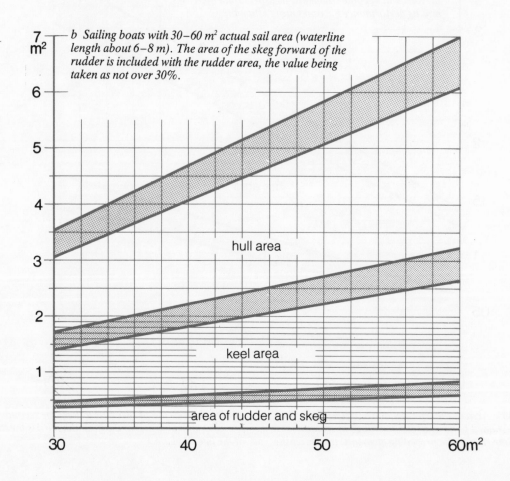

b Sailing boats with 30–60 m² actual sail area (waterline length about 6–8 m). The area of the skeg forward of the rudder is included with the rudder area, the value being taken as not over 30%.

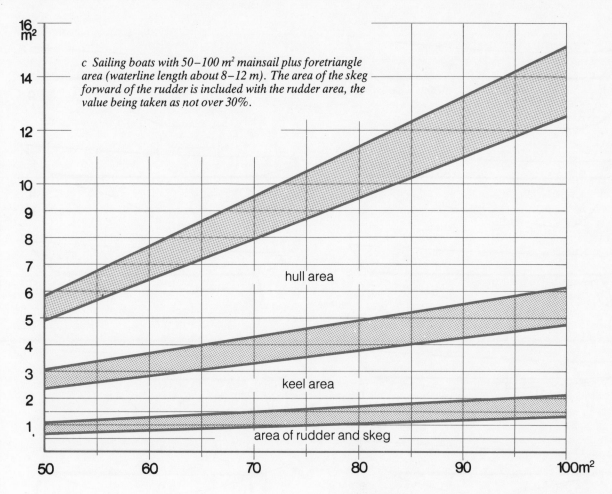

c *Sailing boats with 50–100 m² mainsail plus foretriangle area (waterline length about 8–12 m). The area of the skeg forward of the rudder is included with the rudder area, the value being taken as not over 30%.*

hull area

keel area

area of rudder and skeg

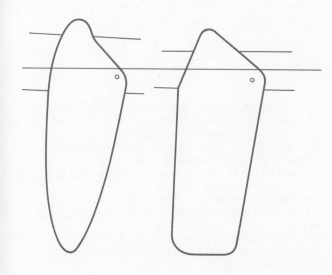

Figure V.50 *Two centreboard shapes, those of the 505 and the Flying Dutchman.*

b The shape of centreboards and ballast keels

This is defined by three main points: their aspect ratio, their planforms and the angles of inclination of the main axis to the vertical (sweep angle). In Chapter II.4d we considered the basic principles governing the first two characteristics. As to their application in practice, the 505's centreboard shows these principles applied perfectly. Its planform is two quarters of an ellipse, and its aspect ratio is 2.8, giving an effective aspect ratio of 4 to 5 (taking into consideration the losses due to the fact that the hull is not deeply immersed), and these are optimum values (fig. V.50). In any case there seems to be no advantage in increasing the aspect ratio; the only result of doing so would be that lowering the centre of pressure would increase the lever arm of the heeling couple.

A simpler shape with comparable performance is a trapezium with a small base/large base ratio of about 0.66. The FD's centreboard approaches this at 0.75.

The shape of the ballast keels of displacement boats has developed enormously over the last few years, the current answer being to have a fin keel that is totally independent of the hull (fig. V.51).

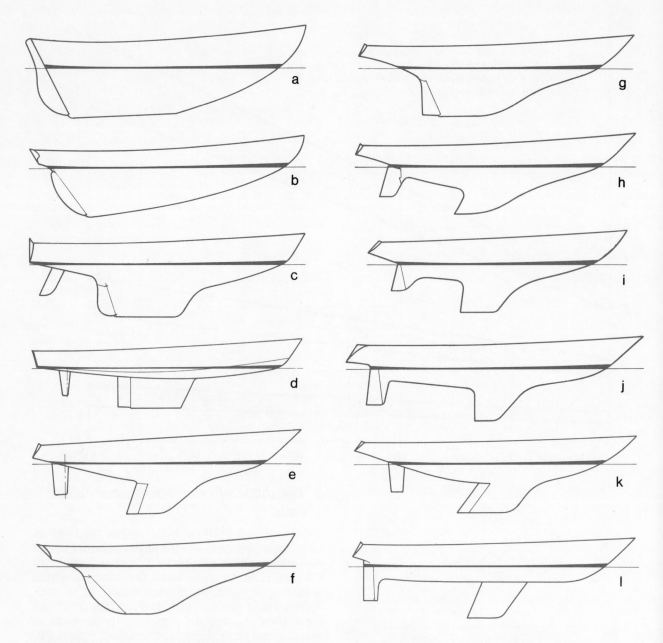

Figure V.51

a Vertue class, 7.66 m long, designed by Laurent Giles in 1936.

b Nina, 18 m LOA, a Starling Burgess schooner designed in 1927. She still won the Bermuda Race in 1962. The centre of lateral resistance is well aft, as is very suitable for schooner rig.

c Feather III in 1963, 10.34 LOA, one of the last plans from Illingworth and Primrose for an RORC rating. The daggerboard aft was needed to provide adequate directional stability when sailing off the wind.

d Zeevalk, LOA 10.67, designed by E. G. van de Stadt. Second, all classes, in the 1951 Fastnet Race and one of the first RORC boats with a short keel and balanced spade rudder; the first to have a trim tab.

e Rasbora, 10.59 LOA, developed from the preceding boat for the 1967 One Ton Cup.

f to j Development of the lateral plane shapes of boats designed by Olin Stephens to compete for the One Ton Cup. All the One Tonner plans are to the same scale.

f Hestia, 10.41 m LOA, old-fashioned RORC type, winner of the North Sea Race in 1964.

g Diana III, 10.98 m LOA, winner of the One Ton Cup with the new formula in 1965.

h Clarionet, 10.98 m LOA, fifth in 1966.

i 5534, 10.23 m LOA, derived from Morningtown, fourth in 1968.

j America Jane II, 11.78 m LOA, eighth in 1974.

k Tina, 11.25 m LOA, began Carter's One Ton Cup winning run in 1966.

l Ydra, 11.28 LOA, ended Carter's run of winners, but should have won in 1972 had a rigging screw not broken.

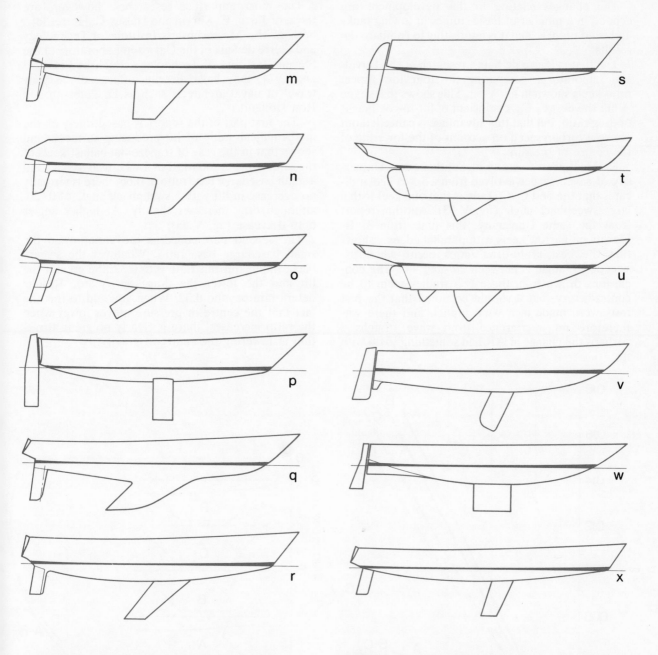

m Ganbare, *10.82 m LOA, the first international boat from the designer Doug Peterson, winner in 1973.*
n Prospect of Ponsonby, *LOA 10.97 m, designed by New Zealander Bruce Farr.*
o Robin Too II, *LOA 11.31 m, one of the last centreboarders designed by Ted Hood for the One Ton Cup. Winner of the 1974 SORC.*
p Terrorist, *10.46 m LOA, centreboarder by Bruce King; very noticeable in the first leg of the 1974 One Ton Cup.*
q CC 46, *14.09 m LOA, one of the last plans from the Canadian naval architects Cuthbertson and Cassian, supporters of the shark's fin-shaped keel.*
r Chance 42/36, *12.85 m LOA, the American designer stayed faithful to the stripped shape with the fin keel fairly far forward.*
s Robber II, *7.33 m LOA; often close to victory, the*

Swedish designers were the promoters of the stripped plans for Quarter Ton Cup boats.
t Finisterre, *11.76 m LOA, without doubt the best-known ballasted centreboarder designed in 1959 for a CCA rating by Olin Stephens.*
u Barlovento II, *21.84 m LOA. This design by Phil Rhodes has two centreboards, the one aft for use mainly to improve directional stability.*
v Red Rooster, *12.56 m LOA, the first and best-known centreboarder from Dick Carter first on points in the Amiral's Cup, and all classes winner of the 1969 Fastnet.*
w Noryema V, *14.94 m LOA, developed from the former. Since then the IOR rating has virtually condemned movable keels.*
x Ondine, *24.10 m LOA, the largest centreboarder designed by Britton Chance.*

The changes relating to this development are echoed in a number of basic studies in towing tanks and wind tunnels, and it is interesting to compare the results.

The first is Pierre de Saix's research at the Davidson Laboratory, comparing the four low aspect ratio keels shown in fig. V.52. This shows that shape A has the best C_L/C_D, coefficient of lift-to-coefficient of drag ratio, but that this advantage is cancelled out above a certain speed on account of the lowering of the centre of pressure.

K. MacLaverty's study at Southampton University of seven shapes evolved from a 5.5 m keel indicates that the best C_L/C_D ratio is that of a keel with a large sweepback angle (fig. V.53). Another report from the same University, this time from J. R. Flewitt on narrow keels with parallel edges, shows that the best lift-to-drag ratios occur when the sweepback angle is between 20° and 40°. The conclusions drawn from these two studies seem to be contradictory, but it should be noted that the first tests were made in a wind tunnel, and there was therefore no interference from wave troughs – perhaps the change in AR had something to do with it.

The most important researches, however, are those of Justin E. Kervin and Halsey C. Herreshoff, both of the Massachusetts Institute of Technology and Pierre de Saix of the Davidson Laboratory at the Stevens Institute of Technology. Published in 1973 and 1974, they have directly influenced the 'new wave' of naval architects such as D. Peterson and Ron Holland.

The first part of the report is based solely on the mathematical study of lift-producing surfaces, and shows that in the case of trapezoidal ballast keels of the same aspect ratio (0.81 or 1.62 effective AR) and a small base/large base ratio of 0.66, there is virtually no decrease in lift with a sweepback angle of 0–20° although drag increases slightly. At higher angles both decrease (fig. V.55).

The second part concerns the variation in the small base/large base ratio. Whatever the sweepback, the nearer this ratio is to 0.32, the greater the lift and the lower the drag (fig. V.56). Results deteriorate beyond 0.32. When you add to this the fact that the centre of pressure moves lower when the ratio increases, there is clearly no great attraction in lowering the centre of gravity.

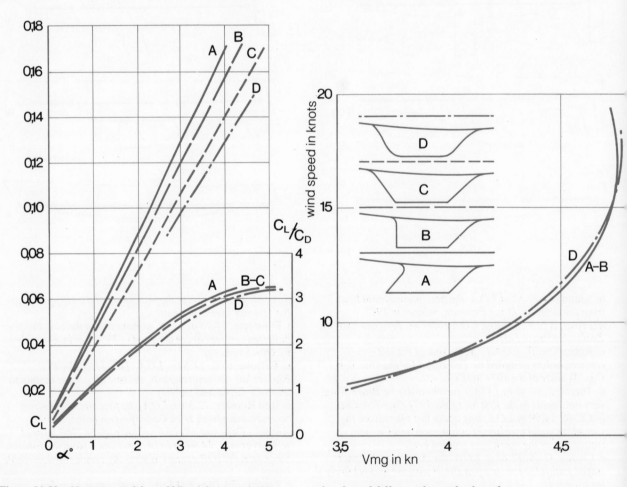

Figure V.52 *Variation in lift, and lift-to-drag ratio of four ballast keels with the same sweepback angle at the leading edge, but of different shapes further aft.*

The second study also relates to a 5.5-metre, with three sets of three trapezoidal keels of varying sweepback and aspect ratio (fig. V.57). One of the first conclusions defines optimum sweepback as a function of aspect ratio. However, because the relative thickness of the profile (10%) is the same for all the keels, those with the highest aspect ratio (and consequently the smallest chord) have least volume in relation to the ballast, and a higher centre of gravity. Given a constant ballast ratio of 55%, the result is a slight loss of stability. Nevertheless Vmg is highest with the highest aspect ratio keel (fig. V.58), although in a following wind, when the boat is neither heeling nor making leeway, the drag of all three keels is the same.

Although increasing the aspect ratio seems to be beneficial, it should not be forgotten that this is linked to a decrease in the angle at which separation

Alignment	0.543	0.855	1.52
Angle of incline	50%	25%	0%

Alignment	0.543	0.855	1.52
Volume in cubic decimetres	102.51	79	60.03
Distance of CG in metres below the waterline	0.47	0.46	0.45

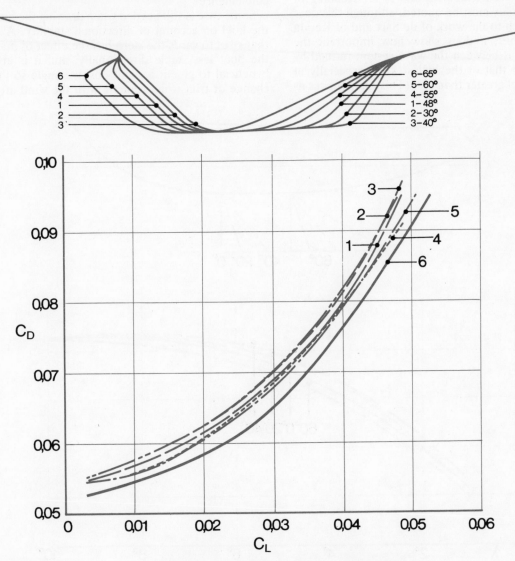

Figure V.53 C_L and C_D values for different keel sweepback angles. Area and mean chord length are constant.

occurs, and that this can be particularly damaging in a seaway.

The third part of the report[1] studies the influence of the shape of the base and its section, and it appears from this that the C_L/C_D ratio is worse when the base is an exponential curve than when it is straight (fig. V.59).

The lift generated by a ballast keel with a squared tip is about 9% higher than that of other shapes, but drag is also much greater and the rounded tip therefore seems to be preferable (fig. V.60). This does not confirm the more theoretical conclusions we reached in Chapter II, and to which the author is still inclined.

The tests with the bulbs are not important on account of their shape and their angle of inclination to the horizontal.

To end this study on the shape of ballast keels, research by W. Beukelman and J. A. Keuning of Delft University must be quoted; although this does not add much to the work of de Saix and of Kervin and Herreshiff, it does show how important the interference is between the wave system formed by the hull and that of the ballast keel, especially at angles of heel greater than 15°. (This again makes us believe in the influence of the Transsonic Area rule.)

The planforms we have considered so far apply principally to lateral planes with an effective aspect ratio of more than 1. When aspect ratio decreases below that figure, greater and greater sweepback angles result in the adoption of an S-shaped curve at the leading edge, as on the 12-metre, and these are not unlike the shape of the wings of an aircraft such as Concorde (fig. V.61); they are shaped like this so as to be suitable for the subsonic speeds (corresponding to the same Reynolds number as a 12-metre) used for landing approach.

All these shapes are dictated by the desire to obtain maximum performance for racing yachts. For a simple cruising boat, other matters are vital and have to be taken into consideration, such as the ability to ground; the shapes chosen will then always be a compromise between performance and convenience.

Some care is still needed when drawing the base of the keel on account of directional stability. A base that rises towards the stern has the effect of making the boat less stable directionally, and it is always beneficial to give it a slight positive angle so that a change of trim when running with the wind aft will

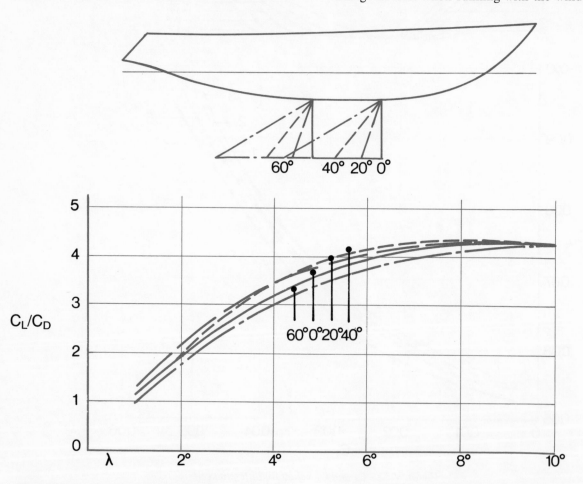

Figure V.54 *Variation of the lift-to-drag ratio as a function of the angle of incidence with different angles of* sweepback for a ballast keel with parallel leading and trailing edges.

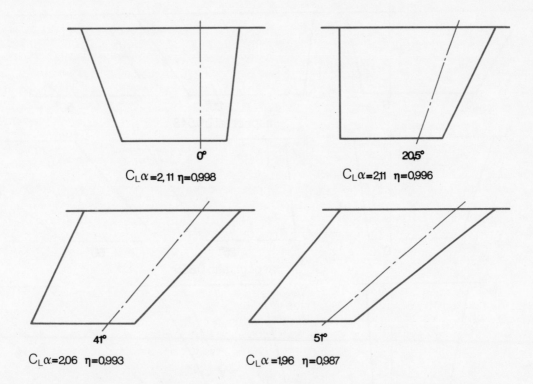

$C_L\alpha=2,11$ $\eta=0,998$ 0°

$C_L\alpha=2,11$ $\eta=0,996$ 20,5°

$C_L\alpha=2,06$ $\eta=0,993$ 41°

$C_L\alpha=1,96$ $\eta=0,987$ 51°

Figure V.55 *Variation of the characteristics as a function of the sweepback angle of the axis, which is one quarter of the way along the chord. The aspect ratio 0.81 and the area are constant. Efficiency is the ratio of induced drag to that of a keel with minimum induced drag corresponding to elliptical load distribution. $C_L\alpha$ is the minimum hydrodynamic drag angle of the fin keel.*

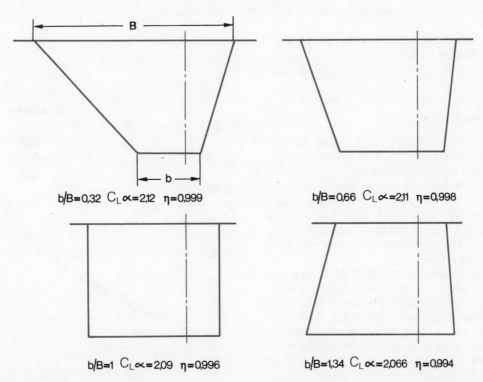

b/B=0,32 $C_L\alpha=2,12$ $\eta=0,999$

b/B=0,66 $C_L\alpha=2,11$ $\eta=0,998$

b/B=1 $C_L\alpha=2,09$ $\eta=0,996$

b/B=1,34 $C_L\alpha=2,066$ $\eta=0,994$

Figure V.56 *Variation of characteristics as a function of the ratio between the length of the base and the top of the fin keel. The measurements are as in figure V.55.*

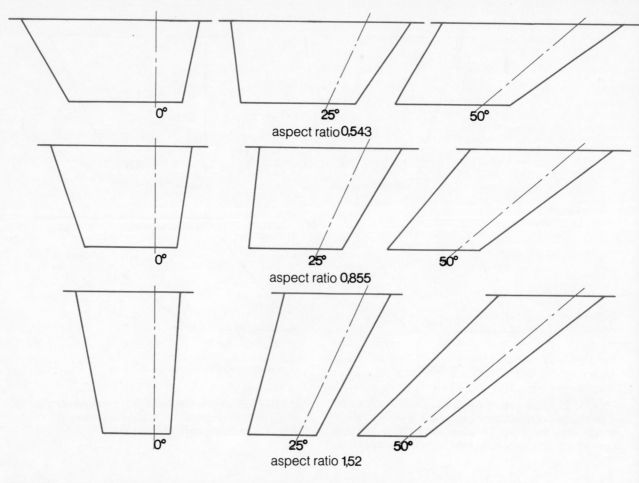

Figure V.57   *Various keel shapes studied by P de Saix at the Davidson Laboratory.*

not make her yaw badly. Cutting away the heel at the end of the keel is extremely prejudicial, as Sir Francis Chichester discovered from experience (fig. V.62).

c The choice of section

This is always very important, and is one of the points to which there is no definitive answer as yet; each designer has his own preference.

At first it might be tempting to use a laminar profile, such as NACA 65, on account of the relatively low Reynolds number of centreboard dinghies, but although this would be advantageous in terms of lower drag, the natural turbulence of the water must not be ignored.

Again, in the optimum conditions of a lake or calm sea, and except for the part situated lower down nearer the tip of the centreboard, it is best to stick to the classic section with maximum thickness one third from the leading edge, of the NACA OOXY type (the two last figures give its thickness as a percentage of the chord); table V.IV gives the dimensions for various different thicknesses.

It is always preferable for thickness to be as small as is compatible with the strength required, because

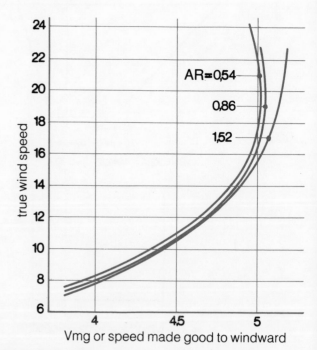

Figure V.58   *Vmg is greatest with the keel that has an aspect ratio of 1.52.*

130

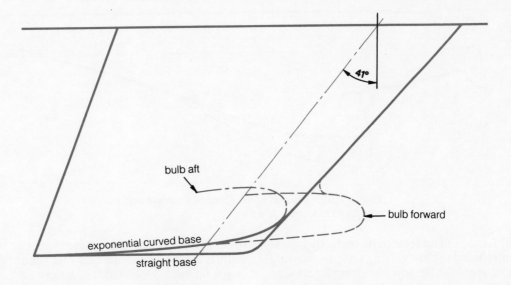

41°

bulb aft

bulb forward

exponential curved base

straight base

Figure V.59 *Different shapes for the base of the keel, studied by J. E. Kerwin and H. C. Herreshoff. The*

inclination of the bulbs causes drag, which makes it impossible to draw useful conclusions.

the C_L/C_D ratio decreases with thickness, and the angles of incidence that are practical are almost always less than the angle at which separation occurs.

Another factor must be taken into account, however. The upper part of the centreboard, near the

bottom of the hull, often has to work at the level of the surface of the water, and the optimum shapes for surface-piercing foils are very different. Instead of a rounded leading edge, a sharp edge is required with the position of maximum thickness further downstream, towards the centre of the foil. GU 2 is one

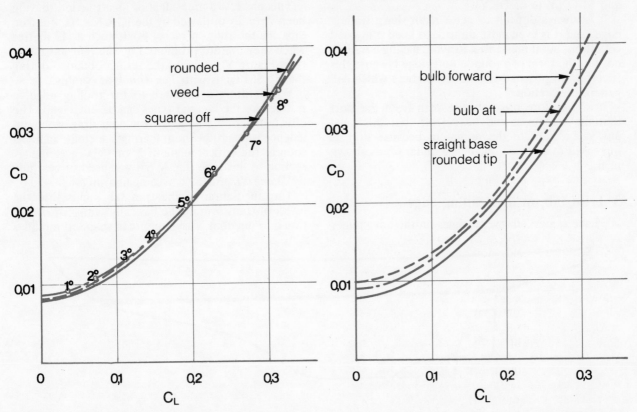

Figure V.60 *On the left are the results obtained for keels with rounded tip sections compared with those that are veed*

and square. On the right are those obtained for the bulbs.

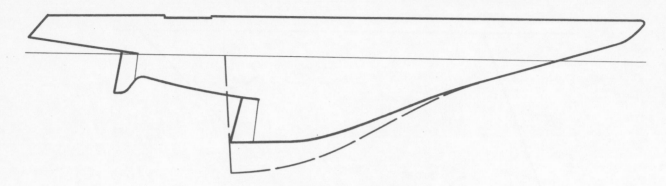

Figure V.61   *The keel of the 12-metre* Courageous
compared to Concorde's wing.

example of these, and it seems to be perfectly logical for the centreboard to have varying sections, starting with a GU 2 profile at the top and changing about a quarter of the way down to the NACA OOXY type which, in the bottom quarter, gives way to a laminar profile of the NACA 65_1 type.

The phenomenon is less evident on keelboats because, due to the greater depth of the hull, the upper sections of the ballast keel will not so often be found near the surface of the water, and the change in the section shape will not therefore need to be so marked. Nevertheless it will still generally be right to start at the top with a 40% profile (series 0012–64 and 64-OXY to 65-OXY).

It is always difficult to get a razor-sharp trailing edge, and it is even more difficult to keep it in good condition, but it is essential to avoid having a trailing edge in the form of a rounded-off ridge because this is certain to provoke alternating vortices which will generate vibration.

It is therefore preferable to plan from the start that the section should be cut off, but this must always be kept to the minimum because drag is increased at angles of incidence under 6°, as shown in fig. V.63.

3 Trim tab on the trailing edge

We have remarked several times on the advantages of cambered sections, but these cannot be used on a normal sailing boat with only one centreboard or a single fin keel. One could, of course, consider constructing a ballast keel, the shape of which could be altered to enable it to take up two symmetrical attitudes, one either side of the centreline, but the main difficulties here would be obtaining a surface that really was continuous, and making the whole device strong enough.

There is a relatively simple way of achieving a curvature of the lateral plane, however; all that is needed is to hinge the after part of the ballast keel so that it acts as a trim tab.

This has lost a great deal of its attraction, having been virtually outlawed by the IOR Mk III, but trim tabs are the rule on racing boats such as 12-metres when they are not prohibited by the relevant rating rule. Figure V.64 shows the results obtained during the ENSM trials with *Pen Duick* at Nantes.

When fitting a trim tab to the trailing edge, a profile like the laminar types can be envisaged. The effect then is to benefit from low drag when incidence is near 0° without fearing a decrease in lift as soon as the critical angle of 2° or 3° is exceeded. A section of this type (fig. V.65) was used successfully by *Dame d'Iroise* for her campaign in 1968.

The angulation of the trim tab almost has the effect of transforming the basically symmetrical section into one that is asymmetric in shape. It modifies

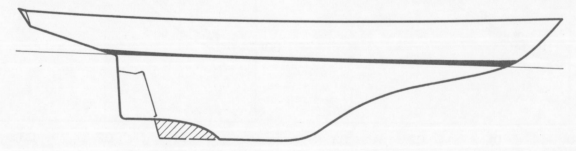

Figure V.62   *During the first half of his circumnavigation of the world, Sir Francis Chichester suffered from a great lack of directional stability in* Gipsy Moth III. *The deadwood piece, aft of the ballast keel, was fitted at Sydney and made a great improvement.*

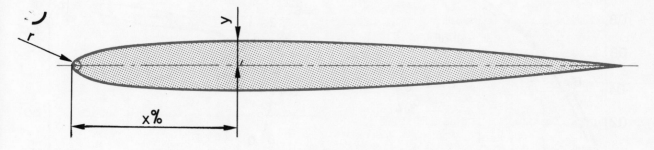

TABLE V.IV

DIMENSIONS OF SOME NACA PROFILES

(The sizes given are the half width y; r is the radius of the leading edge)

% of L	0	1.25	2.5	5	7.5	10	15	20	25	30	40	50	60	70	80	90	95	100	r	Am²/1m
NACA 0006	0	0.95	1.31	1.78	2.10	2.34	2.67	2.87	2.97	3.00	2.90	2.65	2.28	1.83	1.31	0.72	0.40	0	0.40	
NACA 0009	0	1.42	1.96	2.67	3.15	3.51	4.01	4.30	4.46	4.50	4.35	3.97	3.42	2.75	1.97	1.09	0.60	0	0.89	
NACA 0012	0	1.89	2.62	3.56	4.20	4.68	5.34	5.74	5.94	6.00	5.80	5.29	4.56	3.66	2.62	1.45	0.81	0	1.58	
NACA 0012–64	0	1.81	2.45	3.27	3.81	4.24	4.87	5.29	–	5.83	6.00	5.83	5.32	4.48	3.32	1.87	1.03	0.12	1.58	0.0878
NACA 63–006	0	0.77	1.06	1.46	1.77	2.01	2.39	2.66	2.84	2.95	2.97	2.72	2.27	1.67	1.01	0.38	0.14	0	0.30	
NACA 64–006	0	0.75	1.02	1.40	1.69	1.93	2.30	2.57	2.77	2.91	2.99	2.77	2.33	1.74	1.07	0.42	0.16	0	0.26	
NACA 65–006	0	0.72	0.96	1.31	1.59	1.82	2.20	2.48	2.70	2.85	3.00	2.90	2.52	1.93	1.23	0.51	0.19	0	0.24	
NACA 66–006	0	0.69	0.92	1.26	1.52	1.75	2.12	2.40	2.62	2.78	2.97	2.98	2.81	2.32	1.54	0.66	0.26	0	0.22	
NACA 64–009	0	1.13	1.53	2.11	2.55	2.90	3.46	3.87	4.18	4.38	4.49	4.13	3.44	2.55	1.55	0.60	0.22	0	0.59	
NACA 65–009	0	1.06	1.42	1.96	2.38	2.74	3.30	3.73	4.05	4.28	4.50	4.34	3.74	2.86	1.80	0.74	0.28	0	0.55	
NACA 65A010	0	1.18	1.62	2.18	2.65	3.04	3.66	4.13	4.48	4.74	5.00	4.86	4.30	3.43	2.35	1.19	0.60	0.021	0.64	0.0684
NACA 66–009	0	1.03	1.37	1.88	2.28	2.63	3.18	3.60	3.83	4.17	4.46	4.47	4.20	3.43	2.26	0.96	0.39	0	0.53	

Area A is that of a profile 1 m long. A section of any thickness in a given series can be calculated by taking the increase of thickness as proportional and the radius of the leading edge as the square of thickness.

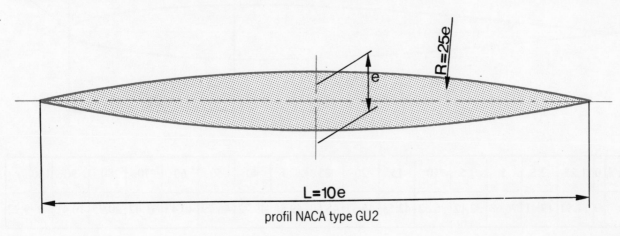

profil NACA type GU2

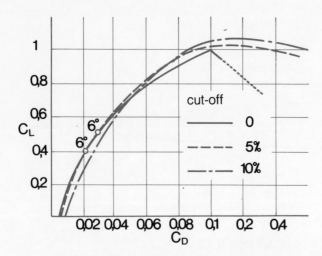

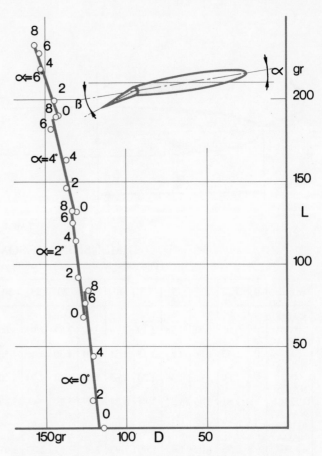

Figure V.63 *A cut-off trailing edge to a section only increases drag slightly, and delays the separation angle. The sections studied here have been reduced to the same length.*

flow over the whole section in such a way that the lift coefficient is increased and the centre of pressure shifted aft. The angle of incidence at which lift is zero is no longer $0°$ but $i_o = \beta\delta_v$ where δ_v is the angle of the trim tab and β a coefficient, the value of which is given in graph 5–66.

The position of the centre of pressure is defined by the formula

$$X_{cp}/L = 0.25 + \cfrac{8.3\,\cfrac{l}{L}}{1 + \cfrac{i}{\delta}},$$

where X_{cp} is the distance from the centre of pressure to the leading edge, L the total length of the section, and l that of the trim tab.

Figure V.64 *Variation of the lift and drag of a keel fitted with a trim tab, as a function of the angle of attack α and of the trim tab β.*

Figure V.65 *Section used for* Dame d'Iroise, *$L = 1\,m$ and thickness = 10%.*

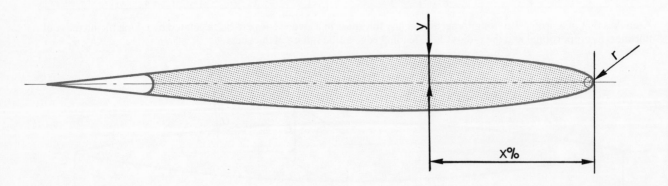

x%	0	1.25	2.5	5	7.5	10	15	20	25	30	40	50	60	70	80	90	100	r
y	0	14.53	19.41	26.68	32.12	36.52	42.53	46.37	48.60	49.86	49.72	46.79	40.43	31.42	20.95	10.41	0	9.22

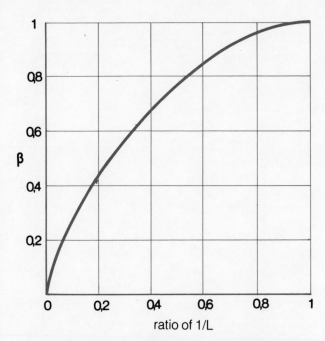

Figure V.66   *Variation of the coefficient* β *with increasing proportion of trim tab breadth.*

VI
Aerodynamic Forces

The aerodynamics that we considered in Chapter II related to a wing, namely to a body that is rigid (up to a certain point), its form defined by the material of which it is made.

Unfortunately the same is not true of our sails, which are made of material that is relatively supple and can change in shape; their cross-section shape can only be that of a cambered plate (so far as the sails in normal use are concerned), which relies on external devices for its support and to maintain its shape.

A Parasitic forces

These external devices, the spars and the rigging, have a definite and generally adverse effect on air-flow over the sail.

1 Influence of the mast

We saw in Chapter II.3f how the Reynolds number affects flow around an elongated cylinder, and the sudden drop in the drag coefficient that occurs at the critical Reynolds number of 300 000 to 500 000.

For a mast, given a chord length of 75 mm, the critical Reynolds number would correspond to a wind blowing at 77.3 m/s, a figure which exceeds the Beaufort scale, or to a force 13 wind, 38.7 m/s, if the length were 150 mm.

It is clear, therefore, that there is generally no chance at all for a normal mast to be in a turbulent regime with a low drag coefficient, and it follows from this that there will always be a zone of major eddies downwind of the mast, the effect of which will spread all over the forward part of the mainsail. This

effect is even more harmful because, as masts do not generally rotate, the turbulent zone extends considerably further on the leeward side, the more effective side, than on the windward side (fig. VI.I).

Croseck's wind tunnel research shows just how harmful this effect can be (fig. VI.2). The masts II and III are already partly rotated, being situated centrally upwind of the sail. In spite of this it is clear that, in case I (without a mast) and II (mast equal to 7.5% of chord), although the loss of lift at 10° angle of incidence is only 4%, the incease in drag is almost 60%. Lift is affected much more when the mast diameter is greater than 10% of the chord, because the loss of lift exceeds 30%.

It can be estimated on average that the drop in performance of a Bermudan sail varies from 10% at its foot to 85% near its head. What can be done to improve this? There are three possible avenues to explore: the reduction of the critical Reynolds number, an improvement in the position of the mast relative to the sail, and the shape and the reduction of the mast section.

On p.43, fig. II.19, we have already seen one of the methods used to stimulate the early occurrence

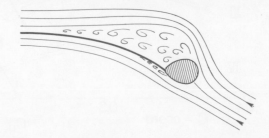

Figure VI.1 *Unfortunately it is on the leeward side, where it is most harmful, that the effect of the mast is greatest.*

of turbulence in the boundary layer, and other methods are used in practice. In the 1974 America's Cup, the American 12-metre *Courageous* had bands of plastic with a zigzag design fitted on her mast. It should be noted, however, that the Australian attempts to stimulate turbulence on *Southern Cross* were judged to be insignificant. This does in fact seem to be a very tricky problem to master, especially out on the water in view of the irregularity of the wind and the motion of the boat.

Rotation of the mast is more effective. In rigs of the simple Finn type, it rotates as the angle of the boom to the centreline changes, but a more sophisticated application is seen in racing catamarans such as the Tornado, or in a few centreboard dinghies like the Tasar. The mast can then be over-rotated to a (controllable) angle which is considerably greater than that of the boom, and thus acts as a lift-producing device at the leading edge of the sail (fig. VI.3). The angle between mast and boom must not exceed 20–30°, however, or flow will separate again at the junction.

The rig invented in the 1930s by B. Ljungström (fig. VI.4) had a sail made in two parts so that it opened out when the boat was running; this rolled round an unstayed rotating mast, and one of the advantages of the rig was that the mast position was then as in IV in fig. VI.2.

Other lift-increasing devices are used (they correspond to the principle of the Handley Page slot at the leading edge of an aircraft wing), for example, the masthead staysail when double-head rig is used, and the tallboy. This raises again the subject of interaction between a number of sails, to which we shall return later.

The shape of the mast section is certainly the factor that has been the subject of most study and thought, but it is also the one about which there is the greatest divergence of opinion. In the first instance, it must never be forgotten that the section must not only meet aerodynamic requirements but those of strength as well, and the two are not always compatible.

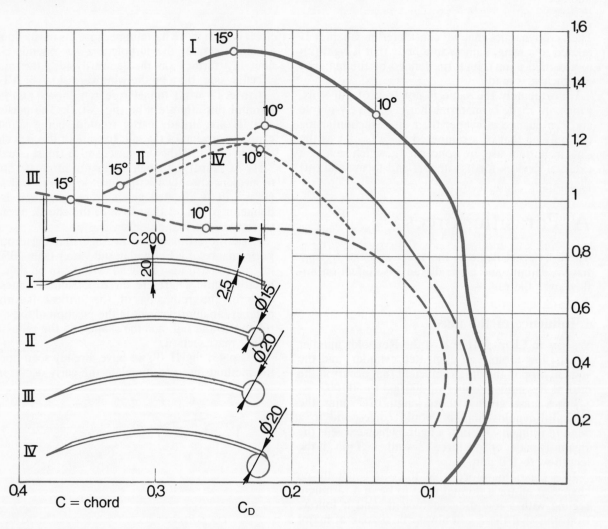

Figure VI.2 *Polar curves of a sail alone compared to sails with various masts, showing the adverse effect the masts* have. *Note the improvement when the mast is to windward of the sail.*

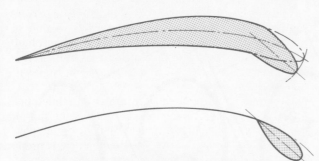

Figure VI.3 *The streamlined rotating mast used on catamarans can be compared to a lift-producing system with a hinged leading edge flap. The angle of separation is delayed.*

Obviously the drag of a streamlined body is less than that of a purely cylindrical body. Thus the coefficient of drag of an elliptical section is nine to ten times lower than that of a circular section with the same frontal area (fig. VI.5) when the Reynolds number is under 50×10^3 and the D/d ratio is between 3 and 4. Even at an angle of incidence of 20° the drag of the elliptical section will not be more than 3/5 of that of the circular section. However, the D/d ratio, which varies with Reynolds number, must not exceed 4; beyond that frictional resistance becomes too great.

It seems that the reduction in C_x is due essentially to the fact that reducing the radius of the leading edge moves the point of separation forward. Consequently pear-shaped sections, which for so long were considered just the thing (have they really disappeared?), have nothing whatever to offer because their leading edge radius is the same as that of a round mast.

Then there are the elliptical sections cut off more or less short at the trailing edge (fig. VI.6). Truncation should be modest because, although up to 30° the drag coefficient is lower than that of the traditional pear-shaped section, it appears that a lift force is developed at the same time, and this is directed to leeward, increasing heeling moment.

Fig. VI.7 gives the polar curves of some typical sailing dinghy spars studied by Robert Froissart at McGill University in Montreal. Section 5 has two wires to stimulate turbulence. The great degree of lift (harmful) generated by the truncated elliptical section is very evident. Froissart also studied the length of the disturbed surfaces to windward and leeward of the sail (table VI.I).

It is unfortunate that a simple ellipse was not included with these sections because this would certainly have been the best compromise. The ellipse has the best ratio of longitudinal and transverse moments of inertia, and is in fact the most suitable shape for masts.

When the longitudinal moment of inertia has to be reduced, for example to make fore-and-aft bending easier, all that is needed is to cut off the trailing edge

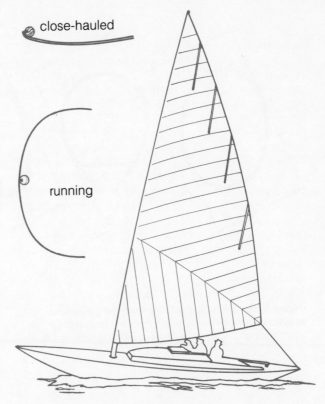

Figure VI.4 *With Ljungström rig, the sail (which is of double thickness so that it can be opened when running downwind) rolls up on the rotating mast.*

of the section to a greater or lesser extent.

Because the mainsail is triangular, it is obvious that the effect of the mast will be progressively more harmful higher up, and every possible opportunity to taper the mast section must therefore be taken. The advantage gained by this is not just aerodynamic, because both the weight and the centre of gravity of the spar are lowered.

The adverse effect of the mast also discourages the use of an excessively high aspect ratio sail, because a

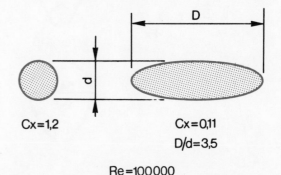

Figure VI.5 *The coefficient of drag of an elliptical rod is considerably lower than that of a cylindrical rod with the same frontal area.*

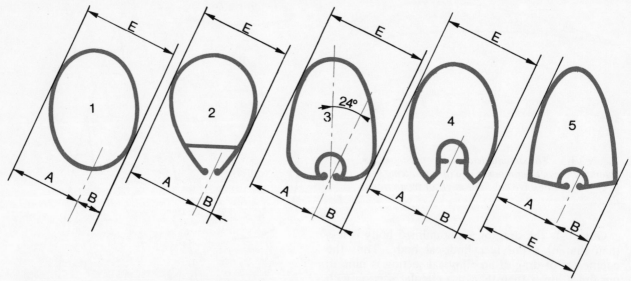

Figure VI.6 *These five mast sections have the same exterior dimensions, and much the same moments of inertia. At an angle of incidence of 24°, it is section 2 that* *has the least total thickness E, but its thickness A is the greatest when the wind is aft; unfortunately the shape of the trailing edge makes it very vulnerable to lateral flexing.*

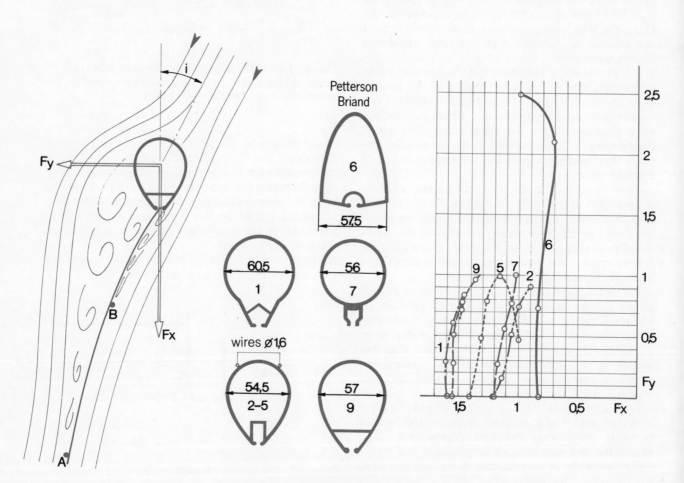

Figure VI.7 *Polar curves for centreboard dinghies' masts. It is clear that profile 6 (elliptical ratio 1/2.75, cut off) has least drag, but it develops great lift.*

TABLE VI.I

	ERMAT	PETTERSON BRIAND	Z SPAR	ELVSTRÖM
i = 20° A	7.0	4.8	7	7.3
B	2.1	5.8	2.5	1.9
i = 24° A	7.3	7	7.2	7.5
B	1.8	6.5	1.8	1.2
i = 28° A	7.9	7.3	7.5	8.2
B	1.1	6.4	1.5	0.3
i = 32° A	8.3	7.8	8	8.5
B	0	6.6	0.9	0

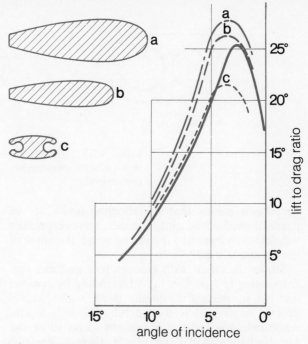

Figure VI.9 *Lift-to-drag ratio of three sails fed into streamlined headfoils compared to a jib hanked to a stay. The three curves show that the separation angle is delayed and the peak of the curves flattened. The profile with the thickness-to-length ratio of 1/3:3 is better than the two others with ratios of 1/4 and 1/2.*

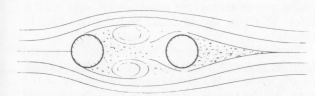

Figure VI.8 *The drag when two wires are fitted in tandem is less than that of one wire alone on account of the re-attachment of the airstream, and this holds good up to the point where the distance between the wires is equal to twice their diameter.*

greater proportion of the sail area will be disturbed, and because the mast wall thickness would have to be increased to maintain the same coefficient of strength. The mast section always needs a great deal of thought and very careful calculation, with a view to keeping its wall thickness as small as possible and its strength adequate but not unnecessarily great.

It is interesting to note in passing the effect that a gap between the mast and the sail can have, as occurs when the sail is held to the mast with slides. The change in the lift coefficient from 0.05 to 0.2 when the angle of incidence is between 0° and 15° is about 10%, and that is considerable.

The aerodynamic study of masts can be combined with that of the grooved headfoils that have appeared in recent years, not only on board racing craft but also in cruising boats because they make headsail changing so much easier. Before looking at their sections it should be noted that the presence of the wire to which the jib is hanked is not harmful; on the contrary it improves flow over the jib. Two wires placed in tandem cause less drag than a single wire of the same diameter, even when the wire further downwind is of smaller diameter, and if the distance between the wires is equal to twice the diameter (fig. VI.8). This corresponds reasonably well with the usual pairing of forestay and luff.

The streamlines that separate from the first wire can be seen to re-attach themselves at the second,

and this not only benefits the sail but makes for a reduction in the volume of the wake, and consequently in drag which decreases by 25%. Even when taking the presence of sail hanks into account, the traditional method would be better, in particular to the hollow stays of the Seastay type, the considerable diameter of which is certainly a disadvantage. It is far from certain that headfoils, which always have a much greater frontal surface than a rod stay, will bring such great improvements in lift as is claimed by many advertisers.

It is as well to note at this point that the drag of a cylindrical rod is 20% lower than that of laid wire rope of virtually equal diameter.[1] In other words, resistance will be equal when the diameter of the rod is 20% larger than that of the wire rope.

Research at Southampton University sheds light on the real value of headfoils. The polar curves of three of the nine models tested are compared in fig. VI.9 with that of a sail hanked to a stay. The tests were made at a Reynolds number near 10^6, with a 1.20 m long sail attached to the headstays. This is a bit short, but the effects were demonstrated. Because the section was always the extension of the sail, it is not the drag resulting from the combination of sail and stay that is most interesting, but the ratio of lift to drag. It is immediately clear that the gain is small, and the main benefits are that the separation angle is delayed, and the peak that corresponds to the maximum L/D ratio is flattened. This characteristic could be expected on account of the thickening of the leading edge, and it is of particular interest

141

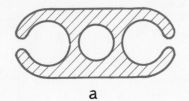

a   b   c

Figure VI.10   *Of these three twin-grooved headfoils, it is c that is likely to perform best — and to function more conveniently.*

because it means that the sheeting angle of the headsail need not be quite so exact; this is especially helpful when trimming the sail to match the angle of the apparent wind.

Stubby headfoils with grooves fore and aft, corresponding to type C in fig. VI.9, should be avoided and so in particular should those with parallel groove, as in fig. VI.10a and 10b. The only worthwhile twin-grooved foil at present seems to be the Headfoil II, sold in France by B. Chéret. The two grooves are in tandem, one behind the other and aft of the stay, and they open out into the same slot (fig. VI.10c).

Headfoils do nevertheless have a certain number of advantages, such as making it easier to regulate tension and to change sails (provided that the system of feeding the luff into the groove is well designed and that the bolt rope fits perfectly.

2 Windage

Apart from the mast, the influence of which is doubly adverse, everything on board that is not a sail acts as a powerful aerodynamic brake, the effect of which is generally underestimated.

The Dragon in fig. VI.11 has a particularly low freeboard and her reasonably well-streamlined superstructure cannot be reduced further, but when sailing close-hauled at an angle of incidence of 25° in a 7 m/s wind of force 4, the longitudinal component of aerodynamic resistance of her hull alone is approximately 1 kg, and the lateral component four times greater. These figures could increase as much as fourfold if the effect of the rigging were included (5.5 kg and 8 kg for F_y). These figures may seem small at first, but it is clear how large they really are when they are compared to the total force developed by the sails which, in the same conditions, amounts to 25 kg for F_x and 105 kg for F_y.

Air drag would then cause over one-fifth of driving force to be lost, if it were not for the fact that, as we shall see later, the presence of the hull has a beneficial effect on the amount of drive produced by the sails.

Nevertheless, even when this is taken into account, windage alone absorbs about one-sixth of driving force when close-hauled — and remember that this is a boat with a particularly small amount of windage. It is easy to imagine how much greater the proporiton will be in the case of a cruising boat with high freeboard, a dinghy on the coachroof, netting and dodgers in the lifelines, etc. All too quickly the figure amounts to one-third of driving force. A choice has to be made and will depend on your own philosophy of sailing, but when you lay your bet it is safety that you should back, and that is allied to speed.

There must then be no compromise; freeboard must be reduced to the minimum, coachroof eliminated, anything that could cause turbulence at the mast, in the rigging or on deck must be removed ruthlessly.

Then there is the crew; the windage of a human being sitting on the gunwale is about 5 times greater than when lying down (fig. VI.12). A member of the crew standing on the deck of a close-hauled sailing boat carrying 30 m² of sail has been estimated to cause her to point 1.5° less high.

The spreaders should be both streamlined (the length/breadth ratio of the section being about 3:5) and set at a negative angle of incidence of 10–15° (fig. VI.13) so as to allow not only for the direction of the streamlines as a function of incidence in the horizontal plane, but also for the rake of the mast and for heeling.

Spreader fittings should be integral with the mast, as should shroud terminals, track for the spinnaker pole, chain plates and fittings of every sort. Sheaves for internal halyards and other parts of the running rigging which are led inside the mast will be at the foot, and the mast should be bare of fittings, cleats and winches. The number and diameter of the pulpit's legs and the number of the stanchions should be reduced to the minimum: no toerails, no netting, no buoys in the pulpits.

The same attention should be paid to the boom, and in particular to the running rigging fittings. The sheet and downhaul blocks should either be recessed in the boom or dropped to deck level by using pendants. Instead of a prominent superstructure the deck may be given considerable camber or have a very low coachroof carried right to the stem, with no ventilators or cowls protruding. The area of the cockpit should be reduced as much as possible, and should preferably open aft at the transom so that the cut-off stern allows for ventilation; alternatively, the

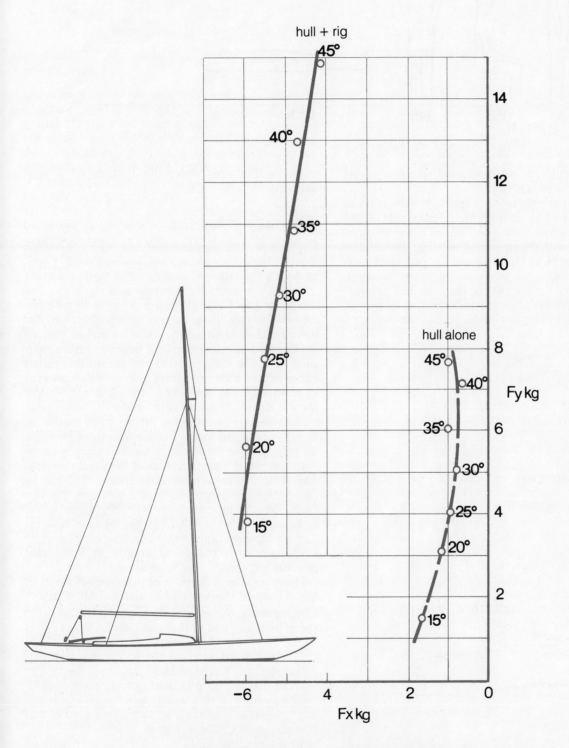

hull + rig

hull alone

Fy kg

Fx kg

Figure VI.11 *Longitudinal and transverse forces developed by the hull alone, and by the hull plus the rig of a Dragon, in a wind of 7 m/s (force 4).*

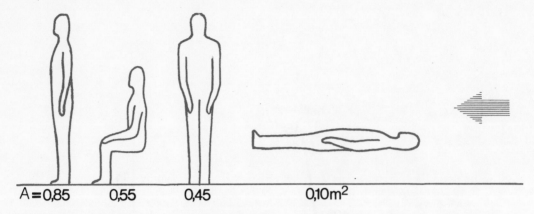

A = 0,85   0,55   0,45   0,10m²

Figure VI.12 *The windage of a human body in different positions.*

transom should be raked forward steeply, joining the deck in a broad curve.

Windage not only reduces speed, however; it can also have a bad effect from the safety aspect. If the area of sail when it has been reefed is too small by comparison with the amount of windage, the result is that the boat lacks manoeuvrability, precluding any hope of working to windward in heavy weather. Furthermore, the position of the centre of pressure will determine the angle at which the boat heaves to, and from that point of view large areas at the extre-

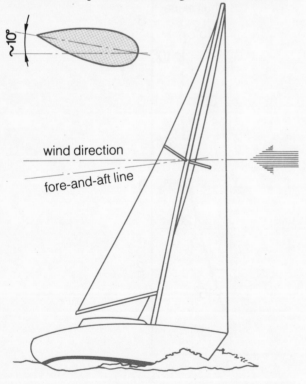

wind direction

fore-and-aft line

Figure VI.13 *The streamlined crosstrees should be raked at a negative angle of incidence of about 10° so as to point directly into the eye of the wind when the boat is close-hauled and heeling.*

mities will always affect the balance of a boat dangerously.

3 Porosity of sailcloth

Up to now, the material that has been considered most suitable for making sails is woven cloth. Cloth alone has the required qualities, the most important of which are flexibility, strength and elasticity. The disadvantage of cloth is that it is made up of criss-crossed threads that are not completely airtight, however closely woven they may be and in spite of coating and calendering. It is understandable that, since it is the difference in the pressures exerted either side of a lift-producing aerofoil which governs its efficiency, any porosity of the cloth will lead to the pressure difference being reduced, and consequently to a decrease in the driving force produced. Every pore in sailcloth is like a nozzle through which air escapes, and the speed at which it escapes varies with the actual characteristics of the sailcloth itself. This is defined by a coefficient of porosity C, and by the difference in pressure, δP, between the two faces. For V in m/s, $V = 4C\sqrt{\delta P}$, given δP in kg/sq m, or $V = 39.4C\sqrt{\delta P}$, when δP is in N/sq m. The coefficient C varies with the Reynolds number. In practice it is the speed of flow at a constant pressure difference that is measured.

However, the difference of pressure δP varies as the square of the velocity of the air, $\delta P \simeq KVa^2$. Consequently the effects of porosity rise as wind speed increases and as the boat luffs up to sail closer to the wind, on which course δP is highest.

Tests carried out at Southampton University established the loss of efficiency due to porosity, and showed that the drop in driving force coefficient C_x can be as much as 10% when close-hauled in a 10 m/s wind, whereas it will stay at 1–2% in a wind of half that strength. C_y drops half as much.

It was also possible to determine a maximum porosity level corresponding to airflow velocity of 0.006 m/s where $\delta P = 24.4$ kg/m².

B Real useful forces

When all these negative elements are taken into account, it is clear that the actual force which a sail can develop at various angles of incidence will not produce as favourable a polar curve as the theoretical rigid profiles studied earlier.

1 The sail alone

It is therefore interesting to compare fig. VI.14 which shows the behaviour of a real sail, a jib as it happens, with fig. VI.29 relating to a thick foil.

In the first phase (a), at angles of incidence below about 5° (depending on the camber of the sail) there is not enough tension in the cloth to maintain the shape of the sail near the luff, and this will flutter or lift. This can often be seen when jibs, and especially spinnakers, lift and shake because the sheet needs hardening or the boat has been luffed up too far.

As soon as the luff is at a large enough angle of attack for a difference in pressure to arise, airflow over the sail becomes normal and similar to that over a thick foil, with a boundary layer that is laminar at the luff and then, after a short transition, turbulent towards the leech (b). Soon after that, at an angle of attack of about 11°, separation occurs near the leech which starts to vibrate (c); beyond the angle of 28°, separation affects almost all of the sail.

The range where the angle of incidence is optimum is actually extremely small, and it is this that makes sail trimming difficult, particularly when it is remembered how the apparent wind fluctuates continuously. Consequently, as with any form of lift-producing foil, it is of interest to delay separation by some means. The latest idea is similar to the vortex generators mentioned in Chapter II. 4h, p.54, but instead of small vanes there is a series of holes arranged similarly, and it is the air coming from the windward face that provokes the formation of vortices. There are no protruberances to create drag and its value is therefore unchanged, whereas the maximum value of lift does increase.

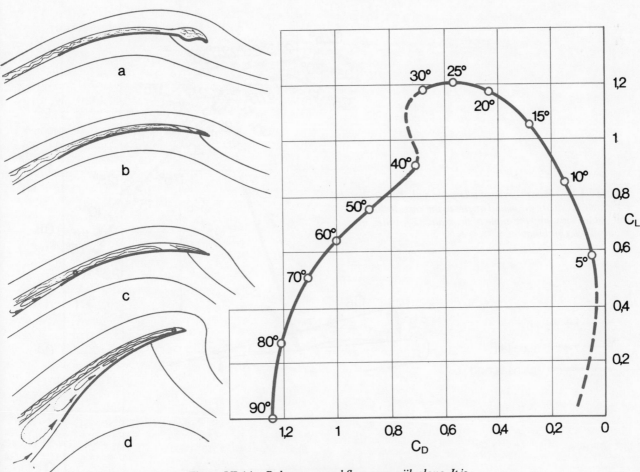

Figure VI.14 *Polar curve and flow over a jib alone. It is assumed that the sail is boomed out at an angle of incidence of over 25°.*

2 Sail interaction

In the same way as with a rigid profile, the presence of another sail, acting like a slap upstream of the mainsail, will move the point of separation downstream. The polar curves in fig. VI.15 are based on measurements obtained from tests made at the University of Southampton, and they verify some points in connection with a traditional sail plan, a three-quarter rigged sloop with jib and mainsail, in this case a Dragon. These polar curves do not indicate the optimum performance obtainable, but provide some very interesting information.

Firstly, it is noticeable how much more regular the curve of the jib alone is than that of the mainsail alone, and this is because there is no mast at the luff. Secondly, it is evident that, although the jib is superior to the mainsail at small angles of incidence (between 10° and 12.5°), it then becomes inferior; this is because it has no boom, and its camber can become excessive.

The curves also show that, up to about 25°, the performance of the two sails combined is inferior to that of each of them taken separately, and this confirms that, given equal total area, a single sail is more effective than two or more because the gap that has to be left between them means that the sail nearer the bow has to work at a lower angle of incidence. We will see later on that the direction of the force developed by the forward sail is nevertheless favourable, so far as driving force is concerned.

At angles of over 25°, on the other hand, the presence of a jib causes an increase in the maximum value of the force developed because the separation of flow from the mainsail is delayed.

The distinction must be made between considering these results from a purely aerodynamic viewpoint relating to all the constituent parts of the sail plan, and the transformation of these results into lateral and propulsive forces. This is why it is interesting, and probably more meaningful, to look at the same combination of sails from the point of view of the propulsive force and heeling force developed per unit of area (fig. VI.16) in, for example, a wind of 7.6 m/s.

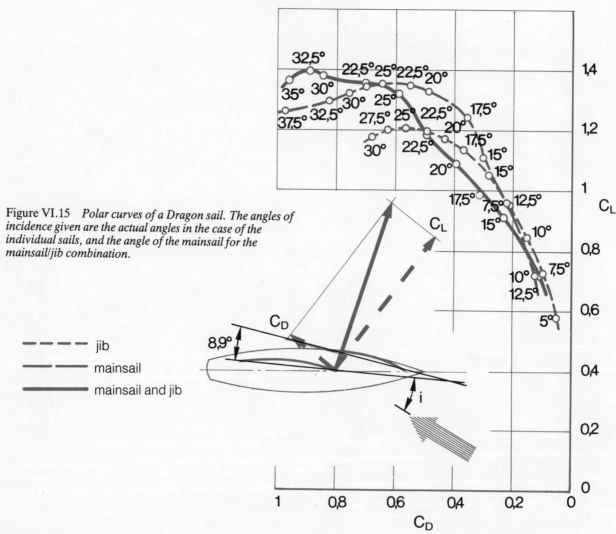

Figure VI.15 *Polar curves of a Dragon sail. The angles of incidence given are the actual angles in the case of the individual sails, and the angle of the mainsail for the mainsail/jib combination.*

- - - - jib
— - — mainsail
——— mainsail and jib

146

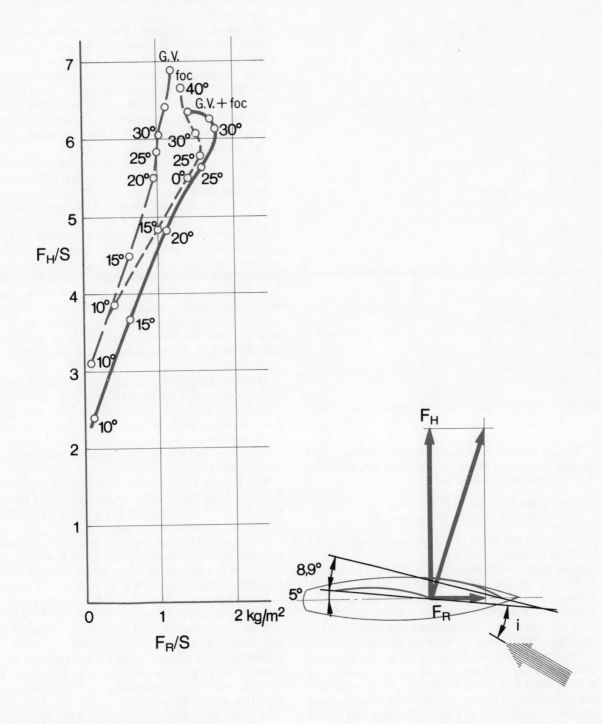

Figure VI.16 *Driving force and heeling force, per unit of area, developed by a Dragon sail in a 7.6 m/s wind. The angles of incidence given are the actual angles in the case of* the individual sails taken separately, and the angle of incidence of the mainsail for the mainsail/jib combination.

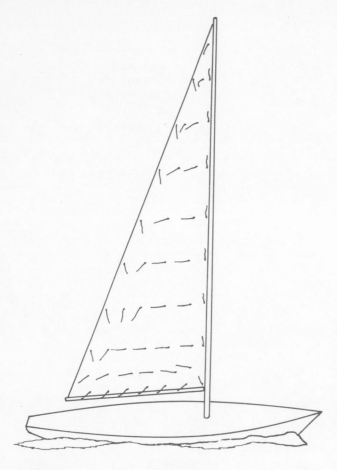

Figure VI.17 *Flow made visible to leeward of a mainsail.*

We will remind ourselves that the propulsive and heeling forces can be calculated from lift and drag with the following formulae:

$$V_x = L \sin (\beta - \lambda) - D \cos (\beta - \lambda)$$
$$V_y = L \cos (\beta - \lambda) + D \sin (\beta - \lambda),$$

$\beta - \lambda$ being the angle of the apparent wind to the boat's centreline.

Here again it is clear to what extent the unit force developed by the jib is superior to that of the mainsail (up to 60%), but we also see that the combined force of the two sails is always greater than the unit forces. We will consider later how the reciprocal adjustment of the sails affects this.

The reasons for the foregoing facts can be better understood by looking closely at the pattern of airflow when it is made visible on sails through the use of woolly streamers or smoke. Full-scale tests carried out in Britain by Lt-Col. Bowden and model tests at the University of Poitiers by the sailmaker B. Chéret provide the information we need. Although there are certain differences in detail when the two are compared, probably due to differences between full-scale and model testing, some interesting information can be extracted from these experiments.

In both, the following phenomena occur when the mainsail is set alone (fig. VI.17):

along the luff, the disturbance caused by the mast converts flow into an ascending vertical current;

over the forward half of the sail, flow is regular on the leeward side of the sail, downwind of the zone disturbed by the mast, whereas on the windward side turbulence is considerable and indicates a much more extensive zone of dead air;

over the after half, airflow becomes regular on the windward side, whereas it tends to reverse over the lower part of the lee side because this part of the sail is at too great an angle of incidence, and this causes circulation from the windward side to the leeward side;

finally, along the foot, the flow of air around the boom to the windward side is a clear indication of induced drag.

If a jib is now set ahead of the mainsail (fig. VI.18), little change can be seen on the windward side of the mainsail, but airflow becomes regular over the whole of that part of the leeward side that is affected by the jib. Above the head of the jib the pattern of flow over the mainsail is unchanged, with flow from the windward side towards the lee side, and eddies forming marginally. Air flows from the lee side to the windward side at the foot of the jib, as well as along the boom as before. Over the rest of the jib, airflow is remarkably stable and regular on both sides.

One conclusion that comes immediately to mind in connection with the mainsail of a fractional-rigged boat is that the upper part near the head should be cut completely differently from the rest, with great twist so that it can adopt the required angle of incidence — and it is far from easy for a sailmaker to do this successfully!

The tests in Poitiers also verified how it is that a build-up of air occurs at the windward end of the slot between the sails, and that there is a major deflection of air upwind of the sails.

The combination of mainsail and jib is of course the most common, but for some years now the trend has been to increase the number of sails set in the foretriangle, and these could be a genoa or a jib with a spinnaker, or variations of the cutter rig now termed double-head rig (figs. VI.19 and VI.20).

It seems, however, that the results obtained are not always as striking as might be expected. To understand exactly what occurs when an extra sail is introduced in the space between jib and mainsail, we have to revert to the method used in Chapter II.4g (figs.II.I, 46 and 48) p.52.

In order to be able to set a staysail (fig. VI.21) the mainsail is hardened 2.5° and the jib eased 5°. It is obvious that if the staysail is trimmed to match the shape of the streamlines exactly, as in a, it will not modify airflow or develop any lift at all, but will have some braking effect on account of friction. On the other hand, if it is trimmed to a different shape, b, we will see what happens. There is virtually no change outside the system, but the streamlines between the staysail and the jib are closer, indicating acceleration of airflow and, consequently, a reduction in pressure on the windward side of the jib. This reduces the difference in pressure between the two sides, and also reduces the force developed.

The opposite occurs between staysail and mainsail; the streamlines are spaced more widely, and speed of flow is therefore reduced, while pressure on the leeward side drops. The difference in pressure between the two sides is again reduced, and so is the force developed.

So far the balance is negative, but there are other compensating factors. For one thing, the sheeting angle of the jib is 5° greater and consequently the force it develops is directed further ahead; this is due entirely to the presence of the staysail because, without it, the jib would have been unable to fill at this angle of incidence without lifting. Likewise, it would not have been possible to change the angle of incidence of the mainsail without separation occurring had the pressure gradient not been lowered as a result of setting the staysail. Finally, there is the force that the staysail itself develops, and this is not negligible.

It does seem, however, that to set a staysail exactly as described calls for very precise trimming, and this is why only very experienced crews are able to reap the benefit from doing so.

The best arrangement for the staysail seems to be roughly as illustrated in fig. VI.19 with the tack about 40% of J (J is the foretriangle base) abaft the stem, the mast halyard sheave at about 10% of I (I is the height of the foretriangle below the topmast stay), and the clew LPIS 110% or 115% of J abaft the forestay.

The effect would be very different if, as is roughly the case with a cutter, jib and staysail were of virtually the same size with their leeches staggered similarly in relation to the mainsail. The mainsail would then react on the staysail and the staysail on the jib in the same way as when there are only two sails; the sail to windward would firstly accelerate flow over the leeward side of the sail that is to leeward of it, and secondly it would cause the apparent wind of the other sail to free. Here again the trimming of the sails furthest upwind and downwind is extremely tricky because the jib will be on the verge of lifting, while separation will occur very

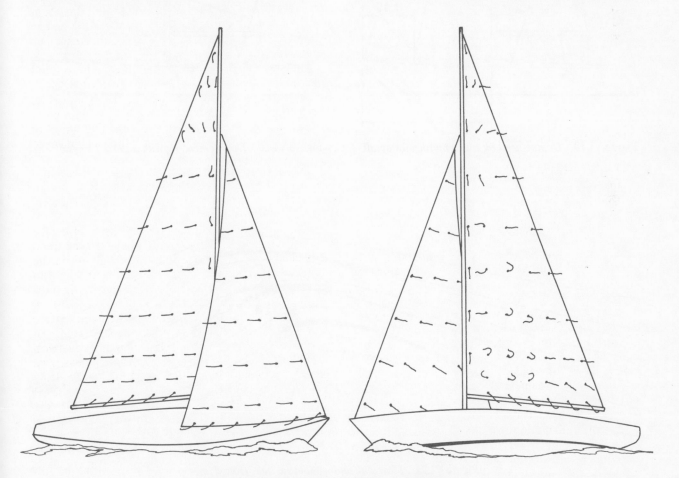

Figure VI.18   *Flow made visible to leeward and to windward of the sails of a three-quarter rigged sloop.*

149

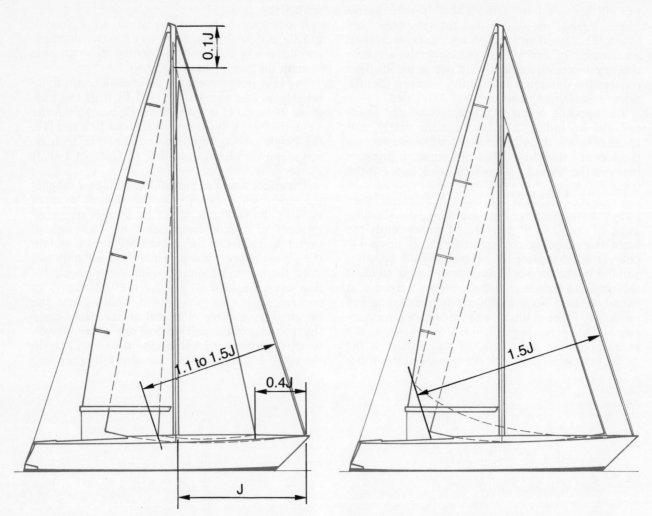

Figure VI.19   *Double-head rig with a masthead staysail.*

Figure VI.20   *Double-head rig with a 150% J staysail.*

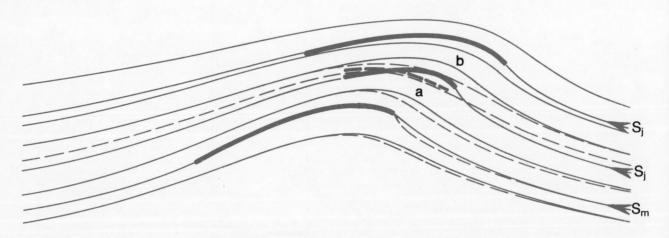

Figure VI.21   *Flow with and without staysail. Dotted lines
indicate flow without staysail: (a) staysail set in line with
flow; (b) efficient staysail.*

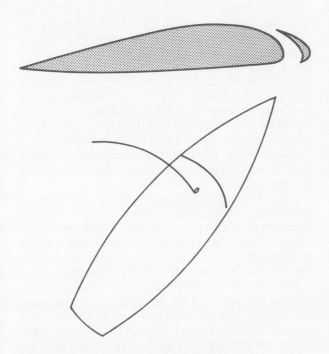

readily on the mainsail; because the unitary output of each sail will always be reduced, the gain can never equal the increase in sail area.

The moment that the boat bears away, the projected area between the sails along the line of their luffs increases, and this makes sail trimming easier. Unfortunately the same does not apply at the level of the leech because, whereas the mainsail leech moves away from the boat's centreline as the boom swings outboard, the clew of the headsail cannot be eased out beyond a certain point due to the position of the sheet lead. The answer is to lead the headsail sheet to the end of the main boom (which necessitates setting a sail with a higher clew, the yankee), and to shift the tack of a staysail further to windward.

In any case, a little squeezing of the slot between the sails at the level of the mainsail will help to prevent too early a separation of the streamlines from the mainsail.

The further the boom swings outboard, the further will the mast cause disturbance to spread over the lee side of the sail, the reason being that the mast section is generally longer than it is broad. A tallboy, tacked down to windward at least 40% of the foretriangle base forward of the mast, helps the streamlines to re-attach quickly (fig. VI.22). When this sail is used in such conditions, its purpose is similar to the Handley Page leading edge slot, designed to create lift on aircraft wings.

The large angle of incidence and great fullness of the spinnaker mean that it is impossible to obtain suitable airflow between the sails, and the occurrence of separation is unavoidable (fig. VI.23). The

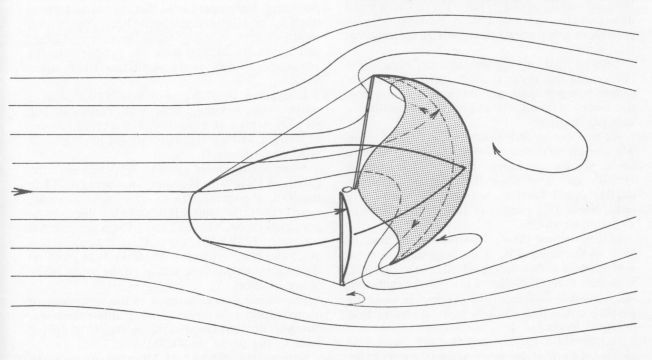

Figure VI.23 *Flow between mainsail and spinnaker.*

aim is to try to delay separation for as long as possible, and here again the presence of a masthead staysail and/or a tallboy will be the most beneficial.

3 Shape and camber

There are major difficulties when testing full-size sails, the three main problems being the gauging of the balances and instruments used to measure the forces, the irregularity of the wind both in strength and direction, and the fact that the shape of the sail and the strength of the wind both have to be measured simultaneously.

With photogrammetry now providing a marvellous way of storing and analysing shapes, B. Chéret has been able to undertake some interesting experiments, as has North in the United States. However, the capital investment involved in buying the instruments and materials, plus the running costs of such a laboratory, still largely limit possibilities in this field.

In model testing, measurement runs into various technical problems connected with the law of similitude.

If flow is to remain similar, the Reynolds number must stay the same and, since it is a function of speed and length, the former varies inversely with the latter; for example, when the scale is reduced to 1/4, speed has to be multiplied by 4. But forces on sailcloth and the rig increase as the square of speed, and the scale of these has to be considerably increased to provide comparable resistance and (for cloth above all) distortion.

All this means that it has been possible to publish only the very few tests and measurements that have been sufficiently precise to judge the relatively small differences that result from varying camber. It is not possible to give precise values, only an indication of tendency.

Tests on rigid sails are unsatisfactory because the phenomena that occur at small angles of incidence cannot be reproduced, nor can those resulting from the distortion of sailcloth and of the combination of sails plus rigging.

All that can be deduced from these tests is that, whereas lift increases with fullness, particularly so far as jibs are concerned, the C_x/C_y ratio will be virtually the same when the mainsails of three-quarter rigged boats such as the 12-metres have either about 12% camber at 49% of the chord, or 10% camber at 43%.[6]

In fact, because the main purpose of the headsail vis-a-vis the mainsail is, as we have seen, to avoid separation of airflow on the lee side of the mainsail, it appears that this condition can only be fulfilled if the maximum camber of the mainsail is as nearly parallel to the jib's leech as possible, rather than abaft the leech.

Nor should it be forgotten that the greater the camber of a profile, the more marked the peak of the polar curve and, consequently, the more crucial does

sail trimming become.

The camber of a spinnaker will of course vary very much according to whether it is to be used when reaching or when running. For a reaching spinnaker the angle of incidence should not exceed 25–30°, the angle at which flow separates totally and causes a sharp drop in the lift coefficient. Camber should therefore not exceed 20%, and this is only possible with very specialized sails that can be used over a very narrow range of angles of incidence. As soon as the angle of incidence is such that complete separation occurs, the object is that the sail should develop maximum drag. The basic shape best suited to this is undoubtedly a semicircle or its derivatives, half ellipses.

One of the factors that complicates the study of sails, apart from porosity which we have already considered, is surface roughness, which can affect the structure of the boundary layer, but present-day cloth is generally well calandered, and has a surface that is smooth enough to avoid problems.

The greatest difficulties are caused by the irregularity of the surface of the sail itself, due to the seams and to the lack of uniformity of thread tensions caused by the seams. Recent photogrammetric measurements made by B. Chéret on 470 sails are very revealing on this point.

4 Aspect ratio

We know that increasing the aspect ratio of a plane surface is one way of increasing the C_L/C_D ratio, although the angle of separation is reduced. Racing ratings generally take the advantage into account by penalizing high aspect ratio rigs, but in fact this is often quite arbitrary and unrealistic: high aspect ratio penalizes itself by raising the centre of effort and increasing heeling moment. Furthermore the advantage is only really significant when close-hauled.

It is quite clear that only one aspect ratio is suitable for a sailing boat with particular hull measurements and, especially, with a certain degree of stability and an optimum ratio of heeling/windward performance.

When the three sail plans in fig. VI.24 are compared, all three with the same total area (RSAT in the IOR, the actual area therefore decreases with aspect ratio), the same LP/JC ratio but three different aspect ratios, 3.16, 2.52 and 1.95 (in this case AR is equal to IC^2/RSAT), the C_x/C_y ratio as a function of C_x and heeling moment M_y depends as much on the sheeting angle of the sails as on the height of the centre of effort.

The author's conclusions as to the superiority of higher aspect ratio seem to be a little premature, however, not in relation to the coefficient of driving force C_x but to the ratio C_x/M_y.

Separate research by J. H. Milgram compares the sail plans of a seven-eighths rigged boat and two

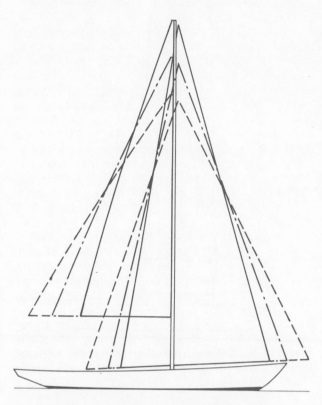

Figure VI.24 *Sails of a masthead-rigged sloop with varying aspect ratios of 3.16, 2.52 and 1.95.*

masthead-rigged boats with different aspect ratio sails of the same area, fitted to a hull of known performance. The actual sail area of the seven-eighths rigged boat is 123 m², and that of the two others is 111 m², while the aspect ratios are respectively 2.75, 3.28 and 3.6. (In this case, height is taken from the base of the jib and the head of the mainsail, and the area is that of the triangles.) The net total gain in speed is a mere 1% in the case of the first two and 1.3% for the last two.

Although these results are rather fragmentary, it can be deduced from them that great caution is required when increasing aspect ratio because other negative effects always result from doing so; the mast has to be longer, and the corollary to that is an increased section, more complicated rigging is required, and there is greater difficulty in setting the sails and in maintaining their correct shape at all heights.

Multiplication of movements of the sail is linked to aspect ratio too, in other words, given that the sheet is eased a certain distance, the higher the aspect ratio the further will the leech move, and the consequence is that it is much more difficult to control the leech.

Then again, the smaller the angle at the head of the sail the more are the forces concentrated over a smaller area, and that means that extensive rein-

forcement is needed, and the sailmaker has much greater difficulty in keeping the correct camber at the top of the sail, in particular because of the large reduction in the fore-and-aft forces that govern this curvature. It therefore seems reasonable not to exceed an aspect ratio of 4 for the genoa, and 6 for the mainsail.

In fact, the gain that results from increasing aspect ratio above 4 is extremely small, as can be seen in the graph, fig. VI.25, because it should not be forgotten that the effective aerodynamic aspect ratio is, in this case, double the geometric aspect ratio. Aspect ratio can be higher for a mainsail because about 15–20% of the area is practically useless on account of the mast.

It is known, however, that the improvement in performance with increasing aspect ratio is linked to induced drag on account of the flow of air from the lee side to the windward side, and we have seen that an artifical increase in aspect ratio can be obtained by preventing this with end plates.

It is indeed hard to provide an end plate at the head of a sail, and tests with 12-metre class mainsails do not seem to indicate significant improvement, probably because of the drag caused by heeling. It is quite different at the foot where the deck acts as a splendid end plate.

The polar curves of fig. VI.26 relate to the Dragon rig of the University of Southampton Report No. 14 and show the difference between the values for the sail alone and for the sail with the boat. It is interesting to note that, because the centre of effort is lowered, heeling moment is not increased as much as would be expected from the increase in lateral force F_x. The increase in heeling moment is actually under 5%.

The adavantage definitely increases as the space between sail and deck is further reduced, and this is why close-hauled genoas have come into contact with decks, and why booms on 12-metres have

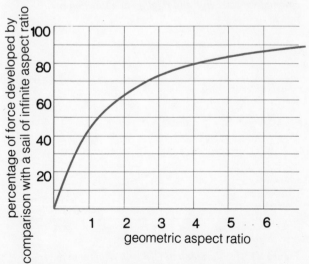

Figure VI.25 *Performance of a sail of a certain aspect ratio as a percentage of that of a sail of infinite aspect ratio.*

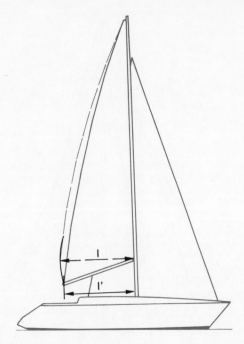

Figure VI.28 *Sail area is lost when the aft end of the boom is lowered because l' is shorter than l.*

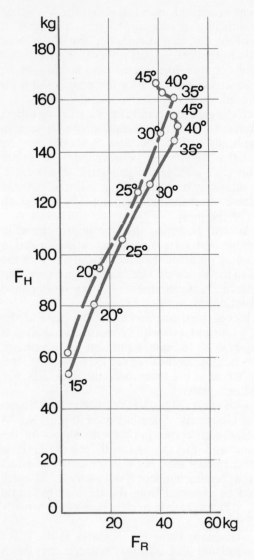

Figure VI.26 *Transverse and longitudinal forces developed on a Dragon rig, for the sails alone, and for the ensemble of sails, hull and rigging, as a function of β − λ.*

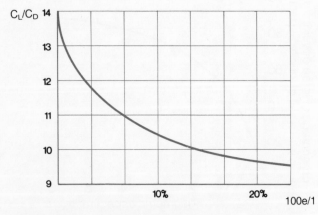

Figure VI.27 *Variation of C_L/C_D in relation to the space between the boom and the deck. Space e is given as a percentage of the length of the boom, l.*

dropped to the point where the crews only have headroom enough to look out over the cockpits.

Two attempts have been made to evaluate the advantage gained. The results of the first on a mainsail alone seem extremely doubtful; no account was taken of the extra area, and this makes corrections necessary, of which the results are that there is almost no difference in the C_L/C_D ratio when the gap between boom and deck increases from 0% to 10% of the boom's length.

The second tests were unfortunately made with a wing mast (which explains the very high values of C_L/C_D), but they do consider the jib and mainsail combination together, and cover gaps varying from 0–23.3% (fig. VI.27).

When racing in classes such as 5.5- and 6- or 12-metres, where the measurement of the maximum height of the sails is fixed, and where sail area distribution favours the mainsail, it is easy (even though inconvenient for the crew) to lower the boom as far as possible.

It is a different matter in offshore racing boats, not only because of the very great inconvenience caused when manoeuvring and sail handling, but because lowering the boom without increasing sail area will lead to much too high an aspect ratio. Sometimes an attempt is made to resolve this difficulty by lowering the clew (fig. VI.28) but, apart from the fact that this arrangement means a loss of sail area because the perpendicular from the lowered clew to the mast will always be shorter than the length of the foot measured along the boom, it is not absolutely certain that induced drag will be improved at all; on the

Figure VI.29   *Sails of a 30 m² Skerry.*

Figure VI.30   *505 sails close-hauled in a fresh breeze.*

other hand, flow over the lower part of the sail will be affected by the boom, and this area will increase as the boat heels further.

5 The shape of the sail

The basic shape of all Bermudian sails is triangular, and this is not at all a bad shape because it is relatively close to a planform with an elliptic load coefficient. If the straight lines that constitute the luff and the leech are distorted by bending the mast and by giving round to the leech, the sail becomes even nearer to the ideal shape.

Ratings, and sailmaking problems, mean that it is almost impossible to pursue the idea of bending the mast permanently, as was the case with the famous Scandinavian Skerry boats (fig. VI.29). It is, however, possible to bend the mast while sailing, an opportunity that is not wasted, in racing dinghies especially, and this may be achieved by varying the tension of the rigging, or by direct pressure of the boom on the mast, as is the case with the Finn.

Together with a considerable degree of rake, this is one advantage of flexible rigs that has perhaps not always been appreciated fully, because of preoccupation with sail camber (fig. VI.30).

The leech roach needs round, and a radius of curvature which decreases progressively towards the head (fig. VI.31), but such a shape can only be obtained when the roach is supported from head to foot, or the upper half at least, by full-length battens. Tension on the leech actually tends to make the large area of cloth forming the roach shift towards the centre of the sail, and this tendency has to be

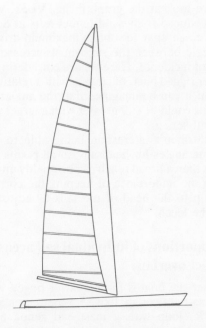

Figure VI.31   *Undoubtedly when designed the most advanced of the fully battened mainsails — that of* Lady Helmsman, *a C class catamaran.*

countered with battens under compression that work elastically, rather than simply by bending as normal battens do.

Due to the compression, these battens yield and take up a specific curvature that is regulated by their varying cross-section, the amount of bend either being determined by adjusting the tension of the cloth over the battens, or by forcing them to bend more by tightening the leech line that passes through the extremities of all of them; the latter enables camber to be modified when under way.

The use of battens, the curvature of which can be regulated, means of course that the shape of the sail can be adapted to a much greater extent. In addition, the rigidity they impart to the after part of the mainsail enables the boat to sail at lower angles of incidence which normally would cause the sail to lift and shake.

On the other hand, the weight of all the battens together can exceed that of the sail itself, and this is why fully battened sails are only really of interest for sailing boats that sail at very low angles of incidence with no urgent need for stability due to weight, for example racing catamarans and ice and sand yachts. In all other cases, battens under compression can only be an inconvenience on account of their weight, fragility and awkwardness.

6 Relative position of the sails

The art of sail trimming is to maintain the correct angle of incidence to the apparent wind of each sail separately, and thereby maintain their reciprocal sheeting angles.

If we look at the graph in fig. VI.32, which has been deduced from wind tunnel tests at Southampton, we see that to obtain maximum driving force the angle between the sails must increase with the angle of incidence. Here we are considering a three-quarter rigged boat, of course, with a relatively small jib, but it can be imagined that the angles between the sails could be still greater with a larger masthead headsail set.

Yachtsmen's interest in being able to use wide sheeting angles for headsails on all points of sailing higher than a broad reach can be readily understood, as can the importance of keeping the correct angle right up to the head of the sails by adjusting twist with the leech.

7 Proportions of individual sail areas, and effect overlap

Whether the boat is three-quarter rigged with a jib that does not overlap, like a 5.5-metre or a Soling, or an IOR sloop with a masthead genoa and large overlap, it appears that, quite apart from any effect a rating may have, the decision as to how to split up the sail area between the different sails is largely a matter of whim.

Initially, knowing that the headsail is aerodynamically superior to the main in the headsail/mainsail combination, one could be tempted into thinking masthead rig preferable, but this would be to forget that the headsail is superior only when the boat is close-hauled, and that when she has borne away and the angle of incidence is greater, the mainsail is superior.

Obviously it is the type of sailing anticipated that will determine the choice of the sail plan, but from experience it is very difficult to isolate the factors linked directly to the type of sailing from the general effects of rating rules and, in particular, of the area allowed for spinnakers.

On the subject of round-the-buoys racing, very interesting information is provided by the British Redwing; the class rules allow any type of rig to be used with a strict one-design hull, provided that the actual area does not exceed 200 ft^2 (18.58 m^2). All

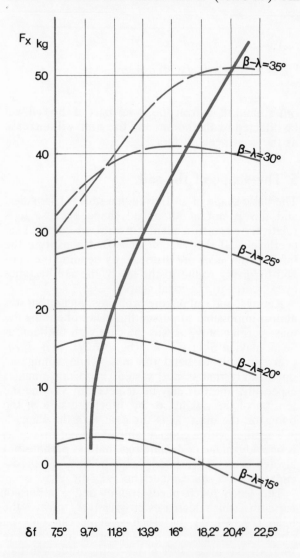

Figure VI.32 *Variation of driving force of a Dragon as a function of the sheeting angle of the headsail. The optimum sheeting angle increases with the angle of the apparent wind.*

156

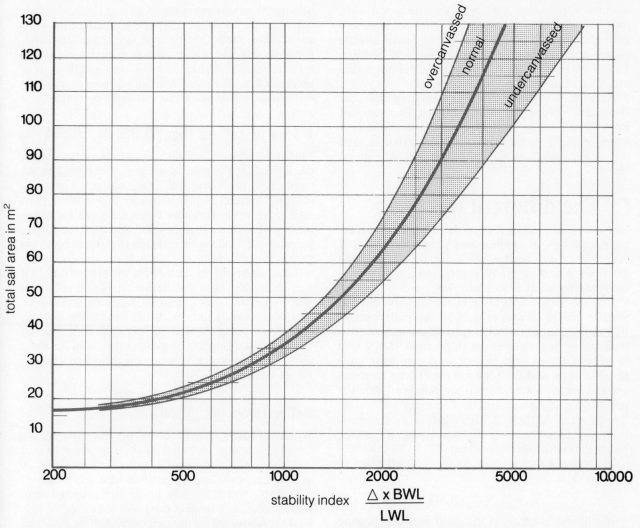

Figure VI.33 *Value of sail area as a function of the index of stability. Exceptional cases are found beyond the limits either side of the normal value. For two-masted rigs,* *an increase of 10–15% in area is allowable, in other words the boats should be in the range above the normal curve.*

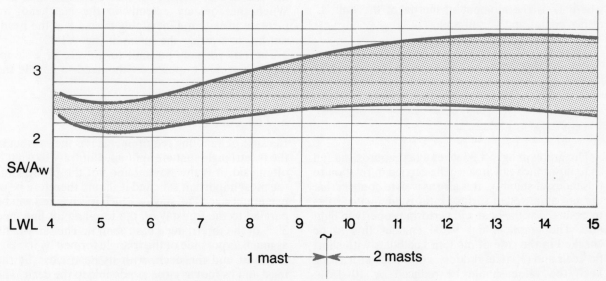

Figure VI.34 *Range of ratios of sail area to wetted area.*

manner of sail plans have been experimented with, including the most extraordinary rigs like an auto-gyro, but the boats have ended up three-quarter rigged with jib-to-mainsail proportions of between 1:2.5 and 1:2.7, a jib that does not overlap, and a mainsail with an aspect ratio of 6 or 7.

As to masthead rig, the final result of the boat speed/true wind speed ratio in tests at Southampton for a One Tonner give an optimum headsail foot value of 165% of the base of the foretriangle, and this is very much in line with the present general trend.

C The different rigs

The above data make it possible to say fairly accurately what type of sail plan and what amount of sail area will be the most suitable for the programme anticipated, and for the type of sailing boat planned, disregarding all questions of rating.

It is clear that all sailing boats must be able to work to windward properly, but it is equally certain that the proportion of time spent close-hauled by a pure racing boat battling on an Olympic course will be very different from that of an ocean-going cruiser. We know that the total sail area that a boat can carry depends above all on her stability, which is primarily governed by her displacement and water-line beam in relation to her length (a light narrow boat should carry less sail than a heavier and/or beamier boat of the same length).

These parameters can be set down as an index of stability V_s

$$V_s = \Delta \times B_{WL}/LWL$$

If stiffness is taken as the ratio between heeling moment and righting moment, and relating all values to waterline length:

$$M_h = L^4 \times B/L = L^3 \times B, \qquad M_r = L \times L^2,$$

where L^4 is the moment of inertia of the hull, L^3 displacement and L^2 sail area.

$$\frac{M_h}{M_r} = f\frac{(L^3 \times B)}{(L^2 \times L)}$$

or

$$f\frac{(\Delta \times B)}{(L \times SA)}.$$

Thus $SA = f\frac{(\Delta \times B)}{L}$.

The graph in fig. VI.33 gives a first approximation as to how much sail area can be carried in relation to this index of stability. It is also as well to confirm that the sail area/wetted surface ratio is adequate, so as to ensure that the boat will perform properly in light airs. The graph in fig. VI.34 enables this to be checked in the case of modern keelboats with short fin keels and separate rudders. For a boat with a long keel, the value should be reduced by 10–15%. Notice how the curve rises for small boats; this is

because the crew are able to sit out.

It depends on the number and strength of the crew as to how well the rig can be controlled and, consequently, the maximum size of each sail and the way sail area is divided. Finally, the length at deck level will limit the ways in which sail area can be split up, and how far apart the stays can be spread.

1 Una or cat rig (figs VI.35, 36, 37, 38)

This is in fact the ideal rig because, as we have seen, per unit of area one sail alone performs better on the wind than the same sail area split up. Clearly a rotating mast is required, preferably a wing mast such as is used on sailing boats designed for maximum performance at very small angles of incidence, for example C class catamarans (fig. VI.31) and ice yachts (fig. VI.39).

The stability of the hull limits the area of sail that can be carried because the height of the centre of effort soon becomes excessive. In normal wind conditions it appears to be virtually impossible to carry over 12 m^2 per crew member, regardless of whether the boat is a monohull or a catamaran, and the main difference is essentially one of aspect ratio, which varies from 4 to 7.

2 The sloop (fig. VI.40)

When sail area is over 10 m^2 per member of the crew, it becomes essential to split up the area and use sloop rig. Given a total area of under about 20 m^2, the non-overlapping headsail of a three-quarter rigged boat will amount to 30–35% of total sail area, and the mainsail's aspect ratio will not exceed 7 (fig. VI.41). Above 20 m^2 the extra area will be obtained by increasing headsail area, preferably by raising the forestay mast fitting, but the aspect ratio of the mainsail should not then exceed 6, and the angle of the luff to the vertical should be no less than 20°. When the forestay extends to the masthead, an increase in sail area inevitably means that the head-sail has to overlap the mainsail (fig. VI.42).

There is virtually no limit to the size of a sloop, other than that imposed by the need to handle the headsails.

3 The cutter (figs VI.43, 44)

Because of handling requirements it is the sails set in the foretriangle that are split up. Contrary to what is often said, it is the staysail and not the jib which is the most important sail, and it should therefore be of maximum size. The stay to which it is hanked will be parallel to the forestay on the fore-and-aft line, and 30% of the foretriangle base abaft it. The sail will fill as much as possible of the triangle formed by its stay, the mast and the deck, with its head close by the mast and its foot as close as possible to the deck. The staysail luff will be equal to three-quarters of the

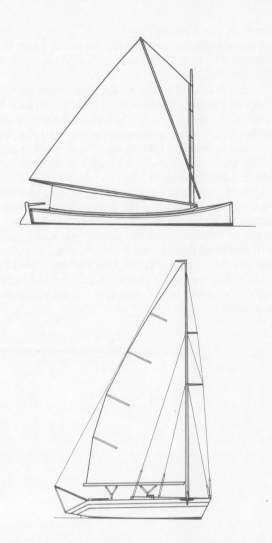

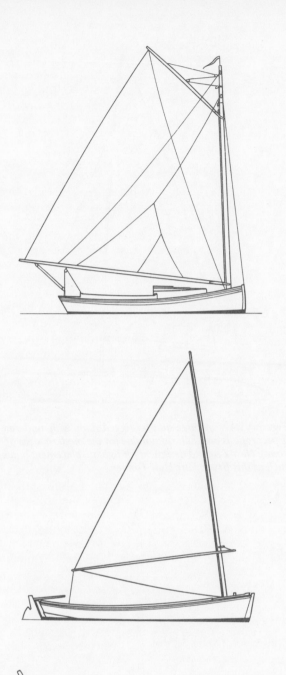

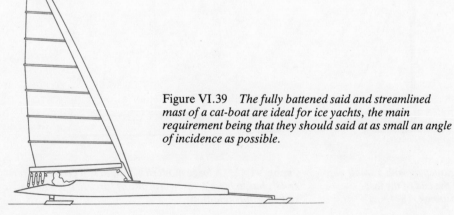

Figure VI.35, 36, 37, 38 *Variations on the cat-boat theme:* Eastern, *an American cat-boat with a classic gaff mainsail (fig. 35); the West Coast* Salmon *with a sprit (fig. 36); the* Eastern Shore of Maryland *(fig. 37), and Patrick Phelipon's modern* Effraie, *the winner of the first Mini-Ton Cup (fig. 38). The rigging always presents a problem, except for the smallest boats where it is simply suppressed.*

Figure VI.39 *The fully battened said and streamlined mast of a cat-boat are ideal for ice yachts, the main requirement being that they should said at as small an angle of incidence as possible.*

length of the forestay.

The ratio of the areas could be taken roughly as mainsail 35–40% of the total, jib 40%, staysail 20–25% (fig. VI. 44).

Today it is hard to define the distinction between sloop and cutter, because it is usual to replace the cutter's jib with a large genoa in lighter winds; furthermore, when a sloop is sailing with the wind free, she normally adds a headsail that reaches to, or nearly to the masthead — hence the modern term double-head rig (fig. VI.19).

In both cases it is possible to provide a reasonable basic sail area which, in the case of a cutter, can be increased either in moderate breezes and on all points of sailing or, for the sloop, only when sailing with the wind free. Local meteorological conditions will decide which of these two options should be chosen. Just as for the sloop, there is no limit to the size of the cutter other than that it must be possible to handle the sails.

Figure VI.41   *A three-quarter rigged sloop with moderate aspect ratio is particularly suitable for the modern ideas of young New Zealand designers for light displacement boats, such as this Bruce Farr Half Tonner.*

Figure VI.40   *Low aspect ratio gunter rig with a small jib; a racing sloop such as was seen at the end of the last century.* Unorna *designed by C. Sibbick, 1894.*

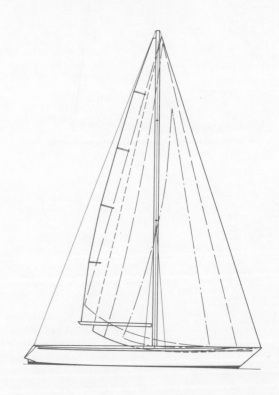

Figure VI.42   *A large modern sloop, here a German Frers Jr 43', has to have a vast wardrobe of foretriangle sails to suit all wind conditions.*

160

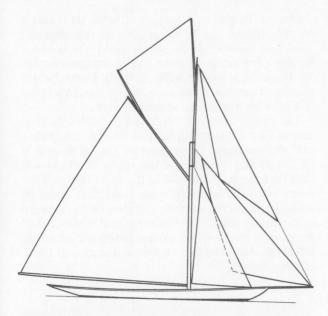

Figure VI.43   *G. L. Watson's* Britannia *is undoubtedly the finest example of a big class gaff cutter, to the length and sail area rule at the end of the nineteenth century. (Launched 20 April 1893).*

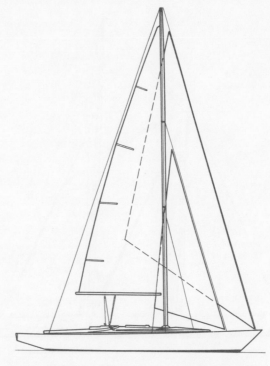

Figure VI.44   *John Illingworth was the most ardent defender of cutter rig during the lasty days of the RORC rating, as here with* Oryx.

4 The ketch (fig. VI.45)

This is the next stage in the division of sail area, and is virtually cutter rig with a mizzen mast added further aft. When its position is taken into account, the mizzen works at a very small angle of incidence on a close-hauled course. It is therefore best to step it as far aft as possible, but in boats with a deck length of under 12 m it is really only possible to do this by providing a bumpkin.

It might seem a pity that a Bermudian mainsail does not make full use of the space between the masts (the same problem arises with schooners) but, rather than reverting to the old gaff mainsail, a wish-bone mainsail can be used, either with a boomed or loose-footed staysail (fig. VI.46) or a quadrilateral staysail as in *Pen Duick III*.

It appears that it is always right to have a large mizzen, not only to compensate to the maximum for the handicap of carrying a second mast with all its rigging, but also because it can have a good effect on the sails that are set further forward, in the same way as a mainsail affects a jib. Its area should therefore be no less than 18–20% of the total area.

The graph in fig. VI.47 also shows that lowering the mizzen causes a very big reduction in driving force, and always much more than would be expected purely from the proportionate size of the areas.

Figure VI.45   *The Bermudan-rigged ketch has become the typical rig for ocean cruising.*

One of the great advantages of ketch rig is that a mizzen staysail can be set as soon as the apparent wind is at some 40° to the centreline. If the distance between the masts is large, as is the case in fig. VI.48, a high aspect ratio staysail could be set sooner. If not, the traditional type of mizzen staysail will provide maximum additional area.

The centre of effort will obviously shift considerably in view of the multiplicity of possible alternative sail combinations. In the case of the rig shown in fig. VI.47, the position of the centre of effort will shift between 0.35 and 0.40 of the space between the masts when the mizzen staysail is set; 0.15 and 0.20 without the mizzen staysail; and minus 0.05 (forward of the mast) without the mizzen, that is about 0.07 forward of the position of the geometric centre of effort (counting the foretriangle and mizzen at 100% of their value).

Figure VI.46   *A wishbone mainsail makes best use of the space between the masts.*

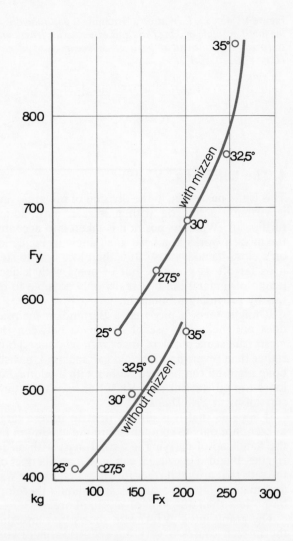

Figure VI.47   *Variation of driving and heeling forces on a modern ketch with a large mizzen, depending on whether this is hoisted or not.*

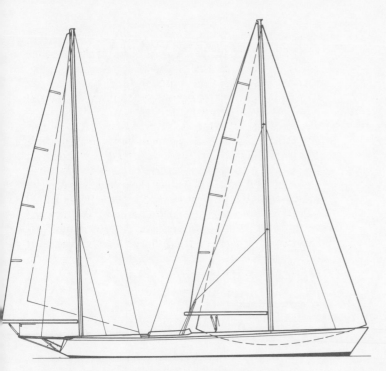

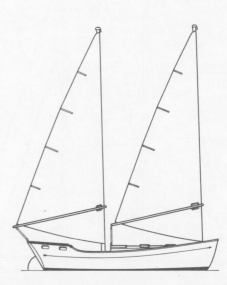

Figure VI.48   *In* Ondine, *Britton Chance tried to step the mizzen as far aft as possible so that a high aspect ratio staysail could be set on a reach.*

Figure VI.49   *The ultimate simplification of ketch rig; the Freedom 40 has two sails on unstayed masts with wishbone booms like the rig of the old Newhaven Sharpies. The sails can be reefed.*

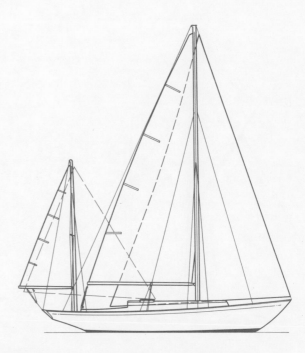

Figure VI.50   *The mizzen of this pretty little yawl is designed essentially, like the roller jib, to make it easy to balance the rig when sailing single-handed.*

Figure VI.51   Finisterre *was undoubtedly the best example of an American yawl to result from the CCA rating rule.*

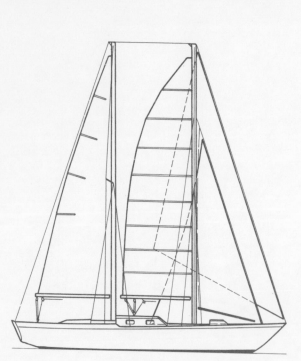

Figure VI.52 Mowgli, *a schooner with masts of equal height and a battened foresail.*

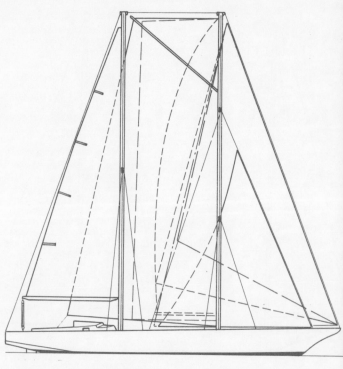

Figure VI.53 *Although E. Tabarly had a battened foresail for* Pen Duick III, *he mainly used two sails with a wishbone gaff.*

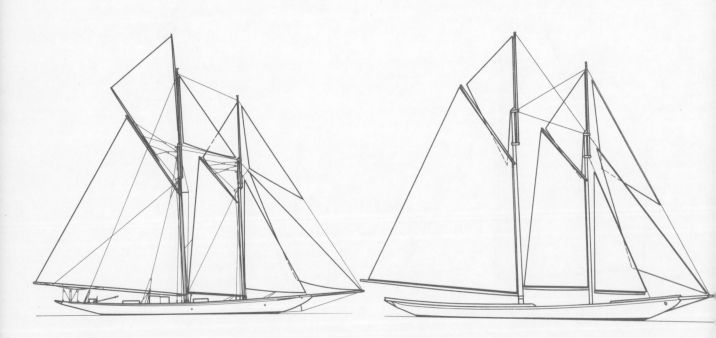

Figure VI.54 Susanne, *designed by W. Fife, is certainly the most superb of the large racing schooners with 'clouds of sail'.*

Figure VI.55 *The Grand Banks schooners were the most handsome examples of this rig in professional use, the* Gertrude Thébaud *being the most elegant of them.*

164

5 The yawl (figs VI.50, 51)

The smallness of the mizzen, which contradicts all that we have just recommended for the ketch, makes this rig absolutely uninteresting by comparison.

6 Schooner with two masts of equal height

Here, on the other hand, is the logical conclusion of the ketch idea, provided that the deck is long enough for the rig to be possible. If the distance between masts is really very great, it is possible to consider setting a main staysail of high aspect ratio permanently; this will act in relation to the mainsail in the same way as the jib of a sloop normally does (fig. VI.48). The four sails will then interact one on the other, and there is no doubt that the variation in sheeting angles will present certain difficulties.

How else to use the space between the masts is always a problem. A fully battened foresail is one answer, but this type of sail is not really very satisfactory for ocean sailing, for which the schooner rig is really suitable (fig. VI.52).

The author would be more tempted to have a wishbone foresail like that set by Eric Tabarly on *Pen Duick III* (fig. VI.53). That the sail is a satisfactory shape can be ensured if the necessary running rigging is fitted to control it, essentially topping lift and sheets, but care is needed because the pull on the leech is very considerable, and it must be possible to move the sheet fairlead in all directions. The only problems are weight, and some difficulty over the strength of the sliding gooseneck.

This arrangement is in any case much superior to the one in which the foresail is replaced by a combination of boomed staysail hanked to a stay, plus a fisherman, because this necessitates extra spars and running rigging, and performance is not so good for windward work, though advantageous for reaching.

7 The classic schooner (figs VI.54, 55, 56 and 57)

Apart from its undeniable aesthetic attractions, provided of course that the hull is in keeping and of equally traditional style and proportions, this rig seems to be just as anachronistic as the yawl.

When the superiority of headsail *vis-à-vis* mainsail is acknowledged, this type of rig seems foreign to all ideas of aerodynamic efficiency. A further inconvenience is that the centre of effort is further aft which, when combined with a modern hull shape with a short central keel, makes for poor balance when the wind is aft.

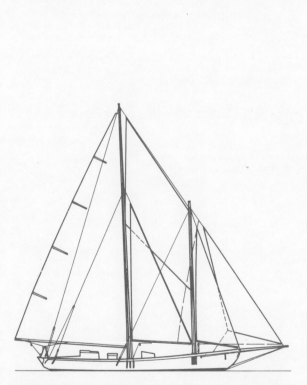

Figure VI.56.*Schooners can hardly be discussed without referring to the famous Starling Burgess-designed* Nina, *undoubtedly the most successful of all the offshore racing boats.*

Figure VI.57 *A modern schooner, the* Grand Louis, *designed by D. Presles, third in the first Round the World Race.*

165

VII
Movement in Waves

A Combined polar diagrams

Knowing the measured values of the forces developed by the sails on the one hand, and those developed by the hull on the other, and having plotted the polar curve for each, it is possible to represent in graph form the two forces F_T and R_T that are involved when a sailing boat moves, and from that to deduce boat speed as a function of the angle of the apparent wind to the course, β. C.A. Marchaj gives an excellent explanation of the method used for resolving this problem in his book *Sailing Theory and Practice*.

Because the sails and the hull work at different speeds and in different media, it is impossible to use the polar curves of the coefficients directly, and instead figures have to be converted to those of the actual forces developed at a given speed, or vice versa.

First, a polar curve of the forces developed by the sails at each selected apparent wind speed is drawn on tracing paper (fig. VII.1). The polar curve of the forces developed by the hull at different speeds and leeway angles is drawn on a separate piece of paper. In order to find the optimum state for close-hauled sailing in an apparent wind of a certain strength and direction, the tangent to the corresponding curve (aerodynamic drag angle) is entered on the first graph. This gives us the value of F_T at which driving force will be maximum and heeling force minimum.

R_T is drawn opposite F_T, and is given the same value as F_T. The hull polar diagram is placed over this, and turned to find the curve which is tangential to R_T at its extremity; this immediately indicates the speed at which the boat will move, and the corresponding leeway angle.

Knowing the speed V_A and the direction β of the apparent wind, as well as boat speed V_S, it is possible, as shown in fig. III.12, p. 00, to calculate the value of the true wind V_T, its direction in relation to the course γ, and the boat's Vmg. All this can equally well be obtained by calculations based on the formulae given on that page.

Following the procedure explained in table VII.I, a polar diagram can then be drawn up, based on this information, to show boat speeds for the various true wind forces (fig. VII.2). These polar diagrams can be used in very many ways, for example to refer to when tuning the boat and, in particular, when deciding which sails to set or what racing tactics to use, as well as to optimize navigational efficiency.

It is also possible to extract more specific curves from them, such as:

Vmg as a function of the true wind (fig. VII.3);

Vmg as a function of the strength and direction of the apparent wind;

Vmg as a function of the angle of incidence and of the direction of the apparent wind, or of the sheeting angle, and so on.

Having established all these facts, it is possible to study the effects that result from varying certain parameters, such as the area or the aspect ratio of the sails, the ballast ratio or, in particular, all that affects stability.

Thus, when the optimum heeling angle at which the hull can achieve maximum speed, and therefore the corresponding heeling force, are known, it is easy to decide what the maximum heeling force developed by the sails should be, and to search for ways of achieving this by making some of the possible adjustments, such as incidence (fig. VII.4), altering camber or reducing the area.

Data processing of measurements of models in towing tanks now enables direct information to be obtained immediately about every possible combination of the measurements obtained, but there is a doubtful area as regards the sail coefficients because these are extraordinarily variable, depending as they do on such a multiplicity of factors, which vary not only with the condition of the sail itself (cloth, cut and so on), but with its controls and supports (mast, rigging etc.).

Professor Davidson's well-known Gimcrack coefficients, obtained in 1936 with measurement trials of a sailing boat of that name, are so old that they can

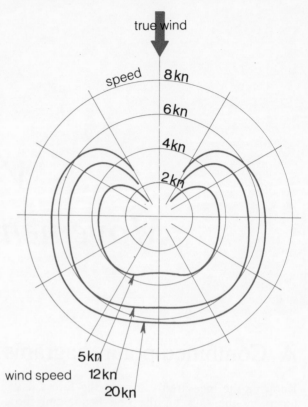

Figure VII.2 *Polar diagram of boat speeds in winds of three different strengths.*

hardly be taken to be representative of modern sails but, since then, the laboratory at Delft, with a series of intensive tests on the American sailing boat *Bay Bea* and on *Standfast*, has brought these coefficients up to date.

B Directional stability

Although the hull/sail combination can be considered in terms of the strength of opposing forces being in equilibrium, their equilibrium can equally well be expressed in terms of direction.

We saw in fig.III.10, p.62, that when a sailing boat is directionally stable forces F_T (sails) and R_T (hull) must not only be equal but must act in the same vertical plane, because otherwise a couple will be formed which will make the boat go off course.

The term balance, which is used in connection with the equilibrium of forces that affect directional stability, indicates how easily a boat can be kept on a given course; she is said to have weather helm if she tends to luff up above her course, or lee helm if she tends to bear away. This does not mean, however, that the rudder should be absolutely neutral, staying in line with the fore-and-aft line without any intervention from the helmsman, and we will see why later.

So many factors can intervene to destroy the equilibrium required that balance is one of the most

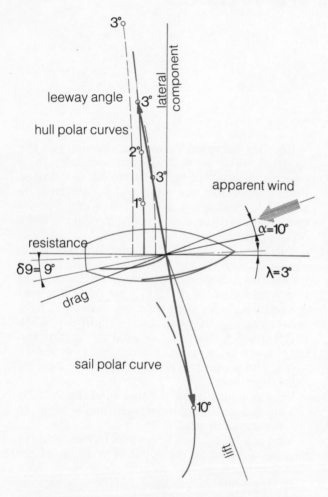

Figure VII.1 *Example of the use of polar diagrams to determine performance. The polar curve of the sail at a selected wind speed indicates the value of the resultant force at an angle of incidence of 10°. When this is plotted on the opposite side on the hull polar curve as the opposing hydrodynamic force, the corresponding leeway angle of 3° and the corresponding values of longitudinal and lateral resistance can be found. The former indicates boat speed and, from the latter, the heeling angle can be found on the stability curve.*

TABLE VII.I

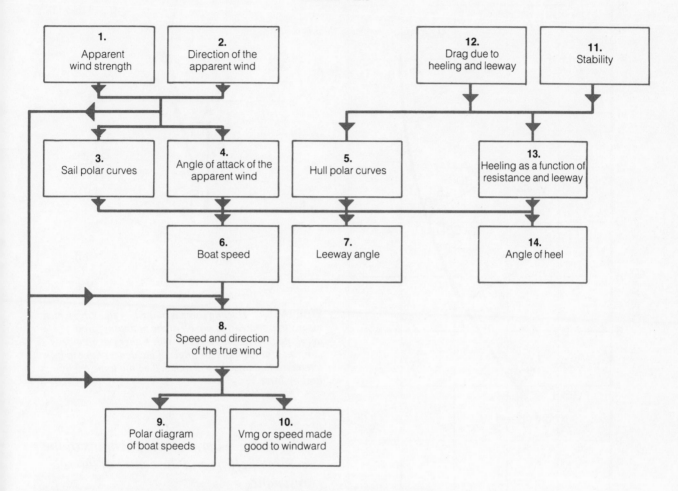

difficult and elusive problems that the designer has to face. A distinction is generally made between static balance and directional stability. The latter is mainly a problem on a run when factors other than those linked to the hull have an effect, and its study is complicated on account of interference with wave systems, so it is on the subject of static balance that we shall concentrate.

Balance may be disturbed for two quite separate reasons: firstly because of the distance between the points at which the forces F_T and R_T are applied; secondly because of the asymmetric shape of the hull when the boat is heeling, and the resulting alteration in the lateral area.

It should also be remembered that, whenever the boat goes off course, the magnitude of forces F_T and R_T will be affected differently according to the point of sailing.

1 Equilibrium of forces

The reason why the distance between F_T and R_T changes differs according to the point of sailing.

a Running

We have already looked at this problem in Chapter IV, and have seen that the only workable answer is to use every possible method of bringing the lines of action of the two forces into the same vertical fore-and-aft plane, *without* helm action and with minimum deformation of hull shape. Obviously this is much more difficult to achieve with una rig than in a boat with a spinnaker set. Luffing up to avoid running dead before the wind would also have the effect of increasing F_T and, consequently, the heeling angle, leeway and turning moment. R_T has to increase equally to counter the increase in F_T, and a leeway angle appears in the same direction as the boat initially deviated from course. When the wind is aft a sailing boat is therefore inherently directionally unstable.

b Other points of sailing

On points of sailing other than dead before the wind, it may be hoped that the two forces F_T and R_T will act in the same vertical plane (fig. VII.5). The centres of pressure, the points at which these forces

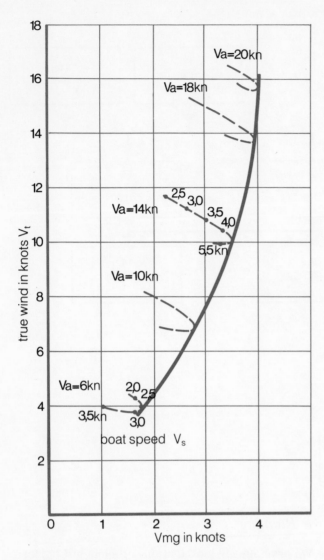

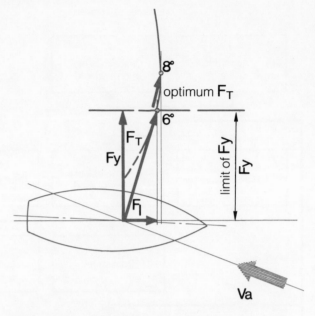

Figure VII.4 *Heeling force is limited by stability, which means that sometimes not all of the optimum force developed by the sails can be used. Either sail area or controls (for example the angle of incidence) have to be altered so that total F_T will match the limit imposed by heeling force F_y.*

c The distance between the positions of the centre of effort and the centre of lateral resistance

The fore-and-aft distance in the horizontal plane between the CE and the CLR is therefore a very important factor when designing a sailing boat, and one where the designer has the least information available to help his calculations. Simply expressed, the greater the angle of heel, the less beamy the hull, and the greater the vertical distance between the CE and the CLR, the greater will be the fore-and-aft distance between them (a disadvantage of high aspect ratio sail plans).

The point about beam is particularly noticeable in the case of catamarans where the fact that the CLR shifts right to leeward means that the centres of pressure are reversed in the fore-and-aft plane, with the position of the CE shifting aft of that of the CLR (fig. VII.6).

When the boat is close-hauled and goes off course by luffing up, the effect is that the angle of incidence of the sails will decrease and the leeway angle will increase. F_T is reduced in consequence, as are the angle of heel and turning moment. If force R_T is to decrease to match the lower value of F_T, the leeway angle has to decrease, and this brings the boat back to her initial course. A sailing boat is therefore inherently directionally stable when close-hauled.

are applied, are called respectively the centre of effort (CE) for F_T, and the centre of lateral resistance (CLR) for R_T.

We know that the true fore-and-aft position of these centres depends on the angles of incidence with the air and the water (Chapter II.4); except in the case of bodies with simple shapes, the positions of the CE and CLR can only be found by experiment, because they are dependent on the character of flow over the whole length of the body. The naval architect is therefore obliged to approximate in deciding their positions and, in any case, except for a sailing boat with a geometrically variable lateral plane (i.e. a centreboarder), the position of the CLR cannot be altered after it has shifted as a result of changing the angle of incidence.

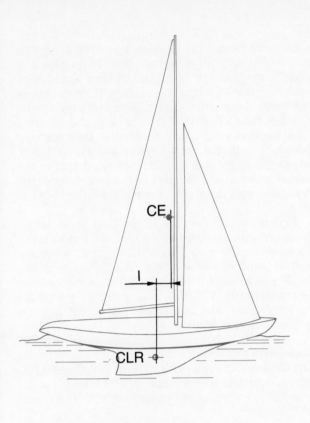

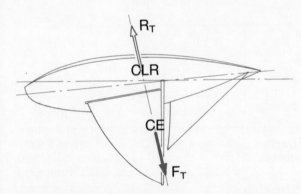

Figure VII.5 *Longitudinal shift of the centre of effort and the centre of lateral resistance.*

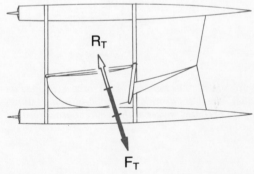

Figure VII.6 *The lateral shift of the centres of effort and of lateral resistance in a catamaran causes their positions to be reversed in the longitudinal plane, by comparison with a normal sailing boat.*

Another point to remember is that, because the sails pivot round when the boat bears away onto a reach, the point where the line of action of F_T intersects the fore-and-aft axis of the hull will shift considerably further aft (fig. VII.7); the result is that a boat which is nicely balanced when close-hauled will have weather helm after she has borne away. The CE can, however, be shifted further forward again by setting a spinnaker to increase the force developed by the sails forward of the mast.

The effect of heeling is particularly noticeable when the angle of heel increases, in a gust for example, with the result that the boat luffs up sharply and may sometimes broach spectacularly. The usual automatic reaction is to put up the helm, which is immediately accessible, so as to bring her

back on course. However, this generally aggravates the situation because, as we have seen in Chapter IV, the side force developed by the rudder includes an additional heeling moment, and this further increases the angle of heel (fig. VII.8). When the heeling moment resulting from the centrifugal force developed as the boat turns is also added (fig. VII.9), it is understandable why broaching can easily lead to a capsize, or at least to a very uncomfortable

171

if not dangerous situation. The lesson to be learned from this is that broaching should *always* be corrected by altering the trim of the sails immediately, and *never* with the helm. Conclusions can be drawn from this: all fittings should be sited where they are readily at hand.

To return to the design of the sailing boat, the CE and CLR are taken by the designer to be the geometric centres of the sail area and of the lateral area respectively, the geometric centres being the centres of gravity of these two areas. In the case of a small sailing boat or of a three-quarter rigged boat with a jib that overlaps only slightly, the areas taken are those of the actual sails, together with their leech roaches (fig. VII.10a). For light centreboard dinghies, the sails have to be considered in their working positions with the mast curved aft. For a larger masthead-rigged sailing boat, the area is that of the actual mainsail and the area of the foretriangle (fig. VII.10b), plus the area of the mizzen if the boat has one.

In determining the CLR, if the boat has a rudder hung immediately abaft a long keel, the rudder is not included in the area (fig. VII.10b), but when the rudder, with or without skeg, is separate from the keel, the whole of this is included as part of the lateral area (fig. VII.10a). This is all purely a matter of convention, and is unimportant except in comparing different boats.

Table VII.II below gives average values for different types of sailing boats for the lead, l, between the CE and CLR as a percentage of waterline length. Here, waterline length is taken as total length at the waterline, including the rudder when this increases hull length.

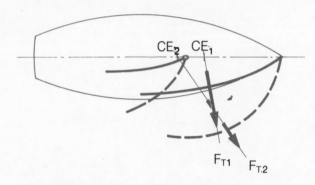

Figure VII.7   *When the boat bears away from close-hauled to a reach, the change in direction of the force developed by the sails causes the centre of effort to shift further aft.*

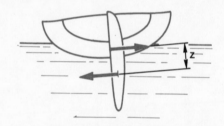

Figure VII.8   *The moment of the force developed by the rudder, which is particulargely noticeable in a sailing dinghy, becomes greater as the centreboard is raised.*

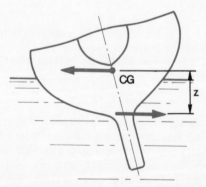

Figure VII.9   *When the boat alters course, centrifugal force and the shift of the centre of gravity and of the centre of lateral resistance create a heeling couple. Here the boat, viewed from astern, is turning to starboard.*

TABLE VII.II

	TYPE	e
Light centre-boarder	cat boat	2 to 4 %
	sloop	6 to 8 %
Keel boats		6 to 8 %
12-metres		6 to 6.5 %
Mast head sloop with separate rudder	$L_f < 5.50$ m	17 to 18 %
	5.50 m $< L_f <$ 9 m	18 to 22 %
	$L_f > 9$ m	15 to 18 %
¾ sloop with separate rudder	$L_f < 8$ m	13 to 15 %
	$L_f > 8$ m	10 to 12 %
Mast head sloop with long keel		13 to 17 %
Ketches		11 to 15 %

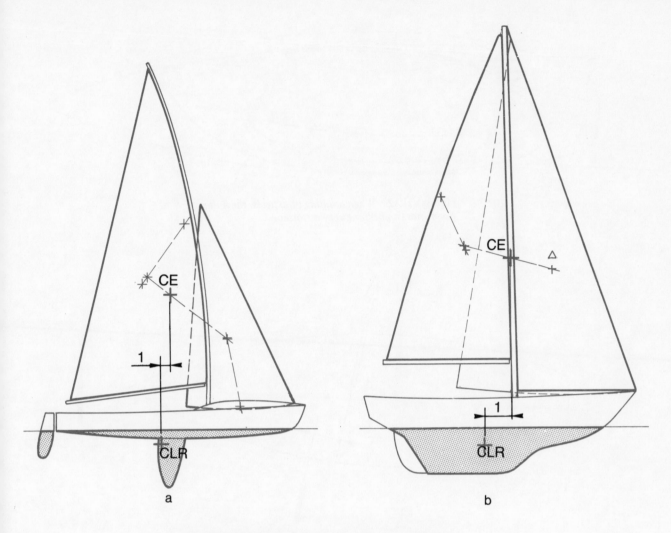

Figure VII.10   *How the centres of effort and of lateral resistance are found depends on the type of sail plan and of the lateral planes.*

It is noticeable that the boats that normally sail at the smallest angle of heel (light centreboarders, bilgekeelers, large cruisers) require the smallest lead. The fact that medium-sized boats with cabins need the greatest lead could be surprising if considered only in terms of their beam, which is as much as one-third of hull length, but it should be remembered that the lead of the CE over the CLR also has to counter the luffing couple caused by the distortion of the hull shape when the boat heels, and this distortion is particularly marked in boats of this size, because of their great beam; the difference in equilibrium at various heeling angles is very evident.

2 Distortion of hull shape when heeling

When a laterally asymmetric body is moved through the water, its course is found to be curved, not straight, and the course will bend in the same direction as the body's average curvature (fig. VII.11).

So, what happens when the hull of a sailing boat heels? Because the waterlines change their curves at different levels (the beamier the hull and the smaller the displacement, the greater the difference in curvature), heeled waterlines all have a more or less pronounced curve (fig. VII.12). The resulting moment tends to make the boat luff up. If the helmsman wants to avoid using the rudder to counter this effect, the only solution is to create an

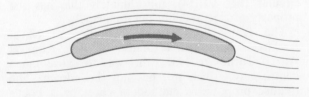

Figure VII.11   *A body moving freely in a fluid will follow a path that is the same shape as its curvature.*

173

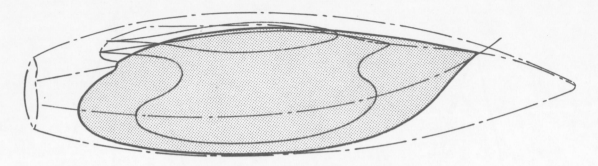

Figure VII.12 *When a sailing boat heels, the hull's waterlines can become very distorted.*

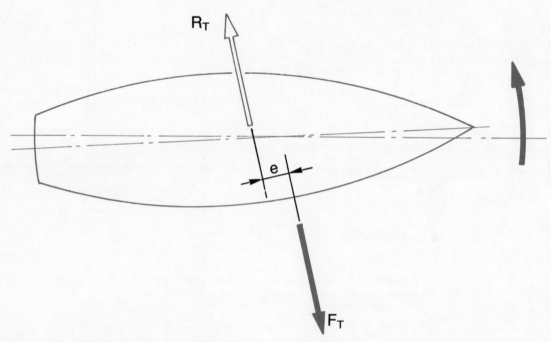

Figure VII.13 *When the boat is heeling, the turning moment caused by the distortion of the hull must be* balanced by an equivalent moment created by the shift, e, of the couple $F_T - R_T$.

opposing moment by shifting the CE further forward (fig. VII.13), but then the boat will have lee helm in light airs when she is not heeling.

Obviously the first step to take to avoid this is to draw the lines of the hull in such a way that its shape distorts as little as possible as she heels, and from this point of view the optimum hull shape would be circular (fig. VII.14); unfortunately this has the property of zero stability due to shape!

The Transactions of the Institution of Naval Architects published a treatise by Rear-Admiral Alfred Turner in 1937; this was to cause much controversy, which still has not died down. The treatise proposed a method of checking a boat's equilibrium when heeled, based on the following procedure (fig. VII.15):

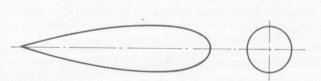

Figure VII.14 *Only a body of circular section stays the same shape regardless of the angle of heel.*

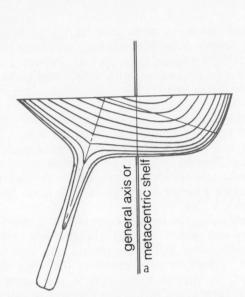

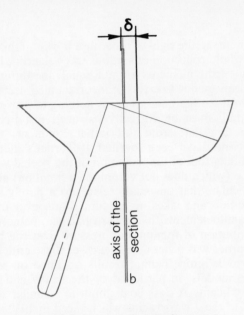

Figure VII.15   *Turner's method. In (a) all the sections together are placed on a knife blade to find the general metacentric axis, the metacentric shelf. In (b) each section* is placed on the blade in turn to find the distance, δ, between the axis of that section and the general metacentric shelf axis.

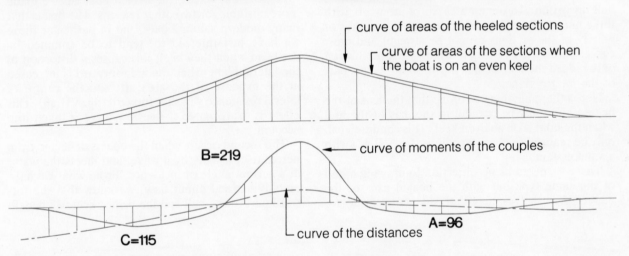

Figure VII.16   *Above, the curve of areas of the sections when the boat is on an even keel and when she is heeled. Below, the curve of the distances δ of the sections, and of* the moments of these sections in relation to the general axis or metacentric shelf.

At the intersection of the waterline at 0° of heel and the vertical through the centre of gravity of the body plan, a heeled waterline is traced on the sections that are inclined at the chosen angle of heel.

The vertical axis passing through the centre of gravity of each heeled section is found (by cutting out each section in board and balancing it on a knife blade).

The metacentric shelf of the entire hull, heeled at this angle, is then found in similar fashion by balancing all the sections placed on top of each other.

The distances between the axes of each of the individual sections and the metacentric shelf of the whole are noted, and are then plotted as ordinates along a longitudinal axis (fig. VII.16). The curve joining the ends of the ordinates can vary in shape, and well may cross the axis at one or two points.

The moment of each section in relation to the metacentric shelf is then calculated and plotted as an ordinate on the same axis (to a scale of some sort) and the curve joining them is traced. Sometimes three areas, a, b and c, are obtained; alternatively there are two areas, a and b, one either side of the axis.

Turner's theory states that a hull is in equilibrium at the heeling angle being considered if a = c = b/2. Obviously, from simple geometry, a + c is then equal to b, and the sum of the moments to the left of the metacentric shelf is equal to the sum of the

175

moments to the right of it because it was on this that the whole collection of sections was balanced. If the sums of the moments are not equal, the difference can only be due to errors or incorrect measurement.

On the other hand, there is nothing to prove that the hull must be correctly balanced just because a = c. Apart from this initial comment, many criticisms have been levelled at Turner's method, including that of the definition of the heeled waterplane (which does not determine a flotation) and in particular, that this study relates to a purely static condition and takes no account whatsoever of the dynamic elements that govern balance, namely the distribution of friction and pressure over the hull.

Turner was never able to answer these criticisms, but took refuge behind results obtained on small-scale models, in particular of the heavy and relatively beamy A class boats, built to a similar rating rule to the J class yachts which raced in 1930, 1934 and 1937 for the America's Cup.

The author's own criticism is that Turner's method does not take account of, and actually introduces, hull distortion. To obtain a curve of moments with three humps, the axis passing through the centres of gravity of the sections cannot be straight and must curve, the concavity being to windward, and this can only reduce the hull's efficiency in so far as it is part of the lateral plane.

Nor is there anything to prove that the axis of the heeled hull must be parallel to the axis of the hull when the boat is on an even keel. This condition can only be realized on scow-type hulls (fig. VII.17) with a square stem.

There seems to be no objection to drawing a hull of the same type but with the heeled axes of the metacentric shelves to either side converging to-wards the stem, as is the case with J. L. Noire's Micro-Tonner *Nuits Blanches* for example. It could be that light racing boats, like *45 Degrees South* designed by Bruce Farr, with their round midships sections and beamy flat afterbodies, also correspond to this sort of preoccupation. When these boats are seen close-hauled it is obvious that they heel with a conical trajectory and are down by the stem.

If a boat of this type has two centreboards, it seems preferable to give them not a positive but a negative angle of incidence to allow for the fact that the hull has a higher drag angle than the centreboard (Chapter V.C1).

Establishing the heeled waterlines of a hull is a lengthy and painstaking affair because a waterline has to be found that is the correct one, and trim should be such that the centre of buoyancy stays correctly positioned in relation to the centre of gravity. Here again, this relates only to a static state which takes no account of the effects of wave-making or of the various pressures and resistances.

Apart from waves, the heeled boat can be made more unstable for two other reasons. The first is that many modern sailing boats, and in particular those we have just referred to, tend to be trimmed by the head when they heel; this causes a distortion of the lateral plane when the area forward is increased at the expense of the area aft, and the centre of lateral resistance will shift forward (fig. VII.18). This effect is exacerbated if the bow wave is taken into account.

The second occurs when the boat is deflected from her course, usually by a wave, and meets the water at a certain angle of incidence. From what we have already learned about flow, we know that the forward part of the hull and the ballast keel will benefit

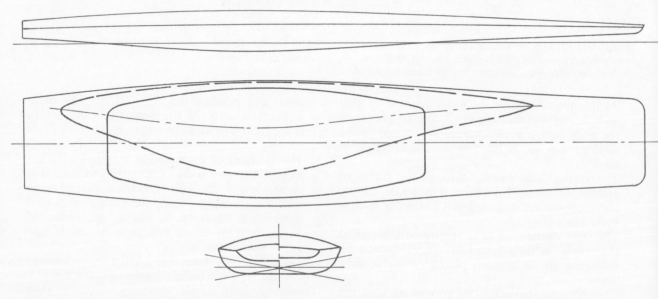

Figure VII.17   *The shape of the American scow, which is sailed on the Great Lakes, provdes favourable distortion of* *the waterlines when heeling, and waterline length is increased.*

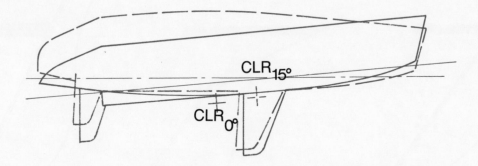

CLR₁₅°

CLR₀°

Figure VII.18   *The shift forward of the centre of lateral resistance when a boat with a flat beamy afterbody heels* *over is not necessarily countered by a matching shift forward of the centre of effort.*

from a 'lift', whereas the after part of the hull and the helm (when it is separate from the keel) will be at a smaller angle of incidence (fig. VII.19). The centre of pressure of the ballast keel is generally forward of the centre of buoyancy, and the natural couple formed, which is a destabilizing couple, increases its effect, augmenting that developed by the hull. (This phenomenon will be analysed in the next chapter, and is particularly noticeable when the angle of incidence is opposite to the heeling angle, i.e. when the boat is luffing.) The rudder must therefore be large enough in area and positioned well aft so that, without the helmsman having to take action, its stabilizing couple is sufficient to counter the sum of the destabilizing couples of the hull and the ballast keel, in spite of the reduction in its angle of incidence.

There is no doubt but that the precise study of these phenomena is so complex in view of the numerous parameters that have to be considered, that little attention has been paid to the problem of the directional stability of a heeled boat, and each designer has to depend on his own skill and experience. This means that the only way that the helmsman can quickly and conveniently correct any lack of equilibrium is to use the helm. The action he takes

should be as effective as possible while keeping to the minimum the price paid in terms of increased resistance.

3 The rudder

The rudder of a sailing boat not only helps to counter leeway (sometimes it is a very important factor, as in the case of a light centreboard dinghy), but has two other main functions: the first, which could be termed passive, consists of keeping the boat on course in spite of external interferences (the tiller is either fixed or left free); the second is active, and puts into effect the manoeuvre desired by the sailor (the tiller is moved by the helmsman). The dividing line between these two functions is not always clear because the helm itself is rarely capable of opposing outside influences without active intervention from the helmsman, but the distinction is nevertheless extremely useful when studying the qualities of the various types of rudder.

Just as for all other foils designed to produce lift at a variable angle of incidence, the efficiency of the rudder depends on the three characteristics of aspect ratio, planform and section.

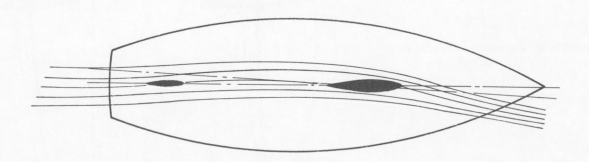

Figure VII.19   *Flow over the various appendages gives 'lift' at the fin keel and 'heads' at the rudder.*

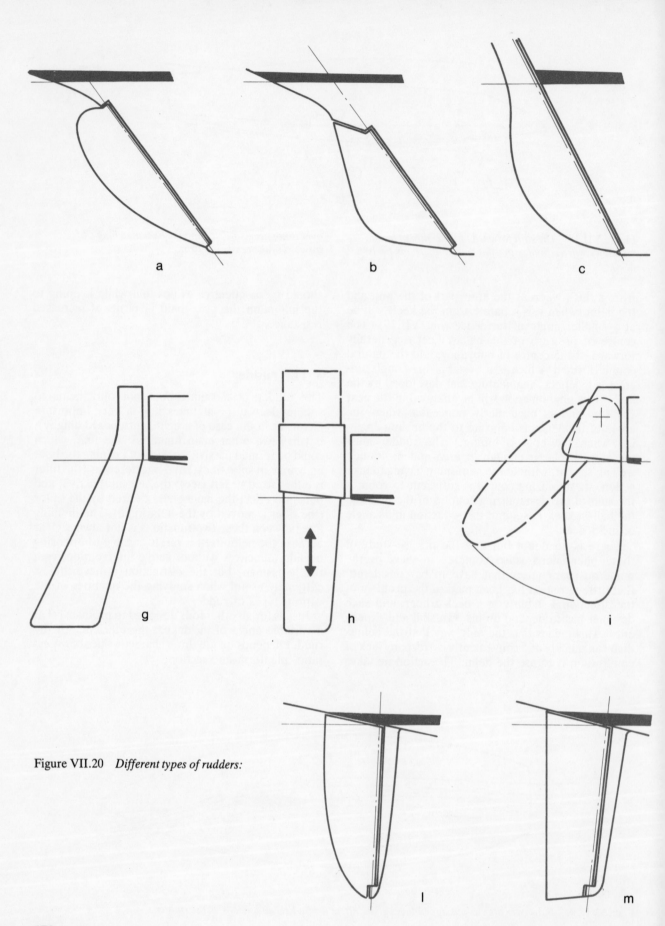

Figure VII.20 *Different types of rudders:*

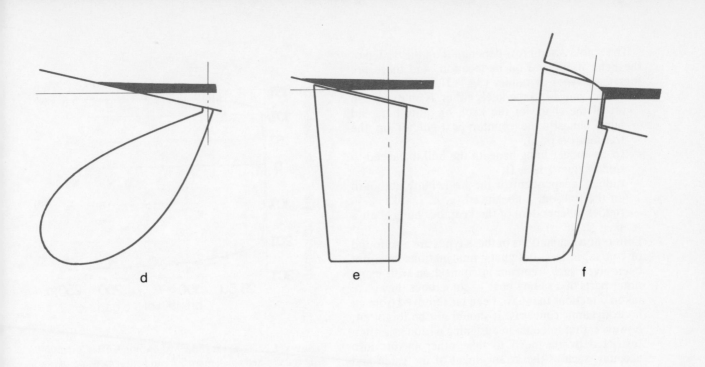

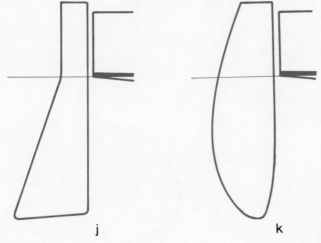

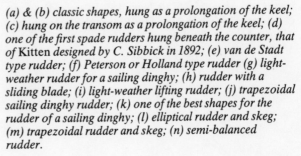

(a) & (b) classic shapes, hung as a prolongation of the keel; (c) hung on the transom as a prolongation of the keel; (d) one of the first spade rudders hung beneath the counter, that of Kitten *designed by C. Sibbick in 1892; (e) van de Stadt type rudder; (f) Peterson or Holland type rudder (g) light-weather rudder for a sailing dinghy; (h) rudder with a sliding blade; (i) light-weather lifting rudder; (j) trapezoidal sailing dinghy rudder; (k) one of the best shapes for the rudder of a sailing dinghy; (l) elliptical rudder and skeg; (m) trapezoidal rudder and skeg; (n) semi-balanced rudder.*

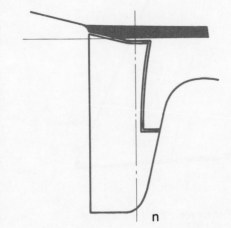

The whole assembly is dependent on the design of the helm itself, and on its location, and there are four main types of rudder (fig. VII.20):
— rudder hinged to the keel, either as an extension aft of the shape of the keel, or quite flat, and hung beneath the counter or right aft on the transom (a, b, c);
— spade rudder hung beneath the hull, balanced to some extent (d, e, f);
— rudder independent of the keel, hung outboard on the transom, unbalanced (g, h, i, j, k);
— rudder independent of the keel, but hung abaft a skeg (l, m, n).

Different combinations of these types are also found of course; in fact, designers' imaginations have not been given such free rein in connection with many other parts of a sailing boat — sometimes they have taken directions that have been far removed from all hydrodynamic concerns. It should not be forgotten, however, that freedom in designing a rudder is often restricted by the need to take other factors into account, such as the arrangement of the cabin and the cockpit, drying out, strength, draught and the position of the propeller.

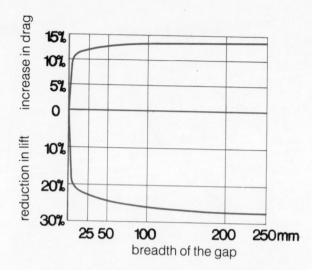

Figure VII.22 *Curves showing how much lift is lost and drag is increased when there is a gap between the top of the rudder blade and the hull. Speed 3 knots, area of the rudder 0.37 m², depth 0.90 m (from A. Millward).*

a Aspect ratio

We have to remember that the effect of increasing aspect ratio is that, although the lift-to-drag ratio is increased, the stalling angle becomes more critical. Aspect ratio must therefore be moderate, especially if the rudder is placed beneath the hull: mirror effect due to the presence of the bottom can then be used to the full by giving the rudder stock suitable rake, so that the upper edge of the rudder blade will stay really close to the bottom while the rudder is being turned to an angle of at least 15° either side of the centreline (fig. VII.21). The flatter the bottom, the easier this is to achieve.

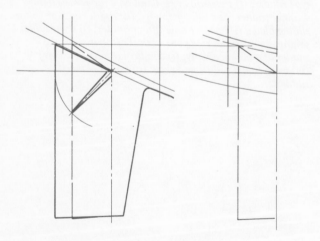

Figure VII.21 *Control of deflection at the top of the rudder blade, close by the bottom of the hull.*

Figure VII.23 *Rudder fence fitted to the top of* Intrepid's *trim tab in 1967.*

The graph in fig VII.22 shows the considerable advantage that can be gained in this way, but we will see later that this path should not be followed too far.

In boats with wineglass-shaped sections and therefore no flat bottom, an end plate, namely a rudder fence, can be provided where the break occurs at the top of the rudder; a fence may also be used for a trim tab on the trailing edge (fig. VII.23), but it is very difficult to decide the exact angle this should be placed at in order to match the path of the streamlines exactly.

b The planform

In the first instance, this is governed by the type of helm selected, and by the practical considerations just mentioned. First we will consider the rake of the stock, because this affects the shape of every rudder, whatever its type.

Raking the stock aft (traditional method) or forward (modern design) involves a reduction in the lateral component, y, and the appearance of a vertical component, z, which is directed downwards or upwards, depending on whether the boat is luffing up or bearing away:

	Bear away	Luff up
Rake aft	z ↑ (1)	z ↓ (2)
Rake forward	z ↓ (3)	z ↑ (4)

The result is that, up to a certain angle of heel (approximately 25°, when the helm angle and rake of the stock are 30°), a rudder with a stock raked either forward or aft is always inferior to one with a vertical stock. Beyond that heeling angle, the effect of the z component will still be unfavourable when it is directed downwards (2 and 3), but will be beneficial when it is directed upwards (1 and 4). (For the amusement of 'mathematicians', lateral force R_{yg} is a function of

$$K(\sin S)(\cos A)(\cos S)(\cos \theta) + (\sin S)(\cos S)(\sin \theta).$$

S = tiller angle, A = rake of the stock, θ = angle of heel. Be careful of the signs of the three angles; A is positive when rake is aft and negative when rake is forward. K depends on the area, the speed and the efficiency of the rudder.)

This just means that a rudder with a stock raked aft will counter a tendency to luff better, but will be less effective when initiating tacking (force z, directed downwards, compensates for this to some extent because it tends to raise the stem out of waves), and then becomes more efficient again when the boat has passed through the eye of the wind. The rudder with stock raked forward, on the other hand, will counter a luff less well, start to go about better (although force z directed upwards tends to bury the bows) and be less effective when the boat has passed through the eye of the wind.

As the effect of rake is minor at a small helm angle, the main aim is to ensure that the top of the rudder sweeps the bottom of the hull. But let us return to consideration of the various types.

Hung abaft the keel These are most often found on older cruising boats; the shape can vary from a graceful curve with maximum breadth at the top of the rudder, and no attempt to match the shape of the bottom (fig. VII.20a) to a trapezoidal shape with maximum breadth low down and the top edge more or less matched to the hull form at the garboards (fig. VII.20b). In both cases major eddies are sure to form where the rudder and hull meet. The force developed by VII.20a will act at a higher point, and heeling effect will be less pronounced, which is an advantage. However, in order to reduce the surface area of the keel as much as possible, the stock may have to be given considerable rake so that the tiller can be positioned normally.

For practical purposes (drying out), the bottom of the rudder has to stop a few centimetres short of the heel of the keel, and it could even be as well to incline it upwards aft, although it is known that this does not improve the performance of the lateral plane or directional stability.

The combination of keel and raked rudder cause the hull to turn because the keel section becomes asymmetric, and a turning couple results. It also causes the centre of lateral resistance to shift aft, which is beneficial when the boat is to bear away, but harmful when wishing to luff up. The continual variation of the position of the centre of lateral

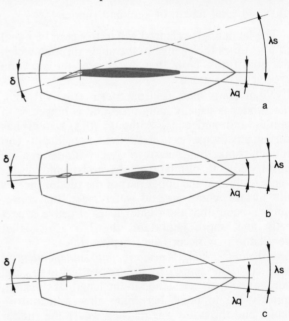

Figure VII.24 *Three different configurations showing the angles of attack and deflection of the rudder:*
(a) rudder hung abaft a long keel; (b) short keel with separate balanced spade rudder; (c) short keel with separate rudder hung on a skeg.

181

resistance, and the modification of flow which causes this, can hardly be said to help the efficiency of the keel. On the other hand, keeping the rudder permanently at an angle a few degrees to leeward makes it act like a trim tab, and considerably increases the lift of the keel/rudder assembly.

A sailing boat with a rudder hung on the keel should therefore normally sail on a close-hauled course with the tiller held 3–4° to weather. The rudder will then be in the same state as the trim tab we considered in Chapter V.C3.

The efficiency of this type of configuration can be determined by calculating the ratio between the helm angle and the angle of incidence resulting from putting the rudder over in order to shift the centre of pressure a certain distance. The higher this ratio, the greater will rudder drag be.

When the rudder is hung abaft the keel, and given a keel with a length equal to 0.75 waterline length, 20% of which is the rudder, for a shift of 10% of waterline length (fig. VII.24a):

$$\frac{\delta}{\lambda} \quad \frac{\dfrac{\Delta X_{cp}}{L}}{0.83 \; l/L - \dfrac{\Delta X_{cp}}{L}}$$

$\Delta X_{cp}/L = 0.133$; $l/L = 0.2$.
    Thus $\delta/\lambda = 4.03$

ΔX_{cp} = shift of the centre of pressure
λ = incidence due to altering course
l = rudder length
δ = rudder angle
L = total length of keel and rudder

The helm angle required will in this case be equal to four times the change in the angle through which the boat turns. Note that the shorter the keel the greater is the angle.

When boats have transom sterns (fig. VII.20c), the rudder is usually hung on it and is hinged with pintles and gudgeons. Although this system has certain advantages as to strength and practicality (no rudder trunk, hinge easy to check, rudder readily unshipped), it suffers from hydrodynamic disadvantages in that the upper part of the rudder pierces the surface where air and water meet, the consequence being that the rudder loses effective aspect ratio and, more important, there is a risk that ventilaton may occur (see Chapter II.3e).
Spade rudder, hung beneath the hull, independent of the keel The search to reduce wetted area, and consequently the reduction in the length of the keel, quickly led to boats becoming almost uncontrollable, and the point was reached where the rudder had to be separated from the ballast keel so that it could be shifted further aft, so increasing the moment of the force developed.

The idea is certainly not new and, although it was E. G. van de Stadt who introduced it in the 1950s with his *Zeevalk* and *Zeeslag*, its parentage should surely be shared with Charles Sibbick, who applied it to his 'One-raters' such as *Kitten* in 1892 (fig. VII.20d) and Nathaniel Greene Herreshoff who used it the year before on *Dilemma*. At that period the rudder blade was swept far aft of the axis of the stock, and there can be no doubt that the moment must have been very great and the effort required at the helm very considerable.

It is to van de Stadt, however, that we owe the more modern type of balanced spade rudder; he took the risk of giving the rudder stock much less rake and, by placing the centre of pressure virtually in line with the stock so that the force on the parts of the blade forward of the stock countered those abaft the stock, he considerably reduced the effort needed from the helmsman (fig. VII.20e). The risk, which is acceptable for a racing boat, lies in the fact that mooring lines, lobster pot gear and floating debris can get caught on the leading edge of the rudder or, worse still, in the gap between the forward part of the rudder and the hull.

Apart from these practical inconveniences, which have been resolved to some extent today in modern boats by reverting to more pronounced rake, by eliminating half of the forward surface of the blade (fig. VII.20f) and by fairing in the rudder, there are some disadvantages to a spade rudder.

When the helm is not being held, and provided that the stock is far enough forward, the rudder will automatically line itself up with the direction of movement; its stabilizing effect is therefore nil, and it has to be manned continuously.

The streamlines will separate at a relatively low angle of incidence of about 11–14°, depending on the section of the blade. This is remedied (to some minor extent) by using a thick section, and this has the advantage of enabling the diameter of the stock to be sufficiently great for strength to be adequate. Drag, on the other hand, is increased.

Generally the feel of the helm is not very pleasant with this type of rudder, especially when the part forward of the stock is large, because the centre of pressure can shift to a position forward of the stock, and that reverses the action of the tiller. This is avoided by never placing the stock further aft than about 20% from the leading edge.

The efficiency of this type of rudder can be found from the ratio δ/λ as before. The formula becomes

$$\frac{\delta}{\lambda} = \frac{\lambda r}{\lambda k} - 1,$$

where

$$\frac{\lambda r}{\lambda k} = \frac{Fr}{Fk} \times \frac{Ar}{Ak} \times \frac{c_r}{c_k}$$

and

$$\frac{Fr}{Fk} = \frac{\Delta X_{cp}}{LWL} \bigg/ \left(\frac{E}{LWL} - \frac{\Delta X_{cp}}{LWL} \right),$$

F being the force developed by the rudder and the keel, A their area, c their coefficient, E the distance between their centres of pressure and LWL waterline length (fig. VII.24b). Given E/LWL = 0.6, Ar/Ak = 0.1 and similarly shaped keel and rudder so that $c_r = c_k$:

$$\frac{Fr}{Fk} = 0.2, \frac{\lambda r}{\lambda k} = 2 \quad \text{and} \quad \frac{\delta}{\lambda} = 1.$$

This is a major improvement over the preceding rudder configuration, and because the improvement will be more marked as the distance between the two centres increases, it is tempting to move the keel forward as far as possible and the rudder right aft. It should not be forgotten, however, that the former should have the effect of reducing stability and that, as regards the latter, the upper part of the rudder of modern boats is often seen to leave the water as a result of heeling and the modification of trim this causes; this is doubly harmful because the effective area is reduced and ventilation is also more likely (fig. VII.25).

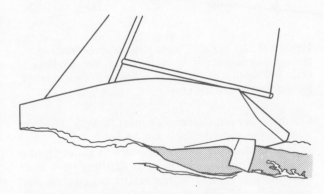

Figure VII.25 *This view of the New Zealand Half Tonner* Rangiri *shows to what point the rudder of a modern sailing boat can lose efficiency when the boat is heeling.*

Rudder hung on the transom, independent of the keel This type of helm is found essentially on sailing dinghies, and the qualities expected from it vary with the speed of flow, except for drag which, of course, should always be as low as possible. The force developed will be reduced at slow speeds, but that is compensated for by the fact that the turning moment of the hull does not need to be very high. As the forces are low, the area of the blade can be shifted further aft in relation to the axis about which it is hinged (fig. VII.20g). Because the boat is frequently trimmed by the head and heeling to a certain degree at the same time, the upper part of the blade often emerges from the water, and the blade must therefore be deep enough.

All this leads logically to a rudder that is roughly trapezoidal in shape, with its maximum breadth near the bottom and aft of the rudder axis. Although a sliding rudder, as used by the Australians (fig. VII.20h), could be of interest with a view to ad-justing the wetted area most efficiently, it seems to the author that a lifting rudder with the pivot very high (fig. VII.20i) is preferable because turning moment can be kept constant while the area is reduced. This is only worth while in calm waters, however, because shifting the centre of gravity aft would have an adverse effect as soon as the slightest pitching motion started. Furthermore, with this lay-out, it is not possible to ensure the equilibrium of the rudder/tiller assembly on the axis of rotation, and this is the basic requirement without which the helmsman will not be able to feel the boat.

At high speeds, this shift further aft becomes detrimental because too much effort is required at the tiller. The force developed is in any case sufficiently great for there to be no need to increase turning moment further by shifting it further aft. The rudder should also be as far forward as possible on account of pitching motion, so that it does not emerge from the water, and so as to shift the centre of gravity back towards the centre again.

The leading edge will therefore be vertical, and the trailing edge raked forward to reduce to the minimum the length of the section at the level where the rudder pierces the surface (fig. VII.20j). Care is needed, however, because the section here must be thick enough to provide the strength required, and because lowering the centre of pressure increases the heeling couple. It seems to the author that it is wiser to use a semi-elliptical shape which will have the advantage of raising the centre of pressure and, in particular, of reducing induced drag (fig. VII.20k). *Rudder abaft a skeg, independent of the keel* The first boat to adopt this type of rudder (although poorly) was probably the *Star*. It took a long time before it was accepted for seagoing boats, and especially for it to become a logical shape. For example, it did not appear on O. Stephens's boats until about 1965–6, when he used it for a variation of the One Tonner Diana, *Josephine VII*. Some extraordinary monstrosities, 'trawler hatches' and 'barn doors', have been seen masquerading as skeg rudders.

When the helm is let free, the results are better than with a spade rudder because of the presence of the fixed skeg, which has the effect of stabilizing the whole. The results obtained from tank-testing this type of rudder flatly contradict actual experience of its use. If the tests carried out by E. G. van de Stadt's helpers at Delft and published in 1977 are to be believed, a spade rudder hung beneath the hull without a skeg will always be superior as regards both lift and drag to a helm with rudder and skeg, the total area being the same.

It is unfortunate that these tests were only carried out on rudders with blade areas equal to or less than 50% of the blade and skeg combined (the interesting range in fact being between 70% and 80%), but even then the results contradict all earlier studies in the field of trim tabs. The author holds to the conclusions published in a report from the Davidson Laboratory, which may be a great deal older but agrees with other studies on trim tabs. The graph of fig. VII.26 makes it extremely clear how the two types perform, namely that the lift coefficient of the rudder without a skeg is limited by early separation.

It is certain that drag must be higher because, using the same formula as previously, this time

$$\frac{\delta}{\lambda} = \frac{1}{\beta}\left(\frac{\lambda r}{\lambda k} - 1\right),$$

β being the coefficient of efficiency of the rudder/skeg combination (see fig. V.66). When the rudder area is 75% of the total area, and all other measurements are the same as before (fig. VII.24c), β is virtually equal to 0.9 and, therefore,

$$\frac{\delta}{\lambda_r} = 1.11$$

or an increase of hardly more than 10% of helm angle.

In this example, the angle of incidence of the rudder/skeg combination is reduced by 25% by comparison with that of the rudder alone, and the drag of the two combined is therefore practically the same (for angles near 10°) as the drag of the rudder alone. This shows just how important it is to keep skeg area very small.

Another factor that encourages us to keep to about 25% of total chord is the fact that this is roughly where the centre of pressure is found (fig. VII.27). The moment of the rudder force about its axis will not be eliminated, but it will definitely be considerably reduced because three-quarters of the force will act on the skeg, even at a large helm angle.

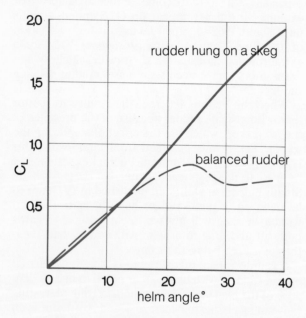

Figure VII.26 *Lift coefficient for a rudder with a skeg, and for a balanced rudder.*

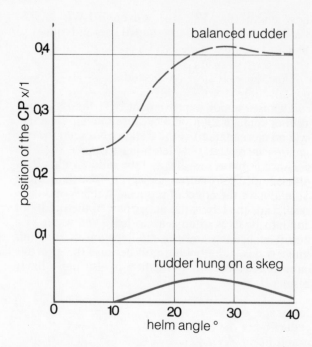

Figure VII.27 *Variation in the position of the centre of pressure as a function of the angle of incidence, in relation to the leading edge of a balanced rudder or to the axis where the rudder is hinged for a rudder hung on a skeg.*

On the other hand, the skeg must be very strong in view of the great loads it has to bear.

The rudder/skeg system appears to suffer from a disadvantage when the helm is fulfilling its role of instigating a change in the boat's course. At that moment the skeg is actually at a negative angle of incidence (fig. VII.28), but if we regard the rudder/skeg combination as a cambered foil, we know that lift is zero at several degrees of negative angle of incidence, and this again means that this configuration is rather better than a pure spade rudder which, in this case, will give the helmsman opposite information when it is deflected through the first few degrees. Note that here too it is an advantage for the skeg to be a small percentage of the chord.

Attempts have been made further to improve the performance of the rudder/skeg combination. Halsey C. Herreshoff has fitted an articulated rudder to several sailing boats; this consists of three parts, the

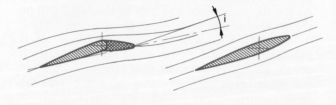

Figure VII.28 *The rudder with skeg develops a little thrust even at a small negative angle of incidence, whereas at the same helm angle and zero incidence the balanced rudder delivers no thrust.*

central one fixed and linked to two movable parts forward and aft (fig. VII.29a). Instead of pivoting like an ordinary rudder, lift is created by altering the shape of the section.

Then there is Georgio Falck who tried to reconcile the advantages of the rudder alone with those of the rudder/skeg combination. His patented rudder consists of three hinged parts with an internal linkage system which enables angulation to increase progressively (fig. VII.29b). The leading edge is therefore never at a negative angle of incidence, and total efficiency is very high. Used by, among others, *Southern Cross* in 1974 for the America's Cup, the results appear not to have been very conclusive. The complexity and fragility of the linkage, the weight and friction of the whole assembly, plus an extra hinge, may at least partly explain why this theoretically interesting helm system yielded inconclusive results.

An extremely important point affecting the performance of the rudder/skeg combination is the reduction of the gap between the two parts, and the graph in fig. VII.30 shows the loss of rudder efficiency with the increase in the size of the slot. In the case of a racing boat, it is essential to fit strips so that the gap between the two is closed.

The planform of the whole assembly can be basically either elliptical (fig. II.20l) or trapezoidal (fig. VII.20m). In both cases it is very important that the upper edge of the rudder blade should almost brush the bottom of the hull when the helm is put over. If the stock is also raked as indicated in Chapter V.C2, p. 000, to match the rake required for keels as a function of their aspect ratio, all the conditions for optimum efficiency of the whole lateral plane will have been fulfilled.

As is the case for ballast keels and centreboards, the shape and vertical cross section of the lower edge of the rudder are very important. Given a trapezoidal planform, the lower edge should slope down aft slightly, and have a 'V' section so as to allow for pitching angles and to reduce induced resistance (fig. VII.31a). However, when the very important vertical component of flow caused by pitching is taken into account, a more curved shape (fig. VII.31b) can be justified.

Occasionally compromise solutions are found, with a skeg forward of the upper part of the blade and the lower part balanced to some degree (fig. VII.20n). This semi-balanced rudder is certainly the worst arrangement that could be imagined. For one thing, on the practical side, the 'shears' formed by the skeg and the balanced part of the rudder excel at catching any cordage or plastic bags in their path, and these effectively jam the helm. These shears are also the cause of major eddies which disturb flow over much of the area. Finally, when one half of the rudder is at the correct angle of incidence, the other half is not.

This system is most often adopted when hulls are made of GRP because construction is simplified.

c Rudder sections

So far as its function of developing maximum lift for minimum drag is concerned, the rudder would be

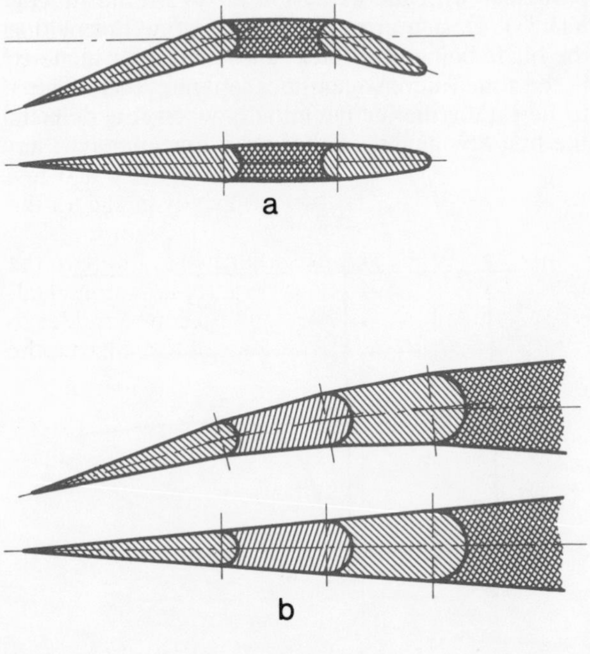

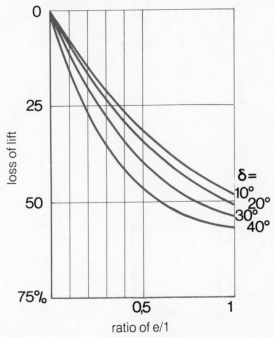

Figure VII.30 *Loss of thrust of a rudder as a function of the helm angle and the ratio between the gap separating it from the skeg, e, to its length, l.*

Figure VII.29 *Two types of articulated rudders: (a) H. C. Herreshoff; (b) G. Falck for the 12-metre* Southern Cross.

fundamentally similar to the ballast keel were it not for the fact that it is required to work at a greater angle of incidence. This is why, in the case of spade rudders without a skeg, there is a temptation to revert to thick sections so as to delay the separation angle, and this also makes it possible to fit a stock of reasonable diameter, as is required to provide adequate strength. It would be a mistake to carry this too far, however, because it must be remembered that drag increases proportionately, particularly at small angles. In practice it seems that optimum thickness is at about 12%, which corresponds to the NACA 0012 section with maximum thickness at 30% and a relatively blunt leading edge (table V.IV, p. 000). It is the latter that in fact enables the angle of stall to be delayed.

However, as with ballast keels and centreboards, interesting results can be obtained with a foil that has a changing section, maximum thickness being nearer the trailing edge at the top than at the bottom of the rudder. This is true of a transom-hung rudder in particular (especially of a sailing dinghy); its section should be lenticular at water level so as to pierce the surface with the minimum of disturbance (page 00). A good way to reduce ventilation and

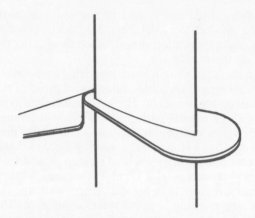

Figure VII.32 *Rudder fence fitted to the rudder of a racing dinghy as the extension of the bottom of the hull, to limit the risk of ventilation.*

improve the effective aspect ratio of these rudders would seem to be to fit a fence, positioned to form a prolongation of the sides of the hull and matched to their shape at the forward end (fig. VII.32). For a rudder with a skeg, the section could change as the ratio rudder chord/total chord changes, assuming that, as is generally the case, this ratio is not constant. The section should not be as thick as in the former case.

It goes without saying that laminar profiles have no application to rudders, which are always situated where flow is more or less turbulent.

Nowadays the upper part of a rudder is often integral with the lines of the afterbody, and in particular with the extension aft of the bustle (fig. VII.33). Design errors here have sometimes led to the blade being very thick, and the rudder then acts in the zone where streamlines separate; this causes it to be totally ineffective initially when it is delected the first few degrees either side. Fortunately, there

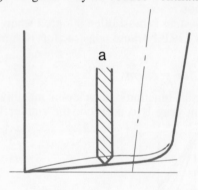

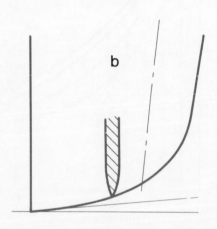

Figure VII.31 *Shapes for the bottom of the rudder: (a) inclined bottom edge with a 'V' section; (b) curved bottom edge with an ogival section.*

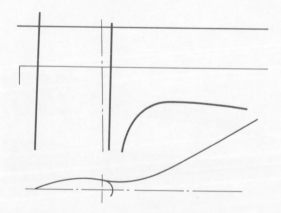

Figure VII.33 *Waterlines between the bustle and the skeg should be concave to encourage retaining the flow and reduce the phenomenon of separation.*

has been a return to a more normal shape, but it is still true that when the rudder is fitted aft of a vertical connection between the keel and the skeg, the connecting part should be thinner upstream of the skeg to encourage re-attachment of flow.

d Propeller apertures

When sailing boats have rudders hung as an extension of the keel, there are several possible positions for the propeller aperture, and this is sometimes also the case with rudders hung on a skeg. The most common arrangement is for the aperture to be midway between the keel and the rudder (fig. VII.34a) so that the propeller can be removed from the shaft when the rudder is put over. The size of the total aperture can then be reduced to the minimum, but rudder performance under engine is slightly worse because the blade barely benefits from the extra speed of the accelerated water from the propeller.

The best solution is to place the aperture a little way forward of the stock (fig. VII.34b), and the water accelerated by the propeller will then affect the maximum area of the rudder. Performance will be equally good on either tack and in either direction forward or backward (apart from propeller torque). The disadvantage is that the propeller shaft cannot be removed from outboard, unless it has been installed at a slight angle to the centreline, which arrangement also helps to compensate for propeller torque.

So as to allow for the rotation of the jet of water from the propeller, the horizontal sections ahead of and abaft the aperture should be bevelled so that they are opposite in shape (as in fig. VII.34e and f). This has a marked effect, and improves the performance of both the screw and the rudder.

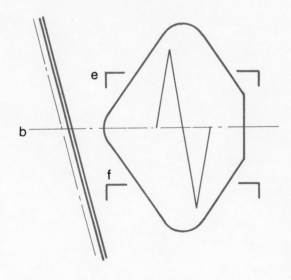

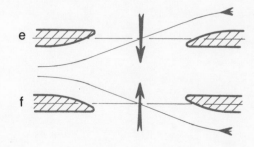

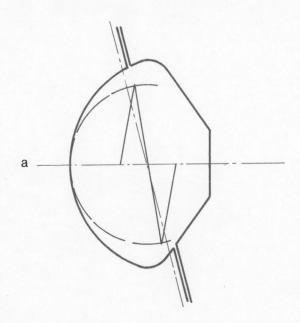

Figure VII.34 *Propeller apertures: (a) the aperture midway between the ballast keel and the rudder enables the propeller to be removed easily from its shaft, but considerably reduces rudder efficiency. (b) the aperture enclosed entirely in the keel is much more efficient, but although the screw can be removed if the aperture is large enough, the shaft can only be withdrawn from inside the hull. The efficiency of the screw is considerably improved by bevelling the edges of the aperture as shown above at e and f, for a right-handed propeller.*

VIII

Combination of Hull/Sails and Balance

1 Defining the hull movements

The motion of a boat's hull can be described in terms of translations or movements along and rotations about three reference axes (fig. VIII.1):

the fore-and-aft or x axis: surge and roll
the transverse or y axis: sway and pitch
the vertical or z axis: heave and yaw

Motion can equally well be referred to three planes (fig. VIII.2):

the vertical/fore-and-aft plane xz: pitch and the combined motion of surge and heave
the vertical/transverse plane yz: roll and the combined motion of sway and heave
horizontal plane xy: yaw and the combined motion of surge and sway.

Obviously it is extremely rare for the hull to react in only one of these three ways because the average direction of wave propagation rarely coincides with the course of the sailing boat; the only exceptions are when both wind and sea are dead astern or perpendicular to her course. It is also very rare to sail in a sea resulting from a single wave system: a sea is usually formed by the superposition of several systems of waves of different sizes and direction (see Chapter I).

The only reason for the reference system just defined is that it makes it easier to analyse the boat's movements when they are related to the axes or to the planes of the hull.

The hull can actually be said to be subject to two types of movements: a circular movement roughly in a plane that corresponds to the average direction of the waves and slightly to either side of this mean direction, a movement that will combine the three translations: surge, heave and sway; and a complex oscillatory movement combining the three rotations: pitch, roll and yaw.

If we remember wave theory (see Chapter I), it is easy to understand that the circular movement is linked directly to the orbital motion of water particles in the wave, while the oscillations are due to the wave slope and the resulting local height of water level. It therefore becomes easier to understand, analyse and define a theory of motion.

In order to do so we will imagine the hull as being made up of numerous vertical cells (fig. VIII.3) which could be compared to a mooring buoy, for example. To study oscillatory movement and circular movement we will start by considering the behaviour of one of these cells.

2 Motion of a buoy

a In calm water

Our buoy, which we will suppose to be cylindrical to avoid complications, has mass and a certain volume. If we exert an instantaneous vertical force on the buoy, it will move downwards and, in doing so, a greater volume will be immersed, resulting in the creation of an additional hydrostatic force which opposes the downward displacement of the buoy. The first force is the exciting force, which provides the buoy with kinetic energy; this energy is absorbed by the opposing work of the hydrostatic force which, in turn, passes back to the buoy the energy needed to make it rise again (fig. VIII.4).

If we record the vertical motion of the buoy (fig. VIII.5), a sinusoidal curve is obtained, with a constant period but progressively decreasing amplitude, because the buoy's movement is damped, first on account of friction between the water and the buoy and, second, due to the formation of a wave-making system which is caused by the variation in the volume of water displaced. Both of these progressively absorb the energy imparted initially.

A body moving in water will obviously carry with it an adjacent mass of water, and the total mass in motion to consider — the apparent mass — will be equal to the mass of the body itself plus the additional entrained mass. The latter is a very important factor when hull motion is studied, and its value depends on the shape of the hull in the direction of movement; the mass is equal to M/2 for a sphere or a vertical cylinder, and to M for a horizontal cylinder. For a sailing boat's hull it can amount almost to 2M when she is rolling.

A simple heave is the movement that we have given to the buoy, and its period (for small amplitudes)

$$T_z = 2\pi \frac{M(1 + X_z)}{c},$$

where M is the mass of the buoy and X_z the coefficient of the entrained mass of water; c is the opposing hydrostatic force, and is equal to

$$\rho \times g \times S$$

(ρ being the specific density of the water, g acceleration due to gravity and S the water plane area of the buoy).

T_z is the period at which the buoy heaves and, as we have seen, its value depends on its mass and shape. For a traditional sailing boat, the period is of the order of 2–2.5 seconds, but it is much less for a light dinghy.

Suppose that we now repeat the force which causes the buoy to move at regular intervals of period T_e. We find that the amplitude of the buoy's

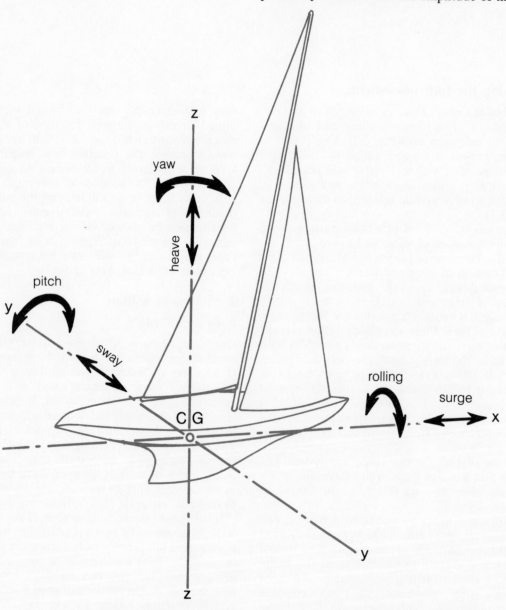

Figure VIII.1   *The motion of a sailing boat in relation to the three axes of reference.*

190

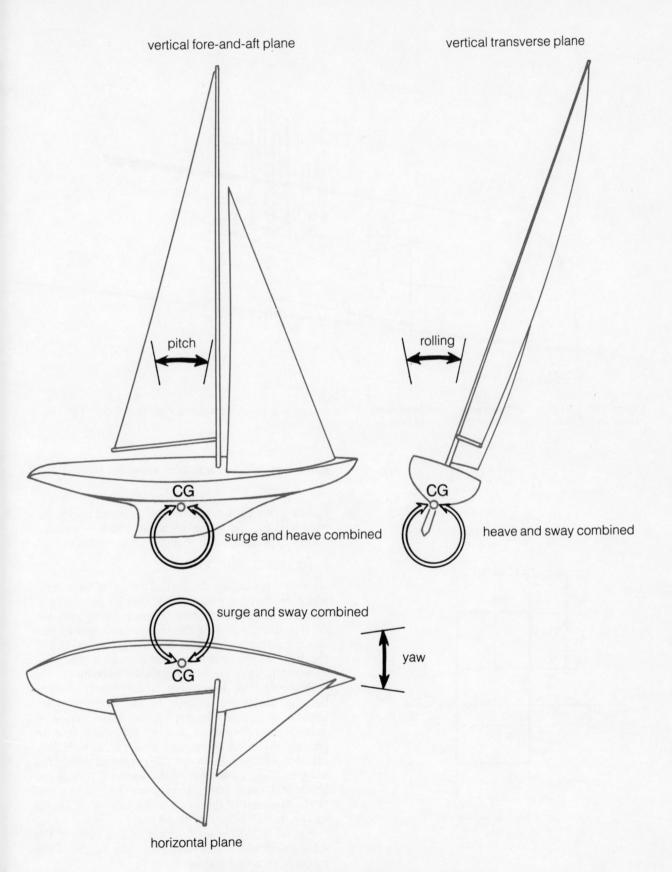

Figure VIII.2   *The motion of a sailing boat in relation to the three planes of reference.*

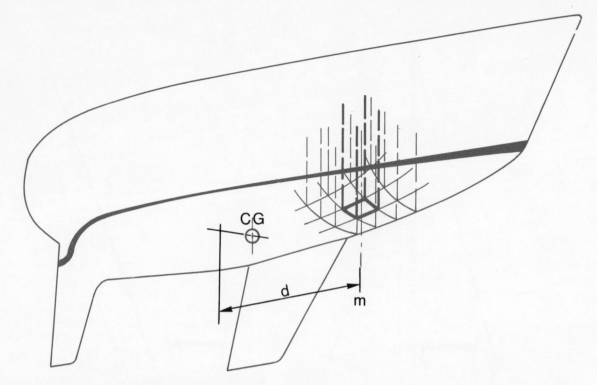

Figure VIII.3 *The sailing boat can be considered as the sum of an infinite number of small cells, each of mass m,* situated at a distance d from the combined centre of gravity.

Figure VIII.4 *Heaving motion of a buoy, excited by an external force.*

movement will be maximum when the ratio

$$\Lambda_z = T_z/T_e$$

is near 1, which is called the condition of resonance (fig. VIII.6); the value of Λ_z at which resonance occurs depends on the damping characteristics.

b In waves

As a boat passes by, she makes a regular wave train which reaches our buoy. It is no longer necessary to excite its movement artifically because the waves will do this. Inertia due to the buoy's mass will in fact cause a certain delay in its reaction to the raising of the level of the water around it, which creates a hydrostatic force that stimulates its movement.

However, this movement is not purely vertical because the orbital motion of the water particles imparts a similar motion to the buoy, which is delayed in relation to that, of the wave (out of phase); the vertical amplitude of the motion is a function of the ratio Λ_z of the period at which the buoy heaves, T_z, to that of the waves T_e, while the horizontal amplitude is simply very close to or equal to the diameter of the water molecules' orbit, that is to say, to the height of the wave.

Fig. VIII.7 gives an example of the ratio of the total amplitude of heaving, Z, to the height of the wave A as a function of Λ_z.

It is instructive to compare our buoy with two extreme and basic cases, one a fishing line hanging

192

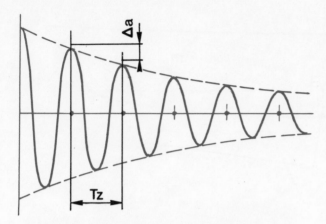

Figure VIII.5 *Recorded movements of the buoy. The linear damping of this movement is indicated by the reduction Δ_a of the amplitude in each cycle at a constant period T_z.*

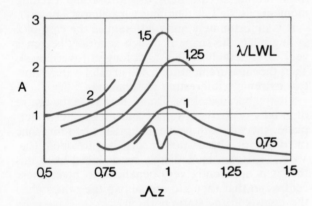

Figure VIII.6 *Variation of amplitude of heave as a function of the ratio Λ_z between the natural period of the hull and the period of encounter of the waves, and for different ratios of the wavelength to waterline length.*

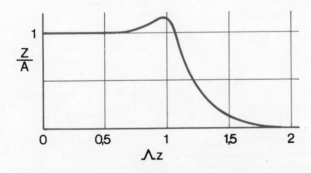

Figure VIII.7 *Curve of the ratio of the total amplitude of heave to the height of the wave as a function of Λ_z.*

straight down with a weight and the other a piece of paper lying on the water. The section of the former is extremely small and, consequently, the exciting force remains virtually zero and the line does not move. On the other hand, although the paper's mass is as small as that of the line, its volume is spread right out over the surface of the water and it therefore exactly follows the movement of the particles on the surface.

3 Pitching

We will now fix two similar buoys at the extremities of a beam. If we excite them with a vertical movement in calm water, they will react together exactly as if each had been excited individually.

It is not the same when the two buoys are among waves. It will not longer be the inertia of their mass alone that delays their being set in motion, but the moment of inertia of this mass in relation to the centre of gravity of the whole, and this moment of inertia is equal to the product of the mass and the square of its distance from the total centre of gravity: $I_g = m \times d^2$ (fig. VIII.8). (The moment of inertia of the buoy itself is estimated as insignificant.)

If we consider that the boat's hull is made up of a multitude of small buoys, each of mass m, and situated at a distance d from the total centre of gravity, then

$$I_g = \Sigma m \times d^2 = Mk_y^2 = \frac{\Delta k}{g} y^2,$$

k_y being the radius of longitudinal gyration of the mass M of the boat.

In the case of pitching, I_g becomes I_y, the axis is y, which passes through the centre of gravity, and the value of k_y is roughly 25% of the total length of the hull.

With regard to the period of pitching, when amplitude is small:

$$T_{\theta y} = 2\pi \sqrt{\frac{I_y(1 + X_{\theta y})}{c}},$$

where I is the boat's mass moment of inertia in relation to axis y, $X_{\theta y}$ is the coefficient relating to the entrained mass, and C the resisting hydrostatic moment equals $\Delta(r_y - a)$, product of the displacement and the longitudinal metacentric height. Equally this can be written as

$$T_{\theta y} = 2\pi k_{\theta y} \sqrt{\frac{1 + X_{\theta y}}{g(r_y - a)}} \text{ because } k_{\theta y} = \frac{M}{I_y},$$

$k_{\theta}y$ being the radius of the gyration of M about y.

The actual period of pitching of a traditional sailing boat is generally slightly longer at about 2.5 seconds than that of heaving, but drops to about 1.5 seconds for a light dinghy.

The coefficient of the moment of inertia of the entrained mass is lower than that of the mass alone. For a Half Tonner, a value of 0.69 has been found as against 1.85 for the mass alone.

193

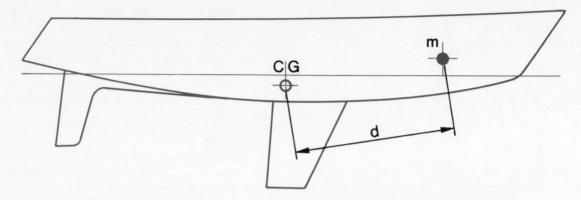

Figure VIII.8 *The moment of inertia in relation to the axis passing through the centre of gravity of a mass m situated at* *a distance d from the centre of gravity is equal to the product of the mass by the square of the distance.*

When the sailing boat is moving at a certain speed, the period of encounter with waves will be a combination of the two speeds:

$$T_e = \frac{\lambda \cos \mu}{V + C},$$

where $\lambda \cos \mu$ represents the effective length of the waves when they are not moving in line with the boat's course. At 0° and 180°, $\cos \mu = 1$, and effective λ is equal to λ; for 90° and 270°, $\cos \mu = 0$, effective λ is equal to infinity, and the boat is no longer pitching, only rolling.

As with heaving, it is in the region of $\Lambda_{\theta y} = 1$ that the amplitude of pitching motion is greatest, as can be seen in fig. VIII.9.

But Λ is not the only parameter that affects amplitude; the ratio between wavelength λ and waterline length LWL depends on speed (fig. VIII.10). It can be noted in particular that the amplitude of the motion only becomes appreciable above a ratio of 0.75.

So far, with a few exceptions, studies elaborating the theory of movement in waves have been related to the hulls of large ships rather than sailing boats. Because ships' hulls generally have almost vertical sides, and the extremities where the shape curves represent only a very small proportion of the total volume of the hull, the forces and exciting moments as well as damping vary almost linearly.

It is unfortunately quite different in the case of a sailing boat, the shape of which generally becomes very considerably wider and longer (overhangs). Thus the measurements of a 470 in calm water show two extremely interesting phenomena.

Firstly, because of the distance between the centre of gravity of the boat's mass and that of her waterplane, she will both heave and pitch when only one or other of these movements is provoked (fig. VIII.11). It can immediately be deduced from this that it is apparently very beneficial to place these centres so that they are one above the other when the boat is in the static position.

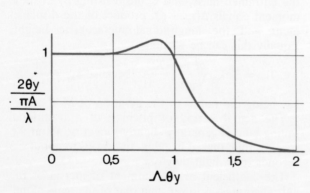

Figure VIII.9 *Curve of the ratio between total amplitude of pitching and the wave slope as a function of $\Lambda_{\theta y}$.*

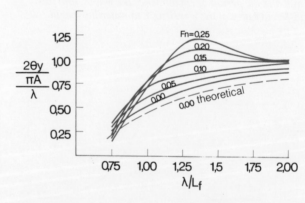

Figure VIII.10 *Curves of the ratio of total amplitude of pitch to the slope of the wave as a function of the wavelength/hull length ratio for different Froude numbers. It will be noticed that speed reduces pitching in small waves, but when waves grow higher speed increases pitching.*

194

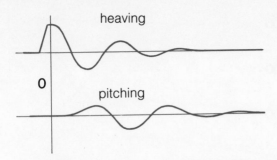

heaving

0

pitching

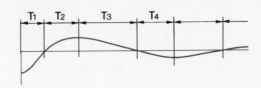

T_1 T_2 T_3 T_4

Figure VIII.12   *The asymmetry of the shape forward and aft of the 470 causes a non-linear damping which is evident from the variation of the time of each quarter of the period.*

Figure VIII.11   *In a hull of asymmetric shape, like that of a 470, a heaving motion causes the associated motion of pitching because of the longitudinal shift of the centre of gravity of the mass of the boat and the centre of gravity of its waterplane.*

Secondly, because the considerable difference between the volumes forward and aft leads to asymmetrical longitudinal movement of the centre of gravity of the waterplane, the shapes of the curves registered are modified very noticeably and, in particular, the various quarters of the phase are of irregular duration (fig. VIII.12).

Because of the boat's own speed, and the interaction resulting from the speed of sea waves and the waves she forms herself (waves of translation), the shapes of the seas are much modified, in particular between the instant that they arrive at one end of the boat and when they leave at the other end; obviously their effect cannot therefore be the same from one end of the hull to the other. In a head sea, particularly, this justifies increasing the volume immediately above the static waterline to a lesser degree forward than near the stern, at least to the extent that the length of the sea wave differs from the length of the wave corresponding to hull speed.

Another factor is always involved when considering pitching in a head sea and the relative size that these volumes should be, namely the direction of the velocity of water molecules in the various parts of the wave. Gilbert Lamboley's study determining the method of checking the centre of gravity and the radius of gyration of a Finn shows this very clearly.

In the first half of the ascending back of the wave (fig. VIII.13a) the direction of molecule velocity thrusts the hull forward and mainly lifts the stern. In the upper half of the ascending wave back, velocity is directed aft, the hull is slowed down, the stern is lifted and the bow tends to bury itself (fig. VIII.13b). Deceleration is greatest at the crest, and extends over the first half of the descending face of the wave; the tendency to bury the bow continues to increase (fig. VIII.13c). It can readily be understood why the crew should shift further aft. Only on the second half of the descending face does hull trim become positive again, and thrust is directed forward (fig. VIII.13d).

As regards shape, therefore, no research so far has enabled criteria to be defined with a view to obtaining a good pitching motion. In a head sea, the volume forward definitely should not balance volume aft, but how great the difference between them should be is a matter that is decided only by the skill and, above all, by the experience of the designer.

The effect of one factor has been established, however, even if its application is not easy, and that is the effect of the moment of inertia.

a Effect of the longitudinal moment of inertia on pitching

In order to delay for as long as possible the time when the natural period of the hull synchronizes with wave period, the hull period can be reduced.

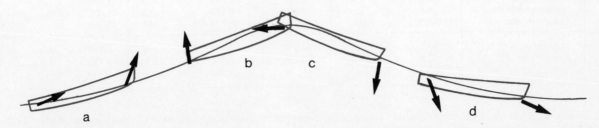

Figure VIII.13   *The direction of the molecules of water in the wave means that different parts of the hull are lifted,* causing the bow to sink at the crest of the wave and the stern to sink in the trough.

If we revert to the formula

$$T_y = 2\pi \frac{\sqrt{I_y(1 + X_{\theta y})}}{c}$$

it is clear that there are two alternatives, either to reduce I_y or to increase C. As C is equal to $\Delta(r_y - a)$ one or other of these two factors would have to be increased. To increase displacement Δ would have the effect of increasing I_y as well, because

$$I_y = \frac{\Delta \times k}{g}.$$

On the other hand r_y, being equal to I_{wy} (I_{wy} is the moment of inertia of the waterplane around the transverse axis), would be reduced (a is virtually constant). An increase in Δ would lead not to a reduction but to an increase in $T_{\theta y}$. It is therefore preferable to reduce Δ, and this would also mean a reduction in the entrained mass of water.

To increase metacentric height $r_y - a$ would again mean increasing I_{wy}, the moment of inertia of the waterplane, but unfortunately the result would be an accompanying increase in the entrained mass, and of its coefficient of inertia $X_{\theta y}$: result nil. The only way therefore is to reduce I_y, that is either M (or Δ) or $k_{\theta y}$.

If the minimum weight of the boat is fixed by a building rule or cannot be reduced without strength being affected, reduction of $k_{\theta y}$ is the only answer, and it is then a question of reducing to the minimum the distance between the boat's centre of gravity and the individual masses that make up the boat, in other words to concentrate weight as near her centre of

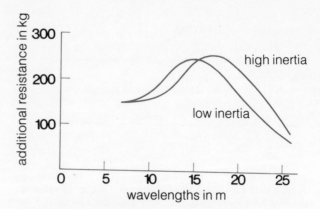

Figure VIII.14 *Variation in additional resistance due to the pitching motion of the two 12-metres whose moments of inertia differ, as a function of wavelength.*

gravity as possible.

The relative influence of the different components of a sailing boat are interesting, and an article that appeared in the American magazine *Sail*[4] gives us details (table VIII.I) relating to a Flying Dutchman measured by the Lamboley method at the time of the 1976 Olympics.

The importance of the mast is very noticeable; although it weighs only 8.4% of the total weight of the boat, it contributes 30.8% of the moment of inertia. The contributions of the sails and the helm are similar. On the other hand, although the crew increase total weight by 111%, they only raise the

TABLE VIII.I

Component	Mass M kg	Mass %	Radius of gyration k m	Centre of gravity h m	Centre of gravity l m	Moment of inertia k_eff m	Moment of inertia I kg m²	Moment of inertia %
Hull	125.1	74.2	1.526	−0.300	2.897	1.571	308.9	50.3
Mast	14.1	8.4	2.068	2.996	3.667	3.664	189.3	30.8
Boom	3.7	2.2	0.821	0.765	2.219	1.263	5.9	1.0
Mainsail	3.2	1.9	1.650	2.933	2.692	3.306	35.0	5.7
Genoa	2.6	1.5	1.424	1.750	3.715	2.350	14.4	2.3
Rudder and tiller	5.1	3.0	0.545	−0.265	−0.050	3.004	46.0	7.5
Centreboard	6.6	3.9	0.387	−0.880	3.000	1.036	7.1	1.2
Anchor, cable etc	8.1	4.8	0.904	−0.220	3.200	1.002	8.1	1.3
Complete boat	168.5	100.0		0.074	2.885	1.910	614.6	100.0
Helmsman	90.0	53.4	0.130	0.150	1.800	0.718	46.4	7.5
Crew	97.0	57.6	0.130	0.150	2.500	0.135	1.8	0.3
Total	355.5	211.0		0.114	2.505	1.390	687.3	111.8

Because the centre of gravity referred to is that of the boat without crew, the calculation of the moments of inertia based on the complete boat has to take into account the change in its position. Thus, given H = helmsman and c = crew:

$$I = I_b + M_b(h_T - h_b)^2 + (l_b - l_T)^2 + M_H\{k_H^2 + (h_H - h_T)^2 + (l_H - l_T)^2\} + M_c\{k_c^2 + (h_c - h_T)^2 + (l_c - l_T)^2\}$$

total moment of inertia 11.8%.

Reduction of the radius of gyration is not only important in theory, but is proved to be so in practice both when it comes to tank testing and on the water.

One of the first studies on this theme[5] carried out on the 12-metre Sovereign at the Stevens Institute shows the difference in added resistance when the hull is the same but the moments of inertia are different (fig. VIII.14).

b Increase in resistance to forward motion due to pitching

Because of pitching, the driving force produced by the sails is reduced on account of the movement of the rig and of the rapid variation in the apparent wind resulting from this but, in addition, there is also an increase in resistance when sailing into head seas.

Movement is virtually proportional to wave height A, but resistance is roughly proportional to the square of wave height (A^2), adjusted for the effects of displacement, the radius of gyration and boat speed.

The graph in fig. VIII.14 shows the increase in resistance as a function of speed for two different radii of gyration, while that in fig. VIII.15 shows the increase of resistance as a function of wave encounter for two different radii of gyration.

J. Gerritsma and G. Moeyes in some very important research at the Delft laboratory analysed the effect that displacement has on increasing resistance. The waterline length of the three hulls tested was 10 m, and they had the same beam, the same draught, the same radius of gyration and the same IOR rating, but their displacements were respective-ly (I) 8207 kg, (II) 9795 kg, (III) 10 670 kg (fig. VIII.16).

The graph in fig. VIII.17 shows how resistance, when heeling and leeway are ignored, increases with the height of the waves. Although the increase is greater when displacement is lower, the absolute value is lowest when displacement is lowest. When we add to this the fact that, when close-hauled, heeling and induced drag increase total resistance by 59%, 66% and 74% for the three hulls I, II and III respectively, the difference in terms of Vmg shows how great the advantage is of the boat with the lightest hull (fig. VIII.18).

Lightening the hull should not be carried to ex-cess, however, because experience shows that at slower speeds a sailing boat that lacks kinetic energy will be stopped rapidly by short seas.

4 Rolling

a Rolling on points of sailing other than with the wind aft

Except when running dead before the wind, or nearly so, it is not usually the motion of rolling that affects a sailing boat most.

The moments developed are small (in proportion to beam), and the whole of the lateral area and the sails have a strong damping effect. Even when the slope of the wave raises the windward side of the hull and tends to increase the heeling angle, the capsizing couple resulting from the wind decreases, because wind pressure is reduced by the sway to leeward that accompanies the movement. In addition there is a very great entrained mass of water on account of the large area of the lateral plane.

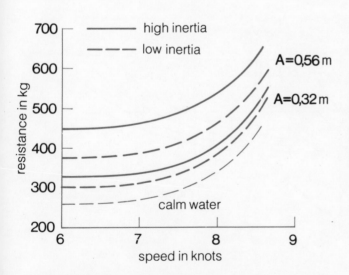

Figure VIII.15   *Increase in resistance of the two 12-metres with different moments of inertia, for two heights of waves which are 20 m in length.*

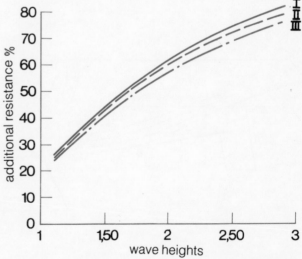

Figure VIII.17   *Percentage increase in the resistance of three models tested at Delft as a function of wave height.*

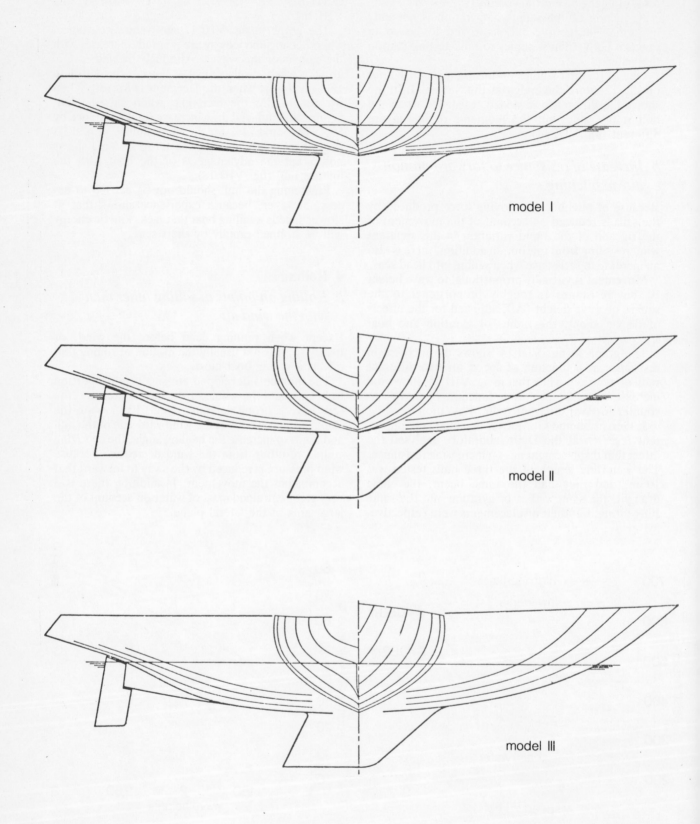

Figure VIII.16   *The three models tested at Delft.*

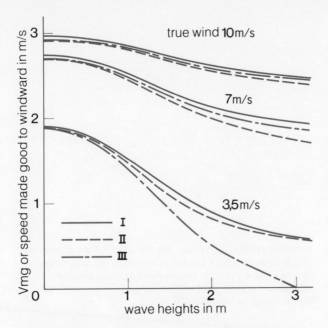

Figure VIII.18 *Variation in Vmg of the three models tested at Delft, as a function of wave heights in three different wind strengths. Note the considerable handicap of the heavy boat in light weather.*

A circular movement accompanies rolling, and is exactly analogous to what occurs when pitching; this time the combination is heave and sway, but it always exists, however much rolling damps itself. When the boat is moving forward, the direction of the streamlines acting on the hull draws nearer to the axis; this increases the lateral components of the forces which contribute to damping the motion (fig. VIII.19). The faster the boat moves, the greater will the damping effect be.

The formulae for roll are as for pitching, but this time

$$T_{\theta x} = 2\pi \sqrt{\frac{I_x(1 + X_{\theta x})}{C'}},$$

where $T_{\theta x}$ is the boat's natural period of roll, I_x the moment of inertia of the mass of the sailing boat in relation to axis x, $X_{\theta x}$ the coefficient of the moment of inertia of the entrained mass, C' the moment of hydrostatic resistance; $\Delta(r_x - a)$ is the product of displacement and transverse metacentric height. Equally, where $k_{\theta x}$ is the transverse radius of gyration,

$$T_{\theta x} = 2\pi k_{\theta x} \sqrt{\frac{1 + X_{\theta x}}{g(r_x - a)}}.$$

The value of the boat's natural period of roll affects the comfort of a sailing boat greatly in a beam sea, particularly when she is anchored. Whereas in the case of pitching the aim is to reduce the period, the opposite is required for rolling. A hull with a short natural rolling period, such as a catamaran, will respond immediately to every action of the waves, and will stay virtually constantly on an even keel. The amplitude of her roll will be equal to the slope of the waves, which is always fairly small. When a crest passes, on the other hand, a movement of little amplitude is produced, but it is rapid and therefore jerky (fig. VIII.20a), causing high accelerations. If the wave height increases, together with the angle of the slopes, the motion can become really harsh, causing fatigue to both crew and rigging.

A hull with a long period (high $k_{\theta x}$ or low metacentric height) has weak accelerations and its angular movements are always much slower, although their amplitude is greater (fig. VIII.19).

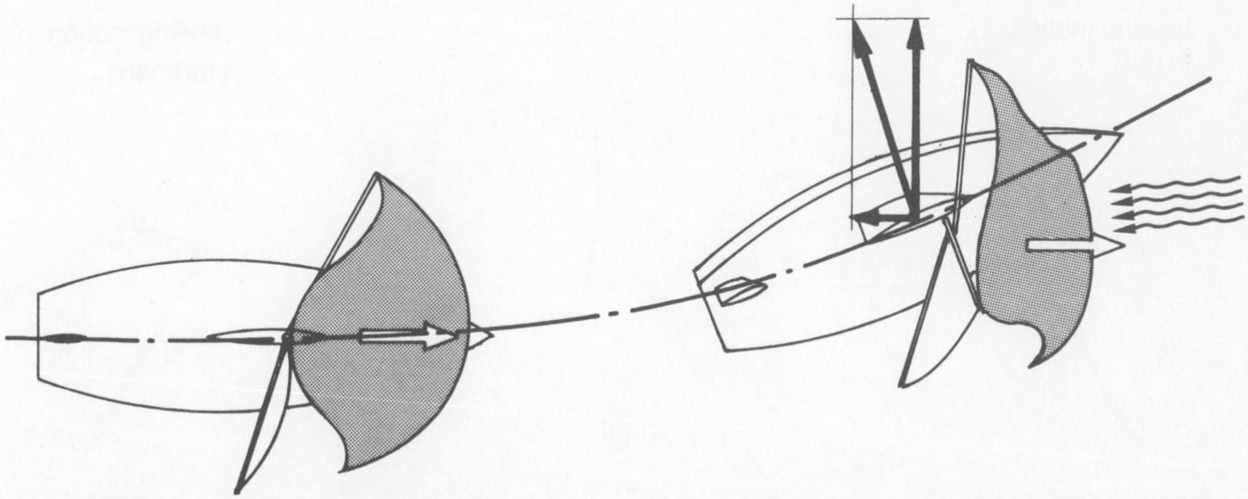

Figure VIII.19 *The moment that the boat starts to yaw, the angle of incidence of the lateral plane causes a lateral force to appear. Heeling is the result of this and, together with the effect of centrifugal force, they shift the driving force to leeward; if the spinnaker starts to lift, even fractionally, the boat will luff more sharply and this cannot be corrected by helm action.*

199

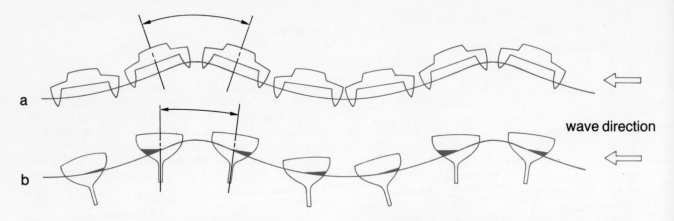

a

b

wave direction

Figure VIII.20   *When rolling, a light hull with great initial stability, like that of a catamaran (a), will follow the movement of the surface of the water almost exactly, and the result is that at the crest there is a movement of considerabe amplitude in a short space of time, and* *therefore great acceleration. On the other hand a classic hull (b), heavier and with less initial stability, will in the same period of time perform a movement of much smaller amplitude; acceleration will be less and the motion felt by the crew will be much kinder.*

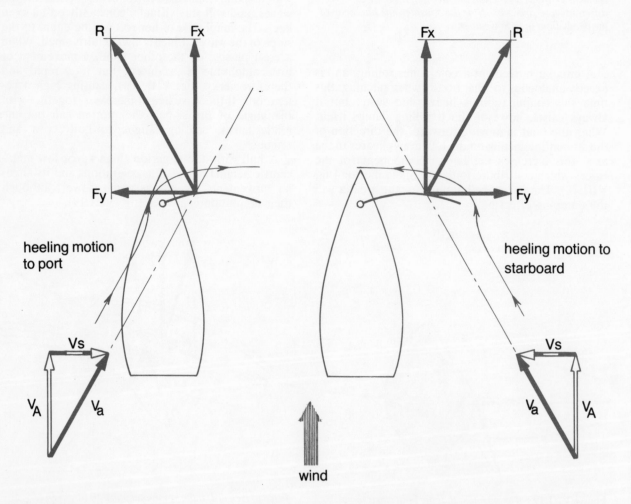

heeling motion to port

heeling motion to starboard

wind

Figure VIII.21   *The apparent wind is changed in strength, and especially in direction, according to which side the boat is heeling, and this has the effect of reversing the flow over* *the sail and of causing a lateral component of driving force to appear which acts in the direction of motion.*

200

Hulls with a very short period therefore have a rolling period very close to or equal to the wave periods, as is the case with pitching. But that of a hull with a long natural period is a combination of its natural period and wave period, the former generally being dominant; the amplitude of roll will be greatest when the two periods are synchronous.

Unlike pitching, rolling can be improved by spreading weight out towards the sides; this is always preferable to reducing metacentric height, which would prejudice stability. On keelboats, metacentric height is generally about 0.90 m to 1 m; if it exceeds 1 m, rolling motion becomes more and more uncomfortable.

When under way in a beam sea, it is possible to avoid synchronization of rolling with wave periods by altering course. Unfortunately the change of course has to be quite large (roughly 45°) to be really effective.

b Rhythmic rolling

Quite apart from any question of comfort, there is one form of rolling that can become very dangerous and compromise the boat's safety; it does not originate from waves, however. This is rhythmic rolling, which generally occurs when running under a spinnaker with the wind aft, and often causes light dinghies to capsize or at least to broach, luffing up sharply to windward; larger boats may heel right over to 90° as they broach. This is every helmsman's nightmare.

The relatively simple causes of rhythmic rolling have been explained by C. A. Marchaj at Southampton University,[7] the main two being of aerodynamic origin:
— First, the self-excited effect of the motion of a wing in its plane by lift (a phenomenon confirmed by insect flight).
— Second, oscillation arising from the formation of Bénard and Karman alternating vortices (see Chapter II. 3f. p.40

The equipment used in a wind tunnel by C. A. Marchaj enabled him to oscillate a sail with dimensions of a Finn sail, scaled down to 1/5 in size; the exciting force and damping were controlled, and the driving force developed was recorded.

The first result obtained was that, even when the amplitude of rolling was great, driving force was not reduced more than 2%. The second was that, once rolling had started for some reason, and in spite of no other external disturbance, the statically stable boat could become dynamically unstable when the demands of the sail exceeded the hull's ability to damp them; in other words, when the lateral component of the energy developed by the sail could not be absorbed by the sum of the hull's potential energy (i.e. righting moment) and kinetic energy (i.e. the damping force of mass inertia, including that of the entrained mass) plus frictional and wave-making forces.

To understand how self-induced oscillation can develop, we will take a una-rigged sailing boat running with the wind aft (fig. VIII.21). If the boat starts to roll for some reason such as a wave, shifting crew weight etc., the force and direction of the apparent wind on the sail will be altered, and this causes the direction of driving force developed by the sails to shift towards the side to which the boat rolls (a), causing a lateral component F_y to appear. (The driving component F_x may well be found to have increased at this moment, particularly when the apparent wind is slight as in light breezes. The increase due to rolling is then very important, and artificial rolling would be widely used when racing were it not forbidden by the racing rules. The gain in driving force cannot all be utilized because of the additional resistance at the hull and appendages which results from their lateral displacement.)

The energy developed by F_y, added to that of the force that started the rolling initially, is absorbed by the potential energy of the hull's righting moment and various damping forces.

The rolling motion will therefore stop at a certain angle of heel before starting off again in the opposite direction in response to stored kinetic energy. Flow over the sail then reverses, as does the direction of driving force (b). The new lateral component adds its energy to the boat's kinetic energy.

While righting moment and the damping forces are able to absorb all this energy, the amplitude of rolling will be decreased (fig. VIII.22a) or at worst remain constant (fig. VIII.22b), and dynamic equilibrium will be stable, but if the amount of energy becomes greater than the hull is able to absorb, the rolling will increase in amplitude (fig. VIII.23), dynamic equilibrium will become unstable, and this will lead to capsizing.

This phenomenon can be illustrated perfectly with the help of a pendulum consisting of a weight suspended on a string. A gentle push sideways on the weight (moderate by comparison with the initial push,) and the amplitude of the swing will diminish progressively. A slightly harder push, and amplitude will remain constant, but push harder still and the pendulum could even swing right round in a circle.

An important factor, which is the sole responsibility of the helmsman, can aggravate the harmful effect of the sails. When the boat rolls, the lateral distance between the driving force and the resistance of the hull will vary, and the asymmetry of shape will lead to a gyrating moment; balance will be modified continually, causing the boat to yaw, her tendency being to alter course towards the opposite side to that in which she is rolling. The helmsman's instinctive reaction is to put the helm over towards the same side to which she is altering course, but as we saw in Chapter VII.1c, by doing this he is unfortunately more than likely to cause an extra capsizing moment to appear, and the effect of centrifugal force will be added to this.

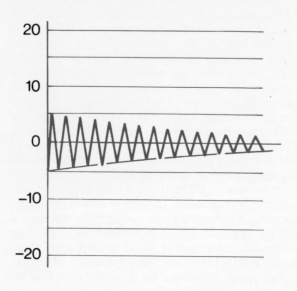

a

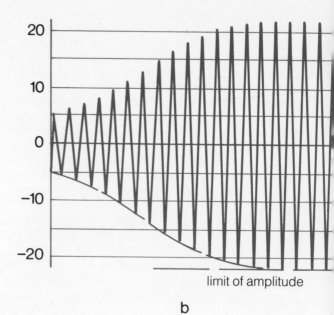

limit of amplitude

b

Figure VIII.22 *Equilibrium is stable when the amplitude of the rolling motion decreases (a), or at worst becomes regular (b).*

In a sailing dinghy, where helm action is instantaneous and easily controlled, and the force exerted by the rudder can be raised sufficiently high by lifting the blade, it may be possible to control rhythmic rolling with the helm. It is not always so in a keelboat, however, and the unfortunate helmsman is often quite unable to check his automatic reactions so as to ensure that this helm actions are out of phase. It is not the helmsman that is best able to reduce rhythmic rolling, but the man trimming the sails.

C. A. Marchaj has been able to extract interesting information from this research as to the effect of altering the sail trim. Fig. VIII.24 shows how it is possible to change from dynamic instability to dynamic stability by hardening the mainsail. A similar result can be obtained by altering course in relation to the wind (fig. VIII.25) and these two possibilities can be used in combination to find the optimum course.

If the boat is so small that the mainsheet can be manipulated rapidly, an alternative 'dynamic'

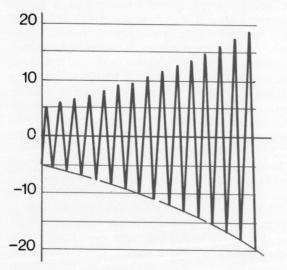

Figure VIII.23 *Equilibrium is unstable when amplitude continues to increase.*

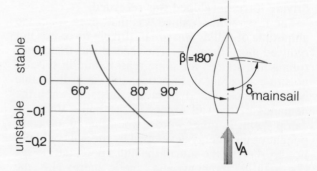

Figure VIII.24 *When the wind is aft, the reduction of the sheeting angle of the mainsail enables the boat to change from an unstable state to a stable state. G.V. = mainsail.*

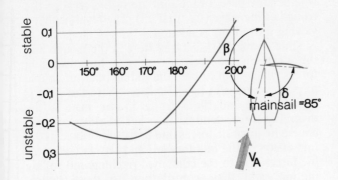

Figure VIII.25 *Changing from an unstable state to a stable state by altering course in relation to the apparent wind, the sheeting angle of the mainsail being unchanged.*

method can be used to control rhythmic rolling efficiently and quickly. This is to harden the sail rapidly when the boat is rolling to windward, and to ease it out when she rolls to leeward. The first action reduces the lateral component of driving force, while the second increases the damping effect of the sails.

It remains to be seen what the 'trouble-makers' are that cause rhythmic rolling, and whether it is possible to avoid its occurrence. (We will study the effect that waves have on the composite motion of the hull in the following section.) Obviously it is necessary to avoid any movement of the crew that could start a rolling motion, but it is undoubtedly airflow over the sails that is the main cause, particularly when a spinnaker is set.

In Chapter II.3f, we saw how, at a Reynolds number of between 150 and 2500, alternating Karman vortices are formed in the wake of a cylinder (fig. II.18, p. 42). The same can occur very easily downwind of a sail, and of a spinnaker in particular (fig. VIII.26). On account of the speed of rotation of the attached vortex, air flowing towards it causes a lateral force to appear. This grows weaker as the vortex is shed, and is then reversed in direction when the next vortex forms on the opposite side of the sail. The spinnaker is thus subject to an alternating transverse force which causes the pendulum motion (fig. VIII.27).

Two factors aggravate this. Firstly, if the spinnaker guy and sheet are fairly slack, and especially if the sail is not fully hoisted, the spinnaker will be free to oscillate to either side and this will increase the variation in the direction of driving force, which has already been modified by the direction of the apparent wind. The first method of reducing the effect of the vortices is therefore to harden in the guy and the sheet, to lower the spinnaker boom and to check that the sail has been hoisted right up to the block.

Secondly, the amplitude of rolling will be all the greater when the period of the vortices is much the same at the boat's natural rolling period. Unfortunately it is difficult to alter this, and little can be done. All that can be said is that a large sailing boat, especially if her natural rolling period is long, will often start rhythmic rolling earlier than a small boat with a short rolling period, but because the latter has a smaller reserve of dynamic stability the effect is sometimes quicker and more serious.

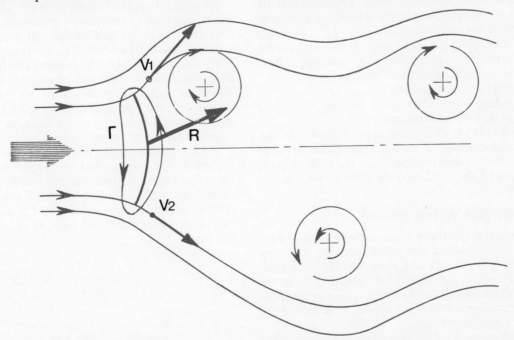

Figure VIII.26 *The formation of alternating vortices downstream of a sail causes a difference in speed of flow between V1 and V2, and this produces circulation around the sail, and the deflection of resultant force R alternately to either side.*

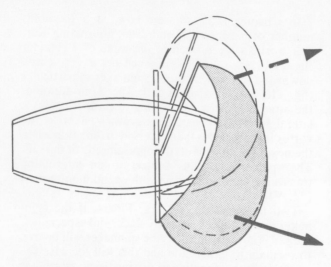

Figure VIII.27 *The change in the direction of driving force caused by the formation of Karman vortices is aggravated by the fact that the sail shape is deformed as it sags towards the side to which the boat is heeling.*

An important way of delaying rhythmic rolling, so far as the sails are concerned, is to set sails in addition to the spinnaker; their presence alters air-flow and discourages the formation of alternating vortices. The tall inner staysail or tallboy can be set, tacked down on the windward rail, but it seems to be the big boy that is the most efficient, acting as an extension of the spinnaker leech, provided that its hoist is not too long which would let it sag too far to leeward of the spinnaker.

Rhythmic rolling is without doubt one of the most difficult problems to resolve when handling a boat because it results from three variables:
    the boat's natural period;
    the period of the alternating vortices;
    the period of wave encounter.
The theory is known; what is more difficult is to find the practical compromise, and this will be different every time because it depends on the type of boat, the force of the wind, and the state of the sea.

5 Composite motion — yaw

At sea, except perhaps when running dead before the wind, and sometimes when reaching, it is very rare for boat velocity and wave velocity to be such that their relative directions are either exactly in the fore-and-aft line of the boat or perpendicular to it; the corresponding motions would then be a pure pitch or roll respectively.

On the other hand, in every case except when the seas are exactly ahead or following, the water moving in its orbit in the wave affects boat velocity, and this varies in relation to the water depending on whether the parts of the hull are in the crest or the trough of the wave (fig. VIII.28). The result is that a yawing movement is created.

Thus, in fig. VIII.28a, the stem in the trough and the stern on the crest are subject to converging forces which tend to take the sailing boat off course to port, whereas in fig. VIII.28b, where the stem is at the crest and the stern is in the trough, the diverging forces tend to turn her to starboard. Of course hydrostatic forces due to the difference in the immersion of the hull forward and aft, and gyroscopic forces due to the combined pitching and rolling motion, add their contribution to these hydro-dynamic forces.

With regard to the gyrostatic force, there are five alternatives:

a When the wave period is less than the period of pitching ($P_w < P_p$), gyrostatic couple is constant in sense, and tends to turn the hull towards a position perpendicular to the direction of the waves.

b When the wave period and pitching period coincide ($P_w = P_p$), the couple varies continually in the same way as yawing motion.

c When the wave period is between the rolling and pitching periods ($P_r > P_w > P_p$) the couple is constant and tends to turn the hull towards the wave direction.

d When the period of the waves and rolling are equal ($P_w = P_r$), the conditions are the same as in (b).

e When the period of the waves is greater than rolling period ($P_w > P_r$) the conditions are the same as in (a).

As with all gyratory motion, this is accompanied by heeling due to centrifugal force and to the fact that pressure either side of the hull is asymmetric.

In the case of figure VIII.28a, the relative speed of the water is reduced at the rudder, and its direction may even be reversed if wave amplitude is very high and boat speed relatively slow; the effect of the rudder will then be considerably reduced, perhaps even reversed, and it is understandable why boats capsize in a heavy following sea.

In such conditions the boat is actually in situation (e) above, the wave period being very much greater than the rolling period; the boat luffs up sharply across the waves, and the sudden heeling which results, added to that caused by the wave slope and orbital motion of the water, plays its part in inverting the boat.

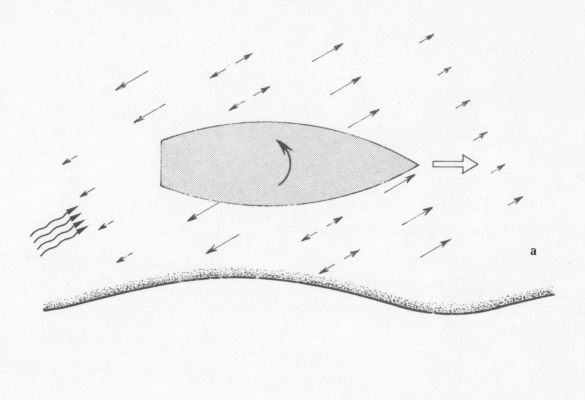

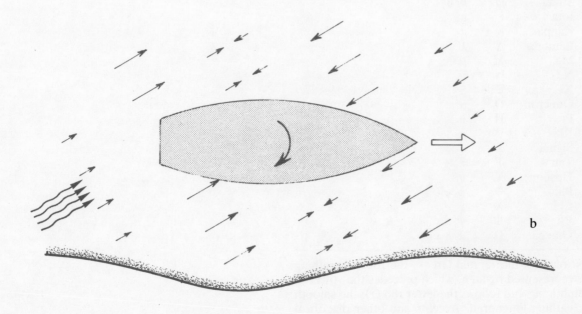

Figure VIII.28 *In a quartering sea, when the stern and stem are on the crest or in the trough of the wave, the forces due to orbital motion of the water particles are successively converging and diverging, and it is this that causes the boat to yaw.*

GREEK ALPHABET AND TRANSLITERATION

Name of Letter	Greek Alphabet		
Alpha	A	a	α^1
Beta	B	β	
Gamma	Γ	γ	
Delta	Δ	δ	∂^1
Epsilon	E	ϵ	
Zeta	Z	ζ	
Eta	H	η	
Theta	Θ	θ	ϑ^1
Iota	I	ι	
Kappa	K	κ	
Lambda	Λ	λ	
Mu	M	μ	
Nu	N	ν	
Xi	Ξ	ξ	
Omicron	O	o	
Pi	Π	π	
Rho	P	ρ	
Sigma	Σ	σ	ς^2
Tau	T	τ	
Upsilon	Υ	υ	
Phi	Φ	ϕ	φ^1
Chi	X	χ	
Psi	Ψ	ψ	
Omega	Ω	ω	

NOTE: In transliterated Greek, the rough breathing is represented by an *h*, which precedes the vowel or diphthong and follows the letter rho (*r*); the smooth breathing is ignored. Accents and other diacritical marks are usually omitted.

1. Old style character.
2. Final letter.

A SHORT GLOSSARY OF MECHANICS AND PHYSICS

Mass   The quantity of matter of a body, expressed in kilograms (kg).

Acceleration (γ)   Rate of increase of velocity, expressed in metres per second per second (m/s^2). Acceleration due to gravity is 9.81 m/s^2 (more accurately 9.806 65) and varies with altitude and latitude.

Force   The effect of an acceleration to which a mass is subjected. An action that alters or tends to alter a body's state of rest or of uniform motion in a straight line, expressed in newtons (N, the SI unit of force). 1 newton is the force that provides a mass of 1 kilogram with an acceleration of 1 metre per second per second. Before the Système International was adopted, force was expressed in kilograms-force, 1 kgf = 9.81 N (or pounds-force, 1 lbf = 4.45 N).

Weight   The force exerted on a mass by acceleration due to gravity; weight should therefore be expressed in newtons. Before SI units were adopted, weight was expressed in kg, and it seems unrealistic to hope that this habit will disappear. The confusion which resulted remains, and the value of the new system (although soundly based in theory) may be questioned for calculations in which acceleration is involved, in almost all cases at its value for altitudes near zero and in average latitudes; 1 kg = 9.81 N.

Density   Mass per unit volume of a homogenous body, is expressed in kilograms per cubic metre (kg/m^3).

Specific Gravity or *Relative Density*   Ratio of the density of a substance and the density of pure water. (Ratio of the mass of two equal volumes of a given substance and of fresh water.)

Moment   In relation to a point or to an axis: the product of the magnitude of a force by its perpendicular distance from the point or the axis, expressed in newtons × metres (Nm, newton metres). A single force causes rotation or translation. Two equal and opposite forces that do not act in the same line form a COUPLE, the moment of which is equal to the product of one of these forces by the perpendiclar distance between the line of action of the forces; a couple only causes rotation.

Centre of gravity   The point of application of the resultant of all the forces of gravity to which the components of a body are subject. By analogy, the centre of gravity of a surface is that of a very thin homogenous solid plate that is the same shape as that surface.

Inertia   The resistance of a body to being set in motion or, if it is already in motion, to resist any alteration in the direction or speed of that motion. The force of inertia increases with the mass of the body and with the speed of the motion applied.

Moment of inertia   The resistance of a body to being rotated; equal to the sum of the products of the mass of the particles that make up the body and the square of its perpendicular distance from the axis about which the body turns. When the moment of inertia of a surface is considered, this is taken as a very thin homogenous solid plate of the same shape as that surface.

Work   The action of a force when it moves the point of application. It is expressed in joules (J), the work done when a force of 1 newton moves the point of application 1 metre in the direction of action of the force. Before SI units were introduced, work was expressed in kilogram metres (kgm): 1 kgm = 9.81 J.

Energy   The capacity to do work, whether mechanical, electrical or thermal; expressed in joules.

Potential energy   The capacity of a body to do work as a result of its position. The potential energy of a weight hung on a string will be released when the string is cut.

Kinetic energy   The capacity of a body to do work by virtue of motion. As the weight falls, its potential energy is transformed into kinetic energy, which is released when it lands on the ground. The sum of kinetic energy and potential energy is always constant. Kinetic energy is equal to the product of half the mass by the square of velocity: k.e. = $\frac{1}{2}mv^2$.

Power   The work done during a given time, i.e. the rate at which work is done or energy expended, expressed in watts (W). 1 watt is the power of an energetic system at which 1 joule of energy is transformed at a constant rate of 1 joule per second. Before the SI was adopted, power was expressed in kilogram metres per second (kgm/s) or in horsepower. 1 kgm/s = 9.81 W; 1 horsepower (metric) = 735.5 W; 1 horsepower (British) = 745.7 W.

Pressure   The force exerted on a given surface per unit area, expressed in pascals (Pa); 1 pascal is the constant pressure exerted by a force of 1 newton on a flat surface of 1 square metre. The bar, which is equal to 10^5 Pa, and millibar are more generally used in meteorology and for fluids. Before SI units were introduced, pressure was expressed in kgf/cm^2 and in mm of mercury. 1 kgf/cm^2 = 9.80664×10^4 Pa, and 1 mm of mercury = 133.332 Pa. Normal atmospheric pressure, 760 mm of mercury, is equal to 101 325 Pa or 1013.25 millibars.

Conversion Tables

Pounds and Kilograms
The central column can be referred to in either direction

Pounds		Kilograms
2.205	**1**	0.453
4.409	**2**	0.907
6.614	**3**	1.361
8.818	**4**	1.814
11.083	**5**	2.268
13.228	**6**	2.721
15.432	**7**	3.175
17.637	**8**	3.629
19.841	**9**	4.082
22.046	**10**	4.563

Feet and inches to millimetres

inches / feet	0	1	2	3	4	5	6	7	8	9	10	11
1	305	330	356	381	406	432	457	483	508	533	559	584
2	610	635	660	686	711	737	762	787	813	838	864	889
3	914	940	965	991	1016	1041	1067	1092	1118	1143	1168	1194
4	1219	1245	1270	1295	1321	1346	1372	1397	1422	1448	1473	1499
5	1524	1549	1575	1600	1626	1651	1676	1702	1727	1753	1778	1803
6	1829	1854	1880	1905	1930	1956	1981	2007	2032	2057	2083	2108
7	2134	2159	2184	2210	2235	2261	2286	2311	2337	2362	2388	2413
8	2438	2464	2490	2515	2540	2565	2591	2616	2642	2667	2692	2718
9	2743	2769	2794	2819	2845	2870	2896	2921	2946	2972	2997	3023
10	3048	3073	3100	3124	3150	3175	3200	3226	3251	3277	3302	3327

Feet to metres, metres to feet

Feet		Metres	Feet		Metres	Feet		Metres	Feet		Metres
3.28	1	0.30	45.93	14	4.27	88.58	27	8.23	131.23	40	12.19
6.56	2	0.61	49.21	15	4.57	91.86	28	8.53	134.51	41	12.50
9.84	3	0.91	52.49	16	4.88	95.14	29	8.84	137.80	42	12.80
13.12	4	1.22	55.77	17	5.18	98.43	30	9.14	141.08	43	13.11
16.40	5	1.52	59.06	18	5.49	101.71	31	9.45	144.36	44	13.41
19.69	6	1.83	62.34	19	5.79	104.99	32	9.75	147.64	45	13.72
22.97	7	2.13	65.62	20	6.10	108.27	33	10.06	150.92	46	14.02
26.25	8	2.44	68.90	21	6.40	111.55	34	10.36	154.20	47	14.33
29.53	9	2.74	72.18	22	6.71	114.83	35	10.67	157.48	48	14.63
32.81	10	3.05	75.46	23	7.01	118.11	36	10.97	160.76	49	14.94
36.09	11	3.55	78.74	24	7.32	121.39	37	11.28	164.04	50	15.24
39.37	12	3.66	82.02	25	7.62	124.67	38	11.58			
42.65	13	3.96	85.30	26	7.92	127.95	39	11.89			

Explanation: The central columns of figures in bold type can be referred in either direction. To the left to convert metres into feet, or to the right to convert feet into metres. For example, five lines down: 5 feet = 1.52 metres, and 5 metres = 16.40 feet.